Dr. Greg Johnson deserves our thanks for writing s
dom and insight. As a model pastor-theologian, G
troversial topic of homosexuality with both pastor:
Drawing inspiration from such evangelical luminat   , ..., Graham,
Francis Schaeffer, and John Stott, Greg makes a compelling case for a "paradigm
of care" as opposed to a "paradigm of cure." The result is an excellent book with an
inspiring gospel vision whatever your orientation—a vision marked not by hope in
heterosexuality but hope in Christ. Highly recommended!

—**Todd Wilson**, PhD, cofounder and president,
The Center for Pastor Theologians

In the suffocating quagmire of the church's debates about same-sex sexuality, Greg
Johnson's *Still Time to Care* is a breath of fresh air. While Johnson unflinchingly documents the failures of the ex-gay movement of the 1980s and '90s, he also defends a
traditional sexual ethic and articulates a "paradigm of care" to counter the "paradigm
of cure" that has harmed so many people. Drawing deeply from history, evangelical
leaders, and Scripture, Johnson articulates a way forward for sexual minorities and
those who love them. Winsome, intelligent, personal, and warm, this book is important and profoundly needed. I want everyone I know to read it.

—**Tish Harrison Warren**, Anglican priest; author,
Liturgy of the Ordinary and *Prayer in the Night*

Greg Johnson offers a fascinating look into the rise of the ex-gay movement and the
reasons for a diminished ex-gay narrative today. He takes the reader back in history
to key voices evangelicals admired to move the reader forward into a vision of biblical
faithfulness and nuanced pastoral care and communal support for those who are both
gay and Christian.

—**Mark A. Yarhouse**, PsyD, Dr. Arthur P. Rech and Mrs. Jean
May Rech Professor of Psychology, Wheaton College

This fascinating book gives a thorough and enlightening account of how the evangelical church has historically mishandled and hurt gay and lesbian Christians. The
damage done over the last forty years is eye opening. While defending the orthodox
biblical sexual ethic, Greg Johnson lays out a healthy path forward for the church
regarding the LGBTQ community that is both biblical and pastoral. Every Christian
(especially leaders in the church) needs to read this book to better understand this
nuanced and complex issue.

—**Becket Cook**, author, *A Change of Affection: A Gay Man's
Incredible Story of Redemption*; host, *The Becket Cook Show*

This book is a lament for an evangelical road not taken. When it came to the pastoral care of lesbian and gay people, rather than heed the wisdom of their own leading lights like John Stott and Francis Schaeffer, many evangelicals opted instead for sexual-orientation change efforts and in the process left a legacy of pain and confusion that haunts the movement to this day. But this book is also a clarion call from a prophetic insider who believes that evangelicalism can change. Anyone wanting to understand better the current evangelical debates around sexuality—from "ex-gay" ministries, to "Side B gay Christians," to "mixed-orientation marriages"—should read this book and consider the costly and courageous witness of its author.

—**Wesley Hill,** author, *Washed and Waiting* and *Spiritual Friendship*

This is a much-needed book for our times. In a refreshing, deeply thoughtful, and engaging style, this celibate pastor shares his experience of living in the tides of secular and evangelical Christian thought, language, and behavior in relation to homosexuality over the last forty years. Here is a strong challenge to Christians to reflect deeply on how we have drifted away from a truly biblical approach. Johnson calls the church back to a more compassionate life of family/community to love and encourage those who are celibate for any reason. You will not regret taking the time to have your understanding and attitude transformed by grappling with the vital issues in this well-researched and excellent book.

—**Richard Winter,** Professor Emeritus of Counseling,
Covenant Theological Seminary

I am in awe of all that Greg achieves so successfully in this incredible book: a critical history of the ex-gay movement, a culturally sensitive defense of traditional sexual ethics, a pastoral manifesto for a better future—all wrapped up in the gospel of grace and accompanied by his own story (and wry sense of humor). I loved every page and am looking forward to seeing the good it will do every church leader and member who reads it.

—**Ed Shaw,** ministry director, www.livingout.org; pastor,
Emmanuel City Centre, Bristol (UK); author, *Purposeful
Sexuality: A Short Christian Introduction*

Greg offers a fast-paced, compelling historical account of the church's failure to engage LGBT+ people. In missiology, we know that it's so critical to learn history or else we'll repeat it. And sure enough, today the church risks returning to culture war over gender identity. While there is still time to care, there isn't much time! And this time, the next steps we take will impact our ability to extend Christ to an entire next generation.

—**Bill Henson,** founder and creator, Posture Shift Ministries, Inc.

As an anti-Christian gay man who decided to follow Jesus, and who was never exposed to the ex-gay world, I welcome this book as a vital contribution through the eyes of another gay atheist-turned-Christian who walked harrowingly through it. Many critiques of the ex-gay world and its theology have been leveraged by those who take its radical opposite position. Greg Johnson is different. He is one who has fought and paid the price to remain close to the Lord and in obedience to his Word and yet to challenge ex-gay theology, dismantle its harm, and face its complicated and flawed humanity. In this rare window into an experience that requires greater understanding, Greg points compassionately and critically to the greater hope of the gospel and the deeper third way that Jesus provides for the LGBTQI+ community in a world addicted to ideological certainty and harmful culture-war divides. A must-read.

—**David Bennett,** speaker and writer; author, *A War of Loves: The Unexpected Story of a Gay Activist Discovering Jesus*

In this eye-opening historical account, Greg Johnson paints a charitable yet harrowing portrait of the ex-gay movement and its residual influence on Western evangelicalism. Better still, he reminds us of the world that existed before the ex-gay movement, a world in which following Jesus and pursuing orientation change were never treated as synonymous. Reading this book has deepened both my sorrow over the past and my unswerving hope for the future.

—**Gregory Coles,** author, *Single, Gay, Christian* and *No Longer Strangers*

Every so often a book comes along of such consequence that it has the potential to reshape the discourse of its subject matter. *Still Time to Care* is such a book, and I pray that it revolutionizes the evangelical conversation about gay people and the history of the pastoral care we have received in the North American church. Combining careful attention to historical detail with incisive analysis of cultural Christianity, Johnson tells the tragic story of how ex-gay theology invaded the worldview of evangelical Christians, laying the foundation for decades of systemic pastoral malpractice. Johnson exposes the theological rot at the core of ex-gay theology, while also identifying the ways it continues to shape evangelical discourse today about gay people and our experience. And as if that were not enough, Johnson draws on his decades-long experience as a faithful pastor to chart a positive path forward so that all of us can grow together to become more like Jesus. *Still Time to Care* is a necessary, challenging, and deeply hopeful contribution to the ongoing conversation about the church and gay people.

—**Nate Collins,** PhD, president and founder, Revoice; author, *All But Invisible*

Still Time to Care is a thoughtful and helpful clarion call to Christians. Throughout this book, Greg Johnson takes you on a journey through the church's controversial approach to the unrelenting gay movement. While mistakes were made and adversaries earned, Greg shows the way back to a path and practice that is both God-honoring and people-loving. Caring for others—it is always the Jesus way.

—Kyle Idleman, bestselling author, *Not a Fan* and *Don't Give Up*

In my city, you can always find a sign proclaiming "Gay Rights Are Human Rights." You need to look no further to fully understand the vitriol against the church. In *Still Time to Care*, you will be discouraged by the history but encouraged for the future. Greg Johnson provides answers and solutions. We have a chance to make things right, upholding God's view of sexuality in a way God wants us to do it.

—Caleb Kaltenbach, bestselling author, *Messy Grace* and *Messy Truth* still time to care

still time to care

WHAT WE CAN LEARN FROM
THE CHURCH'S FAILED ATTEMPT
TO CURE HOMOSEXUALITY

GREG JOHNSON

ZONDERVAN
REFLECTIVE

ZONDERVAN REFLECTIVE

Still Time to Care
Copyright © 2021 by Greg O. Johnson

Published in Grand Rapids, Michigan, by Zondervan. Zondervan is a registered trademark of The Zondervan Corporation, L.L.C., a wholly owned subsidiary of HarperCollins Christian Publishing, Inc.

Requests for information should be addressed to customercare@harpercollins.com.

Zondervan titles may be purchased in bulk for educational, business, fundraising, or sales promotional use. For information, please email SpecialMarkets@Zondervan.com.

ISBN 978-0-310-17637-4 (softcover)
ISBN 978-0-310-14093-1 (hardcover)
ISBN 978-0-310-11606-6 (ebook)
ISBN 978-0-310-11607-3 (audio)

Published in association with Don Gates of the literary agency The Gates Group, www.the-gates-group.com.

Cover Art and Design: Lindy Martin, Faceout Studio

*To every gay person who has ever heard
the call of Jesus and found life.
And to the Christians who love them.*

Contents

PART 1:
The Paradigm of Care

PART 2:
The Paradigm of Cure

PART 3:
The Rising Challenge to a Historical Ethic

PART 4:
A Path Forward

Acknowledgments

There are too many people to name, without which this project would not have happened. I would like to thank Nate Collins for convincing me to write this book. I was lamenting how so few believers understood the context for current discussions about sexual identity and orientation. Nate ran down the qualifications for an author and told me I was it. I'm also thankful to him, Bruce Clark, Ron Lutjens, Mark Yarhouse, Warren Throckmorton, and many others for helpful feedback—and often pushback—where it was needed on the manuscript. I'm thankful for the many, many people who let me interview them, and especially for those who trusted me with deeply personal stories of shame and pain and loss. I also want to thank Ralph Blair. While he and I don't always see eye to eye, he allowed me access to forty years of archives spanning the entire history of the ex-gay movement. I want to thank Don Gates for his encouragement, counsel, and support. And I wish especially to thank the members, staff, and elders of Memorial Presbyterian Church for allowing me the time to write and for picking up the dropped balls that too often resulted. Above all, I want to thank my Savior, Jesus, who saw a confused, gay, atheist kid more than three decades ago and reached down to capture his heart. It has been worth it. I am so thankful.

Introduction

I Used to Be Gay

"You know, Mike, I used to be gay."

Mike stopped moving his paintbrush as the words fell clumsily from my mouth. He was painting the historic Saint Louis apartment I called home in the summer of 1997 as I began working toward my PhD in historical theology. He'd asked me about my schooling, and we got to talking about faith. Mike explained to me how he felt he could never go to church because he was gay. I asked him some questions and listened to his story.

Then I dropped the bombshell. "I know they say that's not supposed to happen," I went on. "But that's my story." Mike stared at me with interest as he set the paint can down, gently balancing his brush on its edge.

Looking back on this encounter, I can see that it had all the trappings of what was known as the ex-gay movement. Most notable is my use of the ex-gay script: "I used to be gay." The phrase implied that I wasn't gay anymore.

To be clear, my sexual attractions at that moment were drawn as exclusively to other men as ever. I was still at the top of the Kinsey scale that researchers since the 1940s have used to classify sexual orientation. What made me ex-gay was that I used the ex-gay script. I was trying to convince myself that I was a straight man with a disease—a curable one—called homosexuality. A condition that was being healed. Alan Medinger, the first executive director of Exodus International, described it as "a change in self-perception in which the individual no longer identifies him- or herself as homosexual."[1] The testimony made the man. And within my ex-gay framework, I wasn't lying.

I was an ex-gay.

A UCLA study in 2018 estimated that 698,000 Americans then between the ages of eighteen and fifty-nine had been through some form of sexual orientation change effort, whether in a church or parachurch ministry, with their pastor, self-directed through books and other media, or with a secular psychologist.[2] That's 6.7 percent of gay, lesbian, and bisexual Americans. If this is correct, then add to that figure all the youth and especially people age sixty and up. When you further consider the many who didn't make it this far because of enemies like suicide and HIV, we may be approaching a million people just in the United States. A great many people experienced their effort at orientation change in that constellation of faith-based parachurch ministries under the umbrella of Exodus International. Ministries with names like Love in Action, Desert Stream, Living Hope, and independent megaministry Homosexuals Anonymous formed the core of what we knew as the ex-gay movement. This movement was born in the 1970s and grew in the 1980s and 1990s before declining and dying.

GAY ATHEIST FALLS FOR JESUS

I wasn't raised Christian. My dad was a senior executive in the federal government, and I was raised in a good secular family in suburban Washington, D.C. I had never gone to church or synagogue. I had never read the Bible. I definitely did not believe that some ancient Near Eastern sky god was secretly pulling the ropes somewhere. A friend named Spencer once told me I was an atheist. I didn't argue.

There were two sons in our happy secular household.

I was the gay one.

Though I made crude attempts to hide it, something was always special about me. At age six I asked for an Easy-Bake Oven and a miniature porcelain tea set for Christmas so I could serve a proper English afternoon tea with my stuffed animals. Somewhere there's a photo of me holding a miniature teacup between my thumb and index finger, pinky sticking out like a rainbow flag. I got my Easy-Bake Oven. But then I was sentenced to Cub Scouts and not one but two terms on a boys' soccer team.

It didn't work.

When I was eleven—puberty came a little early—the realization hit me. I felt toward guys the way they felt toward girls. Exclusively. I was the gay kid. Nineteen eighty-four was a terrible time to realize you're gay. As the year progressed, one hundred gay men in the US were dying of AIDS every week. It would become one thousand per week over the next decade. All the young men like me were getting sick and dying. And the kids around me were cracking jokes about it. The shame was crushing me. I lived in constant dread that someone would find out. The school locker room left me in a state of near panic. What if I saw something? What if it affected me?

On the first day of seventh grade, I sprang into action. I postered the inside of my locker with a dozen shiny yet tasteful pinups of Madonna. I was postering over my shame, fitfully trying to conceal what Alan Downs calls the "velvet rage" of shame and self-hatred, trying to make myself lovable and normal and definitely not queer.[3]

I had no idea Madonna would become a gay icon.

Year after year I poured myself into schoolwork because it was the one thing I did well, the one place where I sensed I could make myself lovable, at least to my teachers.

So there I was. A gay atheist teenager trying to cover my shame.

The thing that began to crack this whole life open happened in the summer of 1988, as I watched pro-life protesters get arrested in Atlanta. I can't say I had any sympathy for their cause at the time, but I was deeply struck that these clean-cut, middle-class people who had jobs were willingly going to jail for something like an embryo. Jail occupied a most terrifying place in my fifteen-year-old imagination. Jail was the place where people like me got raped. Clearly, these Christians were serious about what they believed.

That year, I was assigned a school project to write a paper on a controversial issue. I chose abortion. And as I spent hours researching the topic in libraries, I felt myself sliding down the slippery slope of the moral argument for the existence of God.

Did I believe it was wrong to take human life? If it was okay, then human life had no meaning or value at all. As Sartre said, no finite point can have any meaning apart from an infinite point of reference. But if I concluded it was wrong to take human life, then that would mean evil was real. And if evil was real, then goodness must be real. And for goodness to be real, there must be a ground for goodness.

By the time I graduated from high school, I knew there had to be something to this concept of a higher power. I suspected that the god I was beginning to believe in was the Judeo-Christian God, mainly because I had seen those Christians willingly give up their freedom by protesting against something they believed was wrong and being arrested for their convictions. But I knew nothing about this God. I didn't know any Christians either. At least I didn't think I did. Certainly, no one had ever talked to me about Jesus, except a grandmother years earlier. And I couldn't remember what she'd said or whether it even applied to gay people who had never gone to church.

There was my shame ubiquitously sitting in the middle of it all. No one ever had to convince me that I was defective. No one ever had to convince me that a sexual relationship with another guy was out of the question. Even as an atheist, I could see how male and female reproductive organs were coordinated to create children. No one ever had to tell me I was a sinner. I knew. And I remember begging God to forgive my sin. "God," I prayed, "I don't know who or what you are, but will you please forgive me for masturbating? For being gay? Will you please stop all these fetuses from dying? I'm willing to die for you if that's what you want. But I don't know what's wrong with me or what I'm supposed to do." The shame ran deep.

I learned about Jesus years later, while I was studying architecture at the University of Virginia. There I heard that there was good news for gay people. I heard that Jesus actually favored sinful people, that sinful people were the only class of people Jesus came to save. I heard that Jesus took all the weight of my guilt and shame, and he bore it all in his own body for me so that I didn't have to bear it anymore.

I was so ready to hear this good news. And that gospel gave me the freedom to open up to my campus minister. He was the first person I had ever talked to about my sexuality. He was so compassionate.

At age twenty, I was baptized and became a member of a church in the Presbyterian Church in America (PCA). The following year I moved to Saint Louis to enroll at Covenant Theological Seminary, not because I had any interest in ever being a pastor (that took another decade) but because I wanted to understand the Bible and theology. I had no background in church or Sunday school or youth group. It was there that God broke me of my pride and my anger and began developing in me a gospel-driven spiritual and emotional health I had never known. It was there that I began to really live out the gospel's power to cover my shame. It was there that I fell in love with the church.

LEAVING THE MOVEMENT
BEFORE IT IMPLODED

By the time doctoral studies began, I had started thinking of myself as an ex-gay. The developmental model of homosexuality, which formed the background to many of the ex-gay ministries' methodology, somewhat lined up with my personal experience, and at times I imagined myself one day marrying a woman and having kids. I watched the ex-gay tapes and read the books that assured me I could become straight. But any hope in this life was running up against a disappointing fact. As the years progressed, sanctification for me was not looking like becoming straight, no matter how much I wished otherwise. I could grow in spiritual fruit, self-discipline, personal holiness, compassion, sexual purity, generosity, gentleness, and countless other areas. But I was not seeing my sexual temptations switch gender.

My story was that my heart had been captured by Jesus. He had rescued me, so I deeply loved him and wanted to obey him. That was my narrative.

Whenever I told someone that I used to be gay or that I had left homosexuality, that ex-gay script left me feeling a pang of dishonesty. Who was I fooling?

Conveniently, by the early 2000s reparative therapists were promoting the language of "same-sex attraction." At least that language seemed more honest about my experience than "ex-gay." I have described myself as gay, ex-gay, and same-sex attracted. I can't say that the shifts in terminology made much difference.

My plan remained celibacy unless God led otherwise. Through the decades, there have been seasons when I have reopened the question of pursuing marriage with a woman. After a season of prayer and counsel, I have always felt peace in accepting singleness as a calling from my Savior. Certainly, my faith has cost me more than a tithe, but God's people have not let me be alone.

My narrative was that Jesus captured my heart. He is worth everything.

Meanwhile the ex-gay movement declined.

In January 2012, while addressing the annual conference of the affirming Gay Christian Network (GCN), Alan Chambers, the last president of Exodus International, came clean about the numbers. "The majority of people that I have met—and I would say the majority meaning 99.9 percent of them—have not experienced a change in their orientation." This organization represented more than 270 ex-gay ministries.

It was the first public admission of what a growing number of us had already realized. Real instances of changed sexual orientation were extremely rare. They were like orcs, elves, and pixies. Everyone has heard of them. But do they actually exist? Since 2012, Chambers has clarified that the one woman who represented the 0.1 percent in his GCN address is still bisexual. In 2013, Exodus International closed its doors.

With that, the ex-gay movement officially died. In the early 2020s, you almost never hear of someone identifying as ex-gay.

With so many lives deeply affected by the ex-gay movement, though, this leaves us asking questions. How could this have happened? Is there hope for Christians who are attracted to members of the same sex? For decades the hope was for a cure to homosexuality in this life, so where do we go from here? Even when we autopsy this ex-gay cadaver, in what ways is it still walking dead among us? Did we get the biblical sexual ethic wrong? And what's our path forward with a positive Christian vision for believers who aren't straight?

This book is about how we understand and move forward after the collapse of the ex-gay movement. The opening chapters of this book ask what positive vision Christians had for gay people before the movement. The next section will tell the story of the shift from a paradigm of care to a paradigm of cure. We'll ask why the movement grew and what fissures developed along the way, how it died and why. Three chapters will address current challenges to historical Christian teaching on sexuality. Had we gotten the biblical sexual ethic wrong? Could the biblical writers even have had in mind mutual, monogamous, lifelong gay partnerships, or were they really renouncing pedophilia, temple sex, and male prostitution? And is the biblical ethic inherently violent to gay people? Our final chapters will consider how we can move forward in creating church communities that care for believers who are not straight, even when we have no reliable cure in this life.

A REORIENTED LIFE

I'm Greg. I used to be an ex-gay.

While sexuality has a degree of fluidity in some people, the real change for me has been not in my sexual orientation but in my life orientation. Jesus rescued me. That's everything. Jesus gives me a positive vision for serving him in this life and a confident vision for healing in the age to come.

I want to make sure others have this same chance to have their lives reoriented to Jesus.

We have a culture that tells the gay young man what the good life looks like: You experiment sexually in your teens. You let men buy you drinks in bars. You spend way too much time at the gym trying to build the body that will make you lovable. Gay people excel in every field, driven by a never-ending need to accomplish enough, to be successful enough to become lovable. We decorate our lives to poster over our shame in the hope that we will become lovable. And when those efforts fail us, we turn to drugs and alcohol to self-medicate.

No community in the world longs so strongly for what the gospel alone can give. More than anything, my hope in this book is to cast a gospel vision for gay people: not hope in heterosexuality but hope in Jesus.[4]

A Note about Terminology

This project arose partly out of questions about the terminology of homosexuality. Friends of mine like Becket Cook, Rachel Gilson, and Sam Allberry say they are same-sex attracted. Friends like Wesley Hill, Gregory Coles, and Nate Collins say they are gay. We all believe the same sexual ethic. We're all bound to the same commitment to cultivate sexual desire only within the confines of a marriage between one man and one woman. We all see indwelling sin for what it is. We're all crazy in love with Jesus. We all love each other. We all have very good reasons for why we use the terminology we use.

Yet I have been horrified to watch people play my friends off against each other, weaponizing their testimonies to question the faith of faithful Christian siblings who simply describe their experience using different terms. That doesn't smell of the gospel of Jesus.

One of the questions I have asked is where all this terminology came from. How did it develop? And why are we forced to make terminological choices that will alienate someone whatever term we use? The answer lies buried within the rise and fall of the ex-gay movement.

In mapping all this out for the first time, I have to make choices myself. One of the biggest challenges in writing a Christian book on homosexuality is this question of terminology. The reality is that there is no nonproblematic term to describe people who are sexually attracted exclusively to members of the same sex. To use *homosexual* as a noun today is offensive to most people. It is perceived as insensitive and overly clinical with historical associations with mental illness and criminology. And it flattens human beings into their sexual orientation as if all we are is a lustful mass of sexual sinews and warped synapses.

It does sometimes feel that way. At the same time, though, I have never so much as held hands. That is somewhat rare in my demographic box. But please don't flatten me into "a homosexual." I am a man and I am a Christian. Those are my nouns.

You can choose whatever adjective you like to modify that noun. Goodness knows, we have options. And none of them are fantastic. The shifting meaning of terminology has remained a challenge authors face. Newer editions of John Stott's *Same Sex Relationships* substitute the phrase *gay people* for the original *homosexuals*. Since using *homosexual* as a noun went out of accepted use in the 1990s, that puts Christian writers in a position of having to choose between other terms that all carry a great deal of baggage.

The descriptor *gay* carries a lot of assumptions—and potentially painful memories—depending on the reader's age. Many older readers who see the word *gay* will immediately think of a hypersexualized subculture of bathhouses and sex shops, a political agenda, and/or some highly revisionist biblical interpretations. Younger readers, on the other hand, largely see *gay* as the opposite of *straight* and perceive it as speaking only to sexual orientation.

I most frequently describe my experience using the phrase *same-sex attraction*, but even that has more baggage than the Southwest carousel the day before Christmas. For people who went through reparative therapy, *same-sex attraction* has a lot of baggage. For some it too carries painful memories.

"Don't worry," says my celibate gay Christian friend. "Just say queer."

And seven readers just fainted.

Admittedly, the term *queer* increasingly is the preferred terminology in much of the LGBTQ+ community. The term *queer* does not bias the experience of gay men over that of bisexuals and lesbians the way *gay* does. The problem is that the term at this point is little used in Christian circles. And little understood. And besides, I spent way too much of my life trying not to be called queer.

How about we just use the biblical terms and categories, like *homosexual temptation*? It's a fair question, but it also raises problems of its own. The English term *homosexual* nowhere appears in the Hebrew or Greek Bible. Also, the condition known to modern research as a homosexual orientation is certainly more than just homosexual temptation. The condition carries with it an absence of sexual attraction to members of the opposite sex. (How many straight women go to gay clubs to dance just so they won't get grinded, groped, touched, or otherwise assaulted?) Surely, the lack of temptation to lust after people of the opposite sex doesn't fit under the term *homosexual temptation*. Not every experience linked to a fallen condition is immoral.

We are dealing here with a condition larger than just a temptation. I experience homosexual temptation because my sexuality—whether hardware or software—is bent in a certain way. There are all kinds of fallen conditions not named in the Bible. Think alcohol dependence, bipolar disorder, and every other medical and psychological disorder known to modern medicine. Some of these fallen conditions are morally neutral, while the sexual temptations that flow from mine are not. The Bible does not list every condition, because that is not its purpose. Its purpose is to point us who are damaged by the fall to Jesus.

So how do we proceed?

When we read authors who use language different from what we're used to, we have an opportunity to try to hear what they are intending to say, an opportunity for empathy and what theologians once called the judgment of charity. If any of the terminology in this book triggers you, then I would invite you to simply swap out the triggering term for whichever term you best understand. If this book were an app, the first screen would give you the choice of terminology throughout. We would have both a *gay* version and a *same-sex attracted* version. We might even have a *queer* version for the young folks. I would hate for anybody not to hear how much God loves them just because they can't stomach my often clunky, sometimes dated, and occasionally anachronistic terminological choices.

As seventeenth-century Lutheran theologian Rupertus Meldenius famously quipped, "In essentials unity. In nonessentials liberty. In all things charity."

part one

The Paradigm of Care

one

C. S. Lewis and His Gay Best Friend, Arthur

In homosexuality, as in every other tribulation, [the works of God]
can be made manifest: . . . every disability conceals a vocation, if
only we find it, which would "turn the necessity to glorious gain."
—C. S. Lewis

They grabbed Bedborough and threw him in the choky. That's the slammer to
Americans. It was May 31, 1898, and George Bedborough would be arraigned
for attempting to "corrupt the morals of Her Majesty's Subjects."

A bookseller by trade, he had slipped a hardbound copy of Havelock Ellis's
Studies in the Psychology of Sex Vol. 2 to an undercover investigator pretending
to want to purchase the volume, which included chapters exploring the nature,
prevalence, and causes of sexual inversion—homosexuality. George Cecil Ives,
a close friend of Oscar Wilde, had only recently organized the first group
in England to advocate for the rights of such individuals. Sodomy had been
decriminalized in France a century earlier; the Order of Chaeronea would seek
the same in the United Kingdom. Whether or not one acted on the tendency,
to be sexually inverted in the Anglo-American world was to be mentally dis-
eased and societally dangerous.

Outcast.

After the arrest, George Bernard Shaw and others formed a Free Speech
Committee to work for Bedborough's vindication. The bookseller accepted
a plea bargain and got off with a fine of one hundred pounds—a heavy sum
at the time, equivalent to about fifteen thousand dollars today—for selling a
psychological textbook on homosexuality.

It was into this world the next month that solicitor Albert Lewis and his wife, Florence, announced the birth of their baby boy Clive Staples. The great-great-grandson of a bishop, C. S. Lewis would wander far from God before coming to saving faith in Jesus. And he would model for Christians in the twentieth century a charitable Christian posture toward gay people. He would even add his voice to those seeking to decriminalize homosexuality. This was before the culture wars trained believers to take an adversarial posture toward gay people. Before the ex-gay movement told us they could become straight if they tried.

THE BIG FOUR

Four figures dominated the imagination of evangelicals in the last half of the twentieth century. First, we have C. S. Lewis, who has been identified as evangelicals' favorite Christian thinker of the twentieth century, even though Lewis never identified as an evangelical.[1] Second, we have Francis Schaeffer, whom *Christianity Today* once identified as "Our St. Francis." Schaeffer did more than any other figure to speak into a post-Christian culture and foster the evangelical mind.[2] Third, we have Billy Graham, who was known universally as the Pastor to Presidents and was the ceremonial figurehead of the postwar neo-evangelicalism that arose as a response to the narrowness of American fundamentalism. The neo-evangelicalism that attempted to cast a positive Christian vision for a modern age. Finally, we have John R. W. Stott, the longtime global evangelical leader whom, upon his death in 2011, the BBC hailed as the Protestant Pope.[3]

Lewis. Schaeffer. Graham. Stott.

In the discourse of these four Christian leaders, as in the works of other educated evangelical elites at the time, we see the beginnings of a positive and biblically orthodox Christian vision for gay people who follow the call of Jesus Christ.

For Lewis, this was personal.

HIS GAY BEST FRIEND, ARTHUR

Twentieth-century evangelicals adored Clive Staples Lewis. A 1998 poll of *Christianity Today* readers rated Lewis as "the most influential writer in their lives." J. I. Packer called Lewis "our patron saint." While Lewis taught literature at Oxford and Cambridge, he is perhaps best known for his children's books and his Christian apologetic writing. He is well recognized as the author of the Chronicles of Narnia, *The Screwtape Letters*, and *Mere Christianity*. Lewis never wrote a book or article on the topic of homosexuality. Yet when he did comment on the topic, he did so with a posture of genuine personal humility.

Lewis hesitated to speak authoritatively on matters in which he had little experience. In his preface to *Mere Christianity*, he explains his great dislike of anyone who from a position of safety issues commands to men on the front line. Hence he avoided speaking about contraception. "I am not a woman nor even a married man, nor am I a priest. I did not think it my place to take a firm line about pains, dangers and expenses from which I am protected."[4] As a sexually inactive layperson, Lewis was content to remain silent. He takes a similar stance on the topic of homosexuality. In *Surprised by Joy*, his spiritual autobiography, he labels homosexual sin "one of the two (gambling is the other) which I have never been tempted to commit." He then adds, "I will not indulge in futile philippics against enemies I never met in battle."

When he does discuss homosexuality, Lewis displays a posture of humility, empathy, and compassion. His lifelong best friend, Arthur Greeves, was gay. Lewis called him his "first friend" and made it clear to him that his sexual orientation never would be an issue in their friendship, even though Lewis was straight. Lewis's own weakness as a young man tended more toward sadomasochism; he signed some 1917 letters to Arthur with "Philomastix," or whip lover, knowing that Arthur did not approve. When Arthur came out to Lewis as gay the following year, Lewis felt as though he was in no position to judge. Lewis himself was "affected in this strange way" by the attraction to mix sexual intimacy with the infliction of pain.[5]

My Most Intimate Friend

Lewis adored Arthur, describing him as "after my brother, my oldest and most intimate friend." They had lived across the street from one another as boys growing up in Belfast. Arthur grew up in a very harsh Plymouth Brethren home. Lewis was an atheist from the time he first conceived of religion. Yet Lewis described Greeves as his alter ego.

Writing of his first meeting with Arthur, he states, "Many thousands of people have had the experience of finding the first friend, and it is none the less a wonder; as great a wonder (pace the novelists) as first love, or even a greater."[6]

The two remained close into adulthood, when they were in constant communication even over great distance. A published collection of Lewis's three hundred letters to Greeves is filled with deep affection and runs to 592 pages.[7] These letters provide us with great insight into their relationship.

When Arthur came out to Lewis as gay in 1918, then-atheist Lewis responded with support. "Congratulations old man, I am delighted that you have had the moral courage to form your own opinions <independently,> in defiance of the old taboos." He added, "I am not sure that I agree with you: but, as you hint in your letter, <this penchant is a sort of mystery only to be fully understood by those who are made that way—and my views on it can be at best but emotion.>"[8] Greeves may very well have had a romantic crush on Lewis. If so, though, Lewis never made an issue of it.[9]

Thirteen years later, when Lewis came to believe in Jesus as Christ, Greeves was the first person in whom Lewis confided.[10]

In a December 29, 1935, letter to Arthur, Lewis offers spiritual and relational support during a dark moment in his friend's life. Upon hearing that Arthur had just ended an unhealthy relationship with another man, Lewis takes pains to validate Arthur's feelings of loss. "As regards to your news— sympathy . . . sympathy on the wrench of parting and the gap it will leave" and "I don't think you exaggerate at all in your account of how it feels."

Not the Worst Sin

While Lewis didn't make an issue of Arthur's sexual orientation, he did take issue with those who target people for it. In *Surprised by Joy*, Lewis zeroes in on what he saw as the hypocrisy of those who treat homosexuality as a special category of sin. He points out the homosexual practices that were then common in English public schools like his own, Malvern, which he described using the fictitious name Wyvern, but suggests that there were bigger problems—problems that can't give the sexual stuff "anything like a first place among the evils" of the school.[11] The schoolboys would have preferred girls had they had access to any, Lewis argues. But their options were limited, and their sexual behaviors were mild in comparison with their cruelty, worldliness, and singular focus on self-advancement.

While Lewis viewed any and all same-sex sexual intimacy as sin, he insisted it was not the worst of sins. "There is much hypocrisy on this theme. People commonly talk as if every other evil were more tolerable than this." The sexual sins were hardly the most problematic in his school. "What Christian," he asks, "in a society as worldly and cruel as that of Wyvern, would pick out the carnal sins for special reprobation?" He concludes, "Cruelty is surely more evil than lust and the World at least as dangerous as the Flesh."

This is not to say that Lewis thought the matter morally neutral. Lewis cautions not only against homosexual practice but against same-sex romance altogether. "I am sure that any attempt to evade [bearing his cross] (e.g., by mock- or quasi-marriage with a member of one's own sex even if this does not lead to any carnal act) is the wrong way."[12]

A Positive Vision

In a letter from C. S. Lewis to Sheldon Vanauken dated May 15, 1954 (which Vanauken published in *A Severe Mercy*), Lewis suggests that a same-sex orientation might carry with it a vocation—a positive calling. Vanauken had sought Lewis's advice on how to answer questions from students about homosexuality. Lewis writes,

> I take it for certain that the physical satisfaction of homosexual desires is sin. This leaves the homosexual no worse off than any normal person who is, for whatever reason, prevented from marrying. Second our speculations on the cause of the abnormality are not what matters and we must be content with ignorance. The disciples were not told why (in terms of efficient cause) the man was born blind (John 9:1–3): only the final cause, that the works of God should be made manifest in him.
>
> This suggests that in homosexuality, as in every other tribulation, those works can be made manifest: i.e. that every disability conceals a vocation, if only we find it, which would "turn the necessity to glorious gain." Of course, the first step must be to accept any privations which, if so disabled, we can't lawfully get. The homosexual has to accept sexual abstinence. . . .
>
> What should the positive life of the homosexual be? I wish I had a letter which a pious male homosexual, now dead, once wrote to me—but of course it was the sort of letter one takes care to destroy. He believed that his necessity could be turned to spiritual gain: that there were certain kinds of sympathy and understanding, a certain social role which mere men and mere women could not give. But it is all horribly vague—too long ago. Perhaps any homosexual who humbly accepts his cross and puts himself under Divine guidance will, however, be shown the way.[13]

From Lewis, we see a positive vision for the same-sex-oriented Christian. When we come to Jesus and accept our cross—whether the loneliness, the temptations, or the abuse from the well intended—God can redeem the tears that have accompanied it. We see here a suggestion that God deigns to bring blessing out of a fallen condition, that through a frowning providence God himself will be glorified. We see here a vision for the works of God to be made manifest. That's a positive vision for the gay person who follows Jesus.

For Lewis, the gay person could not be reduced to their sexual orientation or to sexual temptation. Lewis understood that the homosexual Christian's biggest struggle might be not with sexual sin but with despair or pride. In a letter to Bede Griffiths dated May 28, 1952, Lewis writes of "the stories you tell about homosexuals [which] belong to a terribly familiar pattern: the man of good will, saddled with an abnormal desire which he never chose, fighting hard and time after time defeated." But Lewis questions whether Griffiths is missing the obvious. "Is not this continued avoidance either of presumption or despair, this ever-renewed struggle, itself a great triumph of Grace?"[14] To the degree that the gay believer avoids those two pitfalls, Lewis knows that the Holy Spirit is ministering grace. The work of grace is every bit as evident in fostering hope as in addressing sexual sin.

Lewis surely longed for this dynamic in his best friend, Arthur.[15]

FRIENDSHIP AND HOMOPHOBIA

As a nearly lifelong celibate himself, Lewis gave focused attention to friendship, something he had come to value so immensely through Arthur and his other friends.[16] In contrast to lovers who absorb themselves in one another, Lewis saw friendship as sharing common interests that become the locus of the relationship. While lovers sit face to face, friends sit shoulder to shoulder. In opposition to the notion then popular that friendship is merely latent homosexuality, Lewis viewed friendship as a form of love in its own right.

Broadly speaking, Lewis saw homophobia as a threat to friendship. He found the relative lack of physical affection in modern British friendship deeply problematic. The fear of homosexuality, in his view, had fostered a breakdown in platonic same-sex intimacy. "Kisses, tears and embraces are not in themselves evidence of homosexuality," he explained. He commended the much more demonstrative affection among friends of previous eras. "We, not they, are out of step."[17]

HOMOSEXUALITY AND POLITICS

As for political matters, Lewis supported decriminalization of homosexual relationships. In a letter dated May 27, 1960, he writes, "I quite agree with you about Homosexuals: to make the thing criminal cures nothing and only creates a blackmailers' paradise. Anyway," he adds, "what business is it of the State?" He describes his own desire to protect "the persecuted Homosexual" from what he calls "snoopers and busybodies."

At the same time, Lewis felt despised by gay literary critics on account of his Christian commitments. He lamented what he called "the highbrow

Homosexuals who dominate so much of the world of criticism" because they "won't be very nice to you unless you are in their set." And so, he explained, "one is fighting on two fronts."[18]

In the world we inhabit, after the landmark 2015 *Obergefell v. Hodges* case that legalized same-sex marriage in the United States, Lewis's perspective on marriage law may provide a paradigm for Christian political engagement (or disengagement) on sexuality. Speaking about the then-contemporary political push toward looser divorce laws in the UK, Lewis cautioned Christians against using political coercion to force non-Christians to act like Christians. The question of the nature of Christian marriage is one question, he insisted. But a different question altogether is the lengths to which Christians "ought to try to force their views of marriage on the rest of the community" by pushing for strict divorce laws. He explained, "My own view is that the Churches should frankly recognize that the majority of the British people are not Christians and, therefore, cannot be expected to live Christian lives."[19]

In pursuit of common good, Lewis proposed two different sets of laws for two distinct communities. "There ought to be two distinct kinds of marriage: one governed by the State with rules enforced on all citizens, the other governed by the Church with rules enforced by her on her own members." He added, "The distinction ought to be quite sharp, so that a man knows which couples are married in a Christian sense and which are not."[20] Lewis here suggests a model for Christian ministry within a pluralistic context in which followers of Jesus are not a moral majority but a life-giving minority. It's a paradigm that maintains Christian fidelity within the church without making those outside the church feel controlled or condemned by Christians.

Throughout Lewis's writing, we see a personal humility and charity coupled to a desire to support homosexual believers. Lewis sought a positive Christian vision for life in Christ. He sought to defend people like me from snoops and bullies. And he was ready to pull back from political posturing that might interfere with the clarity of the church's evangelistic mission.

C. S. Lewis died in 1963, before flower power, hippies, Woodstock, and the sexual revolution caught the decade up in the turmoil for which it became known. In Lewis's place, another voice was already beginning to speak into the gap between biblical Christianity and secular culture. This voice too would speak a word of compassion and offer gospel hope to gay people.

two

Evangelicalism before the Ex-Gay Movement

The homophile tends to be pushed out of human life (and espe-cially orthodox church life) even if he does not practice homo-sexuality. This, I believe, is both cruel and wrong.

—Francis Schaeffer

"Perhaps no intellectual save C. S. Lewis affected the thinking of evangel-icals more profoundly" than Francis Schaeffer, writes Michael Hamilton. "Perhaps no leader of the period save Billy Graham left a deeper stamp on the movement as a whole."[1] Little can compare with the vibrancy and cultural engagement of transatlantic Anglo-American evangelicalism in the four decades after World War II. In contrast to the negativity, fear, and divisiveness of American fundamentalism, leaders like Schaeffer and Graham trained educated Christians how to counter the secular world's dross with a clear and thoughtful presentation of the truthfulness and brilliant luster of Christian orthodoxy.

And they loved gay people.

OUR ST. FRANCIS

Born in 1912, Francis Schaeffer came to faith in Jesus out of a background of agnosticism. He went on to lead several churches before entering a turbu-lent period of doubt and uncertainty. Through this process, Schaeffer became one of the most profound and effective Christian apologists of the twentieth century. Arguably, no figure has had a bigger impact on the intellectual lives of evangelicals in North America.[2]

Francis Schaeffer studied at Westminster Theological Seminary under Cornelius Van Til and J. Gresham Machen, the lifelong celibate New Testament scholar whose 1923 book *Christianity and Liberalism* crystalized the modernist-fundamentalist debate. Schaeffer then bounced between schools during a season of denominational divisions. After several pastorates, he moved with his family to Switzerland. The hypocrisy he saw among his fellow religious conservatives led him into a crisis of faith in which he rethought his entire faith position. The fruit of that process was the founding of L'Abri Fellowship in 1955. Francis and Edith Schaeffer opened their home to anyone seeking answers or longing for a genuine experience of Christian love. Students and young people traveled from across Europe and around the world to L'Abri in order to live, learn, and wrestle with Christianity. It was at L'Abri that Schaeffer had many conversations with gay people, always pointing them to the "true truth" of a God who is actually there and is not silent. In his view, only Christianity could account for both the glory and the shame of being human, including the glory and shame experienced by people who are gay.

Schaeffer on Not Being Cruel

In his desire to reach young secular people, though, Schaeffer never wavered from a biblical sexual ethic. He saw in homosexuality a breakdown of the biblical distinction between the sexes, a "denial of antithesis."[3] Schaeffer, with all other evangelicals, opposed the ordination of sexually active, practicing gays. His 1970 book *The Church at the End of the Twentieth Century* expressed his shock that mainline denominations were even considering it. Schaeffer foresaw significant cultural battles when in 1984 an Orthodox Presbyterian Church congregation in San Francisco found itself sued for releasing a gay employee who had violated the church's code of conduct.

Yet his posture toward gay people remained one of compassion and empathy.

Schaeffer discussed homosexuality at length in an August 11, 1968, letter to a European pastor.[4] The minister had seen no fewer than six gay people commit suicide. He was wrestling to find a biblical and pastoral response to the pain experienced by believers who were homosexually oriented. Schaeffer's response focused on care. He distinguished sexual orientation—what he called being *homophile*—from homosexual practice. And for Schaeffer, true homophiles were likely born that way. "By definition, to be a homophile is a person who is born so that they have a natural tendency toward affection and sexual practice with their own sex. . . . Not all homophiles practice homosexuality, and not all who practice homosexuality were born homophiles."[5] He understood this as "surely a part of the abnormality of the fallen world."[6]

Schaeffer saw the church at risk from two opposing errors: the error of relativism and the error of fundamentalism. In Schaeffer's view, the first mistake that churches can make in providing pastoral care to gay people "is to fall into the modern relativism that would say homosexual practice is not wrong."[7] Even in the 1960s, Schaeffer saw the cultural handwriting on the wall.

But he saw another error on the opposite side. Schaeffer viewed the church as complicit in the marginalization of its same-sex-oriented members, by failing to distinguish between orientation and practice, saying "that homophile tendencies are sin in themselves, even if there is no homosexual practice."[8] He believed that the consequence of such thinking was disastrous. "Therefore the homophile tends to be pushed out of human life (and especially orthodox church life) even if he does not practice homosexuality." He concluded, "This, I believe, is both cruel and wrong."[9]

It's unclear whether Schaeffer was denying that indwelling sin was involved in homoerotic temptation, or was instead arguing that homophiles didn't choose to be that way and shouldn't be treated as if they were committing willful sin. But what is clear is that Schaeffer insisted that experiencing sexual temptation—homosexual or heterosexual—was not the same thing as committing sin. "In neither case should it be called sin."[10]

A Posture of Humility

Schaeffer was adamant that "in approaching these people . . . we do not compromise our Christian absolutes—that is, that we say what the Bible says, which is that homosexual *practice* is wrong."[11] But, like Lewis, he advocated that Christians keep a humble tone when they speak of this truth. "It is equally important that they feel within themselves that we do not count ourselves better than they." He added, "Their sins are no greater than our sins." And for those facing a possible future of celibacy, he went on to say, "We may cry with them concerning this."[12]

He speculated about the possibility of cure for those who merely had some homophile tendencies—for those Kinsey would have rated lower on his scale. Some might become able to marry. But for those whose homosexual attraction was exclusive—those whom Schaeffer called "real homophiles"—Schaeffer viewed celibacy as a calling from God. "In this case they must face the dilemma of a life lived without sexual fulfillment."[13]

For such a calling to be possible, Schaeffer insisted the believer needed the church to be the church and to help "the individual in every way possible."

Indeed, Schaeffer's ministry became a magnet for gay people wrestling with Christianity.[14]

In a 2008 interview on NPR, Francis's son Frank described his father's Swiss L'Abri as a place "where pregnant girls are coming to . . . that will accept them to have a baby" and "where homosexuals—both lesbians and gay men—are welcomed." He added, "No one's telling them they've got to change [become heterosexual] or that they're horrible people. And they go away, you know, having found my father wonderfully compassionate and Christlike to them."[15]

Defender of Gay People

Edith and Francis also listened to gay people share their perspective. "Not only did they believe them, but Dad defended them against people who would judge or exclude them," stated Frank. Francis was critical of anyone thinking that Christian conversion cures homosexuality. "Dad thought it cruel . . . to believe that a homosexual could change by 'accepting Christ.' . . . Dad often said, 'Salvation is not magic. We're still in a fallen world.'"[16] And Schaeffer cautioned against marriage as a means of orientation change. "Dad always counseled gay men and women against getting married to a heterosexual if they were doing it in the expectation that it would change them."[17]

When Jerry Falwell in private brought up the issue of gay people with Francis Schaeffer, Schaeffer commented that it was a complicated issue. Falwell shot back a rejoinder: "If I had a dog that did what they do, I'd shoot it." There was no humor in Falwell's voice. Afterward Schaeffer said to his son, "That man is really disgusting."[18]

Grace and Peace and the RPCES Report

Schaeffer was an ordained minister in the northern Reformed Presbyterian Church, Evangelical Synod (RPCES), a denomination that in 1982 joined the predominantly southern Presbyterian Church in America (PCA). The combination effectively doubled the denomination's number of clergy and brought Covenant College in Lookout Mountain, Georgia, and Covenant Theological Seminary in Saint Louis into the PCA.

Schaeffer's denomination also brought with them into the PCA a position paper on homosexual Christians.

This report offers yet another window into educated conservative evangelicalism before either the culture war or the ex-gay movement had picked up steam. The denominational study committee included a theological ultraconservative in Dr. Robert L. Reymond, professor of systematic theology at Covenant Theological Seminary and later at Knox Theological Seminary.

A supralapsarian ultra-Calvinist with a PhD from Bob Jones University, Reymond was paired to produce the report with Egon Middelmann and other men. Middelmann, who served as committee chair, was also brother of Udo Middelmann. Udo, who was Schaeffer's son-in-law, had worked with Schaeffer to raise the evangelical consciousness about environmental stewardship and creation care in a 1970 book they cowrote.[19]

At thirty-eight years of age, Egon was the German-born, celibate, closeted gay pastor of Grace and Peace Fellowship in Saint Louis. Founded by followers of Schaeffer in 1969 in a house and soon moved to a storefront, the church had a reputation as a hippie church with deep relational connections to Schaeffer's L'Abri. To start the church, seventy members moved en masse into a then-marginal urban Saint Louis neighborhood. Members of Grace and Peace eventually started a homeless shelter and food pantry and a community housing corporation to renovate low-income housing for the poor.

Grace and Peace became a magnet in the 1970s for gay believers seeking to find community and support in living lives of celibacy. People moved to Saint Louis from across the country because the congregation was known as a safe church for orthodox Protestants who were same-sex oriented. There were experiments in communal housing to provide intentional community—chosen family—for Christians who were celibate or otherwise single.

In July 1980, during its annual meeting at Seattle Pacific University, Egon, Reymond, and other members of the denominational study committee presented their report to the RPCES general synod.

We see in their report on homosexuality a clear statement of the biblical boundaries of sexual behavior within monogamous heterosexual marriage. We see the gospel of Christ and its corresponding call to faith, repentance, and a new obedience. From so conservative a denomination, these we would expect.[20]

And we see other things we might not expect.

Our Homosexual Brothers and Sisters

The report spoke affectionately of "our homosexual brothers and sisters."[21] It grounded unspecified nonnormative experiences of sexuality in those whom Jesus said were born eunuchs. Citing Paul's thorn in the flesh, the report stated that gay people who follow Jesus shouldn't assume that sexual orientation change will be possible. The report praised David and Jonathan as an example of what non-romantic, nonsexual commitment can look like with members of the same sex.

The report rejected any categorical exclusion to church office on account of sexual orientation. Three years earlier, in 1977, the Presbyterian Church in America had itself declared only that "practicing homosexuals"—by implication distinct from nonpracticing homosexuals—were not suitable candidates for ordination.[22]

And the report offered what was one of the first denominational confessions of sin against gay people from an evangelical denomination. The first had been the Christian Reformed Church, whose approved 1973 position paper on homosexuality had stated, "It is one of the great failings of the church and Christians generally that they have been lacking in sympathy and concern for the plight of the homosexuals among them." The paper continued, "It has been said that the homosexual has been far more sinned against than he has sinned. In the light of our understanding of homosexuality today, Christians bear a great burden of guilt relative to such persons."

Seven years later, the 1980 RPCES report stated, "In the context of our concern for the homosexual in our congregation . . . our congregations have at times acted more out of fear and lack of compassion than offering long term friendship, care, and openness." It was a more concise acknowledgment than the Christian Reformed Church's, but the RPCES report itself was a more concise document.

We do hear biblical orthodoxy in this report, but we hear flowing from that orthodoxy a sorrow over the way the church has not loved its nonstraight members.

This is Schaeffer's denomination. Empathy for gay people pervades much of the report. A primary concern noted by the 1980 report was the fear experienced by so many gay people, specifically including "the fear of 'coming out' or being 'found out'" and "the fear of loss of job [or loss of] reputation."[23]

The report also cast a larger vision for gay people in society. Quoting the *Westminster Confession of Faith*, it charged church members to "publicly and privately protect those struggling with homosexuality in and outside of our congregations 'in such an effectual manner as that no person be suffered . . . to offer any indignity, violence, abuse, or injury to any other person whatsoever.'"

In a historic vote, the body of the report was approved by the synod.[24]

When the RPCES joined the PCA in 1982, the PCA voiced no objection to the new RPCES report on homosexuality. To the contrary, the PCA General Assembly voted to receive the report and other RPCES reports as part of the PCA's history to be "valuable and significant material which will be used in the perfecting of the Church."

A Suicide in Saint Louis

In 1994, the year I moved to Saint Louis as a Presbyterian seminarian, twenty-six years after Egon planted Grace and Peace Fellowship and fourteen years after the RPCES report on homosexuality, tragedy struck Saint Louis. Egon Middelmann had fallen into sexual sin. He had told no one. In despair, he committed suicide. He had spent decades helping carve out an emotionally safe space for gay people who become Christians and want to be faithful to the historical biblical sexual ethic. Certainly, there were those in his church and presbytery in whom he could have confided. But Egon had never opened up to anyone about his own sexual orientation. Or about his struggles with mental health. He was either too fearful or—perhaps more likely in his case— too proud. Still, it was his suicide that prompted his local presbytery to begin serious work to create safe spaces for Christians who are oriented to members of the same sex.

I remember visiting Grace and Peace Fellowship in Saint Louis a few months after Egon's death. I remember sharing my story with one of the deacons there that day. They were a grieving congregation who had loved their pastor. Now they were struggling to figure out what they believed. The man who preached the gospel to them had fallen victim to the lie that speaks into the mind of every gay person who meets Jesus. It's the lie that the gospel is true for everyone except me. I think a lot of folks like me struggle with that lie.

Christians need to know that the gospel is true for them too.

BILLY GRAHAM ON A GOSPEL POSTURE TOWARD GAY PEOPLE

As for proclaiming the gospel, Billy Graham was the twentieth century's most prominent evangelist. Born and raised in rural North Carolina, Graham received a degree in anthropology from Wheaton College in 1943 before becoming a pastor and then president of a Bible college. He gained national notoriety in 1949 during his Los Angeles Crusade, with help from aging newspaper mogul William Randolph Hearst, who that year sent a two-word telegram to all his editors, instructing them to "Puff Graham." With word from the boss to promote his ministry, Graham became a headline in newspapers across the country as well as in *Life*, *Time*, and *Newsweek*.

Throughout his career, Graham would preach to 210 million people in 185 countries. He served as spiritual advisor to every president from Harry Truman to Barack Obama. Graham's earliest recorded comments about gay people may very well be in the recording of a phone call to the White House. It was during a gay sex scandal involving a top aide to the president of the United States, which unfolded just weeks before the 1964 presidential election.

Billy Graham and the Big Gay Sex Scandal

Walter Jenkins had been born in a town named Jolly in the great state of Texas. The forty-six-year-old World War II vet was a convert to Roman Catholicism and a father of six. He had worked as Lyndon B. Johnson's top assistant for most of the previous twenty-five years, following Johnson from the House to the Senate and on to the White House. And Jenkins had a secret: in 1959, he had been arrested for an incident involving another man.

After Jenkins was arrested a second time on October 7, 1964, the press at first suppressed the story. But on learning of the previous incident, newspapers broke the story a week later. It blew up like a nuclear bomb over Washington. Top presidential adviser Walter Jenkins had been arrested a second time for having gay sex in the same Washington, D.C., YMCA men's room where he had been busted five years before.

President Johnson agonized over the potential political fallout at the polls. Homosexuality was still considered a mental illness in 1964. It was also still a crime. Jenkins resigned immediately.

Republican Barry Goldwater's campaign issued bumper stickers: "All the way with LBJ, but don't go near the YMCA."

Five days after the scandal broke, Graham called President Johnson to offer his support and advice. In the recorded phone call, Graham charged President Johnson to show compassion to Walter Jenkins. "You know," Graham began, "when Jesus dealt with people with moral problems, like dear Walter had . . . he always dealt tenderly. Always. This is the way he handled it. And that's the way I feel about it." Graham stressed to the president his own moral solidarity with Jenkins as a fellow sinner. "I know the weaknesses of men, and the Bible says we're all sinners. . . . I just hope if you have any contact with him, you'll give him my love and understanding."[25]

While Billy Graham's moral convictions never wavered, his dual sense of the sinfulness of his own sin and the beauty of the gospel moved him to compassion, solidarity, and empathy. It moved him to plead with others for such empathy. It compelled Graham to leverage his powerful connections to plead for a closeted gay man with a wife and kids who'd been busted for having gay sex in a public toilet. This was 1964. Graham put his own name on the line to be a friend to the friendless.

"Graham Backs Ordaining Homosexuals"

But the learning curve would be steep for Graham. In response to one 1973 letter from a young Christian woman asking about her attraction to another woman, Graham bluntly warned her that such a path leads to destruction.

He warned her of judgment and pointed her to conversion and regeneration, even though she seemed to indicate that she was already converted.[26] I can only imagine that his comments might have left her questioning her salvation.

Two years later, though, Graham shocked the world. A 1975 headline in the *Atlanta Journal-Constitution* declared, "Billy Graham Backs Ordaining Homosexuals."

Graham had been asked at a Eurofest campaign in Belgium whether he would support the ordination of a gay man to the Christian ministry. Graham had replied that they "should be considered on individual merit" based on certain qualifications. Specifically, the article mentioned "turning away from their sins, receiving Christ, offering themselves to Christ and the ministry after repentance, and obtaining the proper training for the job."[27]

A week later the newspaper printed a letter to the editor from a Mrs. Rae Ansley, chiding the editors for their misleading headline. "Dr. Graham favors considering *repentant* homosexuals for the ministry *after* they have accepted Christ."[28] You can imagine the backlash from fundamentalists who already viewed Graham with suspicion. Yet even under pressure, Graham refused to issue any public retraction that might appear to treat homosexual sin differently from other sin. Graham believed that homosexual orientation was something people are born with. He said as much in a 1994 interview with Larry King.[29]

Depoliticizing the Gospel

Graham continually made it a point to avoid the political adversity of the culture war.[30] At a 1992 crusade in Portland, Oregon, Graham was asked about his support for an upcoming statewide referendum prohibiting government support of homosexuality. "I intend to stay out of national and local politics while here," he said. "God loves all people whatever their ethnic or political background or their sexual orientation." He went on to say, "Christians take opposing views on many issues. . . . Those on both sides of the issue must love each other."[31]

There were some stumbles. The following year in Columbus, Ohio, when asked whether AIDS might be a divine judgment on sins, Graham voiced an uncertain, "I could not say for sure." Graham then hesitated. The wages of sin is death, after all. Since the garden, all death has been judgment on sin in general. Graham added cautiously, "But I think so." The backlash was fierce. Graham's comment played out on network and cable news with all the theological nuance of a gorilla on meth at a tea party with the queen.

Graham was grieved. Shortly thereafter he apologized for the remark, saying he was sorry he said it. He had forgotten his own maxim to always remember he's dealing with people. He issued a clarification with his apology. "To say God has judged people with AIDS would be very wrong and very cruel."[32] He didn't want anyone suffering from the disease to see in the face of God an angry ogre shaking his fist at them. God is not cruel. Graham wanted them to see the gospel.

This remained Graham's priority. At a news conference before his 1997 San Francisco crusade, the evangelist commented to a reporter that he was tired of people trying to get him to criticize gay people. "There are other sins. Why do we jump on that sin as though it's the greatest sin?" Graham asked. The day of the crusade, he said, "What I want to preach about in San Francisco is the love of God. People need to know that God loves them no matter . . . their sexual orientation." The Southern Baptist preacher raised in 1920s North Carolina added, "I have so many gay friends, and we remain friends." Speaking to a crowd of ten thousand that night in the Cow Palace, Graham declared, "Whatever your background, whatever your sexual orientation, we welcome you tonight."[33]

A Gospel Focus

There can be no doubt that Graham's moral convictions had not changed since he warned that young woman in 1973 about the dangers of homosexual sin. But Graham remained steadfast in the same gospel posture toward gay people he first showed while interceding for Walter Jenkins back in 1964. Lead with empathy and compassion. Focus on the gospel. Remember your solidarity as a fellow sinner. Appeal for forgiveness. Remember these are people. Tell everyone God loves them. Be a friend to gay people. Stay out of politics. Don't make an issue of sexual orientation. Speak up when people treat homosexual practice like it's worse than their own sins. Be prepared to take flack for showing solidarity. Don't be surprised when God converts gay people and they repent and come to Jesus. Don't be surprised when they end up in ordained ministry. Always trust God with the results, because only he can change the heart. Lay out the welcome of Jesus to sinners whatever their background. This was Billy Graham's posture toward gay people who need Jesus.

It was a beautiful gospel posture toward people in some ways very different from himself.

Meanwhile, across the Atlantic, Graham's friend and colaborer John Stott would take many of these same ideas and weave them together into a larger vision.

three

John Stott:
Architect of the
Paradigm of Care

At the heart of the human condition is a deep and natural
hunger for mutual love, a search for identity and a longing
for completeness. If gay people cannot find these things in
the local "church family," we have no business to go on using
that expression.

–John Stott , *Issues Facing Christians Today*

It was 1969. The Stonewall riots raged in New York City. It was the first mass uprising to demand equal rights for gay people, and it thrust that fight onto the global scene. Young men hurled beer bottles and protesters gathered as police with truncheons dragged off patrons of the mafia-run gay bar at the center of the conflagration. This defining moment led to massive social upheaval over the next half century. In the process, Western cultural norms were rewritten as gay people transformed in the American psyche from shamed deviants carving out spaces on the fringes of society to a protected and celebrated class of iconic cultural leaders.

While Stonewall was raging, across the pond, one of transatlantic evangelicalism's preeminent publishing houses was drawing up plans to release a new book. The pseudonymous *Returns of Love: Letters of a Christian Homosexual,* released by InterVarsity Press in 1970, would place orthodox Protestantism at the center of the conversation about how the church can care for gay people who have fallen in love with Jesus.[1]

A CHRISTIAN HOMOSEXUAL

The Returns of Love would be rumored to have been written by celibate evangelical Anglican John Stott. It was not, though he commended it for aiding his understanding of those who felt the pain of being celibate on account of one's sexual orientation. The book dove deep into the emotional longing, angst, and spiritual reality experienced by those who inhabit the no-man's-land between two very different worlds: Christian and homosexual. Additionally, the book would explore the dialogue between two theologically astute celibate men who believed the Bible to be the inerrant word of God. Jesus Christ was their Savior.

But they weren't straight.

As the world awoke to the presence of nonstraight people in our midst, Christians could begin to recognize that our siblings in our pews were suffering and needing our care.

This was before the ex-gay movement, before the culture wars. This was back when our paradigm for the same-sex-oriented Christian was not cure but care. More than fifty years ago, Christianity's leading voices were already casting a vision for the gospel's work among people like me.

In the decade and a half after the 1969 Stonewall riots, orthodox Protestants wrestled with how best to care for gay people who seek to follow Jesus in joyful lives of sacrificial obedience. In this period, we see key leaders within transatlantic neo-evangelicalism bringing a gospel-centered paradigm of spiritual care. More than any other single figure, John Stott would lay out the paradigm of care. But he would be building on foundations laid by Lewis, Graham, Schaeffer, and others.

THE PROTESTANT POPE

When *Time* magazine named John R. W. Stott one of the hundred most influential people in the world, it was Billy Graham who did the write-up.[2] No figure had a larger impact on late-twentieth-century global evangelicalism than John Stott. Dubbed variously the Protestant Pope or the Evangelical Pope, Stott was the son of a Harley Street physician and spent his life pastoring the same church in which he grew up, All Souls, Langham Place. Stott and Graham were influential in laying the foundation for the First International Congress on World Evangelization at Lausanne in July 1974. In 1982, Stott would found the London Institute for Contemporary Christianity. Stott authored more than fifty books. His *Basic Christianity* sold two million copies. That's not bad for a Christian book.

It was Stott who led the discussion of sexuality among the Anglican evangelicals in the years following Stonewall. His leadership role among evangelical Anglicans meant Stott had huge influence among American evangelicals, since at that time educated American evangelicals looked to evangelical Anglicans for scholarly leadership.[3] Anglican evangelicalism sneezed, and campus ministers across America caught cold. This relationship gave Stott a powerful reach.

In 1980, Stott convened a gathering of Anglican evangelicals to map out a pastoral approach to homosexuality. Remarkably, they led with public repentance for their own sins against gay people. In a formal statement, this gathering of leaders declared, "We repent of the crippling 'homophobia' . . . which has coloured the attitudes toward homosexual people of all too many of us, and call our fellow Christians to similar repentance."[4] It was a staggering confession at a time when popular opinion was still biased strongly against gay people. Remember, this was not the twenty-first century, when Christian leaders repent in order to look progressive, relevant, and inclusive in a culture that celebrates all things fabulous. Stott and these evangelical leaders were truly grieved for the ways they had injured their neighbors and siblings in Christ.

Participants were intrigued by recent psychological theories about the development of homosexuality. Elizabeth Moberly, a pioneer researcher in reparative therapy, was invited to participate. Yet they cautioned against claims of people being "instantly and fully 'cured' of their orientation" through nascent Christian ex-gay ministries. The statement called specifically for qualified nonpracticing gay people to be received as candidates for ordination to ministry.[5]

THE 1978–79 SERMONS

In a series of sermons addressing issues facing Britain in 1978–79 later collected under the title *Issues Facing Christians Today*, Stott provided a masterful defense of a two-thousand-year Christian consensus on same-sex relationships.[6] He inductively examined the six biblical passages that appear to explicitly prohibit sex acts between members of the same sex (the Sodom narrative, two Levitical texts, and the three Pauline injunctions in Romans 1, 1 Cor. 6:9–10, and 1 Tim. 1:8–11). He argued that these negative views on homoerotic behaviors flow from the Bible's positive vision for marriage in the opening chapters of Genesis, a vision affirming the complementarity or diversity of the two sexes within marriage.

Stott didn't rule out church discipline in cases in which members refused to repent of homosexual sin, which was the same standard to which he held heterosexual members.[7] "If we waver in our belief that God has spoken to us in the Scriptures, then we are left with conjecture and opinion," he explained. Yet Stott wedded his orthodoxy with compassion, empathy, and infinite respect for the dignity of gay people. He appealed for "an unusual degree of sensitivity" when discussing sexuality, arguing that in creating us as sexual beings, God placed sex "close to the center of our personality."[8] Stott pleaded for Christians not to "stereotype and stigmatize" gay people but instead respect them. "We have no liberty to dehumanize" people who aren't straight, he preached.[9]

Stott, like Graham, Lewis, and Schaeffer, stressed the commonality we all experience as sexually fallen beings with disordered sexual desires. He also insisted that no one has a right to be morally superior: homosexual sin was no different from other sexual sin. "Christians should not therefore single out homosexual intercourse for special condemnation." He emphasized that every kind of relationship and activity which deviates from God's revealed design displeases God.[10] "Sexual sins are not the only sins, nor even necessarily the most sinful," he wrote. "Pride and hypocrisy are surely worse."[11]

Part of Who They Are: Sexual Identity and Orientation

Stott too distinguished between homosexual practice and homosexual orientation, arguing that the Christian is not responsible for their sexual orientation. With this, he was acknowledging that orientation is generally unchosen, unwelcome, and for most relatively fixed. For the Christian, Stott assumed, orientation remains a part of one's identity, or constitution.[12] "We may not blame people for what they are, though we may for what they do," he explained. "In every discussion about homosexuality we must be rigorous in differentiating between this 'being' and 'doing,' that is, between a person's identity and activity, sexual preference and sexual practice, constitution and conduct."[13]

For Stott, a homosexual orientation was part of the believer's identity, part of who they are, part of their constitution. It was a fallen part of one's identity that the gospel doesn't erase so much as it humbles. That humbling opens up the door to distinguish constitution from conduct. At the same time, Stott cautioned against sexual orientation being given too central a place in defining us. No one should be flattened into their sexual attractions. "There are only people, human persons made in the image and likeness of God."[14] He added that we all share in the "glory and tragedy" of human experience.[15]

The Idol of Romance

Stott didn't demonize those with whom he disagreed. He displayed a sensitivity toward gay couples even as he argued against same-sex coupling for Christians. "I do not deny the claim that homosexual relationships can be loving," he wrote.[16] But love, he continued, is insufficient to sanction such relationships for the Christian. "[True] love is concerned for the highest welfare of the beloved. And our highest human welfare is found in obedience to God's law and purpose, not in revolt against them."[17]

Stott rightly perceived within Western culture an unhelpful elevation of the romantic and sexual. The secular West had taken these good things and made them ultimate. So Stott emphasized how sexual experience was not essential to human fulfillment. While sex is a good gift of God, it is not a gift given to all, and it is not indispensable to our being human. "Jesus Christ was single," Stott noted, "yet perfect in his humanity."[18]

As in the report from Francis Schaeffer's denomination, Stott saw biblical precedent for gay people who follow Jesus in celibacy. He tied our experience to those born eunuchs in Matthew 19. "For some," Stott explained, "it is 'because they were born that way' . . . with a physical defect or with a homosexual orientation." He added, "Such are congenitally unlikely to marry."[19] But this didn't mean that the believer who couldn't marry was relegated to a seat in coach while the married folks flew first class. Stott spoke from experience as one with a rich understanding of the high calling of celibacy.[20]

A Vision for Life

Stott set out to cast a positive vision for homosexually oriented people. He spoke of the gay person's life of faithfulness as a calling from God. He pointed to the encouragement and support the church will have to offer as people like me live out lives of fidelity to Christ. He then pointed us all to faith, hope, and love. By this, he meant the faith to accept both God's standards and his grace. It meant the hope to look beyond this present life of struggle to our coming future glory. And it meant love—specifically, love from churches that have historically failed to give such love to believers who aren't straight. Jesus, Stott charged, is calling his church to love its nonstraight members.[21]

As to whether orientation change can be had in this life, Stott discussed popular theories and expressed skepticism about it for those who were exclusively homosexual—what he called "the invert."[22] He concluded, "Complete healing of body, mind and spirit will not take place in this life."[23] Stott instead pointed to the wellspring of Christian hope, a hope that lies not in this world but in the coming age when Jesus will make all things new. The locus of hope for the homosexual Christian was not change in this life but transformation in the life to come. "Some degree of deficit or disorder remains in each of us. But not forever! For the Christian's horizons are not bounded by this world."[24] He mentioned stories that were circulating of Christians being healed of homosexuality but concluded that "it is not easy to substantiate them."[25]

Like Lewis before him—also celibate most of his life—Stott viewed friendship as central to a gospel vision for the homosexual Christian. Also, like Lewis, Stott expressed concern that the biblical vision of friendship was threatened by homophobia. "It is sad that our Western culture inhibits the development of rich same-sex friendships by engendering the fear of being ridiculed or rejected as a 'queer.'"[26] Stott cited biblical examples of committed friendship: Ruth and Naomi, David and Jonathan, Paul and Timothy. These relationships were nonerotic and nonromantic but involved deep affection and strong commitment. In the case of David and Jonathan, Stott noted, they were even "demonstrative."[27]

A SIMEON MAN

Stott modeled his life and ministry after his eighteenth- and nineteenth-century forbear Charles Simeon of Cambridge, Stott's alma mater. Stott frequently described himself as a "Simeon man." Also an evangelical Anglican with a commitment to expository preaching, Stott would share Simeon's passion for global evangelization as well. Simeon had developed a reputation as a dandy from his school days at Eton and was known for fussing ever so about his carpets.[28] But we must remember that being a dandy in the 1780s had more to do with projecting a cultured appearance. Dandyism did not carry assumptions about one's sexuality until later in the nineteenth century. And celibacy remained a requirement for Simeon's role as a Fellow of King's College, Cambridge. Still, Simeon did face suspicion on account of his continued reluctance to take a wife. In a letter to Robert Noble, Simeon explained that he felt his usefulness to God required his celibacy. "I have never regretted it." He continued, "If . . . you determine on a life of celibacy, God can and will support you, and you will be blessed in the deed!"[29] Stott might have found in such words great encouragement.[30]

As with Simeon and just about any unmarried man in Protestant ministry, Stott's own sexuality would at times be the subject of speculation. Stott's biographer Tim Chester notes that Stott "had had schoolboy crushes on girls and remained somewhat dazzled by beautiful women throughout his life."[31]

Opinions about Stott's sexuality have ranged from definitely straight to possibly gay—but nonpracticing. Others saw him as something of a nonsexual person, like the Doctor Who then airing Saturday evenings on the BBC. Some of Stott's associates commented that whatever shape sexual temptation might have taken for him, he was an incredibly disciplined and regimented man. Stott is known on two occasions to have considered pursuing a relationship with women he considered attractive. But he never had peace about it, so he never so much as dated. Commenting on Stott sometime after 1958, Australian Anglican primate Marcus Loane wrote, "In those days John was said to have been more willing to run a mile than to meet a girl."[32] He was already committed to celibacy.

Called to Christian Celibacy

Stott placed the reason for his celibacy in God's will for his kingdom.

> During my 20s and 30s, like most people, I was expecting to marry one day. In fact, during this period I twice began to develop a relationship with a lady who I thought might be God's choice of life-partner for me. But when the time came to make a decision, I can best explain it by saying that I lacked an assurance from God that he meant me to go forward. So I drew back. And when that had happened twice, I naturally began to believe that God meant me to remain single.
>
> Looking back, with the benefit of hindsight, I think I know why. I could never have traveled or written as extensively as I have done if I had had the responsibilities of a wife and family.[33]

And there is context for Stott's celibacy.

Stott was one of Bash's boys. Stott was sixteen years old when, with the encouragement of Eric Nash—nicknamed Bash—Stott dedicated his life to Christ. It was Nash, also a lifelong celibate Anglican clergyman, who became the single biggest influence during Stott's early years as a Christian.[34] Seeking to reach young men in the leading British schools, Nash mentored an estimated two hundred men who later entered ministry in the Church of England. Among Bash's boys were preacher Dick Lucas—also celibate—as well as writer-evangelist Michael Green and hymn-writing bishop Timothy Dudley-Smith. Stott certainly had in Nash a model for Christian celibacy in service to Christ. Nash wrote to Stott weekly for his first seven years as a Christian. It should come as no surprise that this celibate servant of God might become a model for John Stott.

But curiosity about Stott's celibacy came to a head in 2016.

An Educated Wrong Guess

That year, a prerelease edition of a book by Andrew Brown—religion correspondent for the *Independent*—and religious scholar Linda Woodhead identified John Stott as the author of *The Returns of Love: Letters of a Christian Homosexual.*[35] The rumors concerning Stott's involvement were not without reason. The pseudonymous author of *Returns* was celibate like Stott. He was apparently theologically trained like Stott. He was an evangelical Anglican like Stott. He was possibly a clergyman like Stott, given how he used details of the Anglican marriage rite to illustrate a point. He even wrote at times in numbered paragraphs like Stott. His arguments sometimes paralleled Stott's later arguments elsewhere. Both he and Stott had InterVarsity Press as their publisher. The similarities are noteworthy. Brown was convinced it had to be Stott.[36]

The problem was that it was not Stott.

They got it wrong.

And there was proof.

In the midst of the uproar surrounding the prerelease of Brown and Woodhead's book, a witness close to the *Returns of Love* project produced a signed affidavit proving definitively that Stott was not the author. The publisher hastily recalled the review copies and pulled and pulped all copies of the book. It was then rereleased without listing Stott as the author of *Returns of Love.* It did however include the comment, "When we consider the great evangelical revolt over homosexuality, it is important to remember that evangelicals . . . were disproportionately likely to be gay."[37]

Perhaps. But I would think the Anglo-Catholics might be in the running.

The fact is, we can't know anything about the form of sexual temptation John Stott faced. Anyone to whom he confessed his sins remained as loyal as Stott would have been.[38] What we can say is that John Stott gives us an enduring model of a Christian who found human longings fulfilled in Christ and the friendship of his people, even with a lifelong calling of celibacy. The model of a heterosexual Stott could be even more valuable to believers with same-sex orientations than would that of a nonstraight Stott. It would be a lot easier on gay people who become Christians to embrace celibacy if they could look around and see straight believers also following Christ in celibacy in response to Jesus' words in Matthew 19:12 and the apostle Paul's in 1 Corinthians 7.

More than anyone before him, through his teaching and through his celibacy, John Stott mapped out a positive Christian vision for all people—including gay people pursuing celibacy—to find abundant life in Jesus Christ. More than anyone, Stott was the architect of the paradigm of care.

GETTING REAL WITH *LETTERS OF A CHRISTIAN HOMOSEXUAL*

While we do not know whether John Stott played any background role in bringing the book to market, he commended *The Returns of Love*. He wrote, "Nothing has helped me to understand the pain of homosexual celibacy more than Alex Davidson's moving book."[39] This pseudonymous 1970 InterVarsity Press book subtitled *Letters of a Christian Homosexual* set forth an incredibly honest description of the author's life. We read of his fear when he realized he had fallen in love with his friend (and possibly mentor). Such carnal interest threatened their friendship. We read of his confused relief to learn his feelings were unrequited. He described his longing for an exclusive one-on-one relationship, and his equally strong conviction that for him such a relationship with another man—even if nonsexual—would be wrong on account of its exclusivity.[40] We know the author was celibate, a theologically trained evangelical Anglican, and still a virgin at the time of writing. The recipient of his letters, possibly a mentor, was much the same—celibate and an evangelical Anglican, though less sentimental than the author. While the author was still a virgin, his recipient was not. He mentioned that the recipient had lived for a time in an all-male environment, and contrasted his own sinful fantasies with the recipient's sinful activities, now long since forgiven.[41]

Like Lewis, Graham, Schaeffer, and Stott, the author distinguished homosexual practices from his "homosexual constitution," which he described as a "disease."[42] His conclusion was that being attracted to members of the same sex is not in itself morally blameworthy; at one point he compared his "abnormal affections" to left-handedness.[43] This is not to say that the author of *The Returns of Love* believed that everything about his sexual orientation was morally neutral. He called his affections abominable. His point was that his condition was unchosen. He could distinguish between the misery of the fall—what we might call the damaged hardware and software, or damaged nature and nurture—and the way indwelling sin made use of all of that.[44] The author of *Returns* elsewhere observed how indwelling sin was enmeshed in his experience of his sexual orientation. Still, he stressed that his underlying sexual orientation, while evil, was not a sin.[45] The indulgence, the passion, the selfishness were all sin. But beneath these was his underlying condition. He wrote, "The homosexual condition is to be classified with disease, weakness, death, as an evil; not with gluttony, blasphemy, murder, as a sin. Both sin and evil are the work of Satan, were brought into the world at the Fall, and will one day be destroyed by Christ, but they are not identical."[46] He speculated about whether psychotherapy might bring some level of orientation change, but he tried that route himself to no avail. "I never asked to be born or raised with such inclinations," the author wrote bluntly.[47]

The Complexity of Good Longings and Indwelling Sin

The author described an incredible complexity in which good desires are bent, the same feelings reflecting simultaneously the Christian graces and the reality of indwelling sin. He sounded very much like Lewis in the way he was looking for God to bring good out of a difficult calling. He explained,

> I know that some would say that homosexuality, not only the practice but also the condition, is morally reprehensible and should be abhorred and fought in all circumstances, and that I am wrong even to acquiesce in it, let alone to expect good to come out of it. In a way, I agree; one should groan over it as a sample of the perversions evil has wrought in the world, and long for something better. But if in spite of everything it is there, and the Lord apparently sees fit to leave it there, then surely my concern is to see what he can make out of such unpromising material. Paul's "thorn in the flesh" came from Satan, and Paul longed to be free of it; but the Lord let it remain, and made it a means of blessing.[48]

What He Needed Most from the Church

In this calling to handle such a thorn, the author explained what he wanted from his church. He wanted a pastor who cared for him. He cried out that his pastor "even if he offers no cure" might "at least offer care. Yes, you turn to your minister. And if you can know in advance that he will give you what you need, the limitless sympathy of a caring pastor, then you're a lucky man indeed."[49] The author described feeling spiritually neglected by clergy but loved by a Jesus who spoke into his shame. It's a gospel-centered vision focused on Jesus. "*He* calls me by name: 'Alex—sinful, hypocritical, embarrassed, homosexual Alex,' He calls; and in doing so He demonstrates both that He knows all about me and that He still loves me in spite of it."[50] This is to be both seen and loved by Jesus. The author longed to be known also by a caring pastor.

And he longed for brothers who truly knew him. With isolation his constant companion, he described a hunger to be known. "You leave your friends, too, at the garden gate; and you're going to be on your own in the house tonight. And brother, it's so *lonely*."[51] He explained, "All I want is a brotherhood open-hearted enough to encourage one to open up one's own heart within it."[52] He described how his loneliness bred bouts of introspective self-pity as well as sexual fantasies and immoral liaisons. "A tremendous help is a wide circle of friendships."[53] He followed Lewis in seeing friendship as being about something other than each other, two friends preoccupied with a third matter of mutual concern.[54]

While homosexuality was a major part of the author's story, he questioned, "Why should I let myself be persuaded that it is the biggest thing in my life?" It's not Jesus. "It has to be put in its place."[55] And, the author of these letters of a Christian homosexual found his hope not in this life but, like Stott, in the age to come. "One day my sanctification here will end and I shall be glorified in heaven, and . . . under the hand of God the finished product will be a splendor for angels to marvel at." He added, "In light of the next world I see that the torments which make me rebel, because God won't explain them, are mere details in the grand purpose which He *has* explained, the bringing of yet another son to glory along the same path by which the eldest Son went, the path of maturity through suffering."[56]

This is a Christian vision for gay people, a vision developed among evangelical Anglicans in Britain in the 1960s and '70s. Under the symbolic leadership of John R. W. Stott, the evangelical Anglicans—so influential among their siblings across the pond—offered a paradigm of care with a vision of God's bringing many sons to glory through Jesus Christ.

four

A Positive Gospel Vision

The church's sponsorship of openly avowed but repentant homo-
sexuals in leadership positions would be a profound witness to
the world concerning the power of the Gospel to free the church
from homophobia and the homosexual from guilt and bondage.

—Richard Lovelace, 1978

C. S. Lewis asked, "What should the positive life of the homosexual be?"
That's the question any gay person who comes to faith in Jesus will ask. Too
often the answer we hear is simply, "No."

No sex. No dating. No relationships.

That leaves people like me hearing that we have, in the words of Eve
Tushnet, a "Calling of No."

What is a calling of yes?[1] That's the question we need to ask. When God
calls us to himself, what does that look like? What is the positive Christian
vision the gospel gives for gay people?

A VOCATION OF YES

Let's think about Lewis, Schaeffer, Graham, and Stott. What positive vision
for gay people do we see among these leaders who were most respected among
evangelical Protestants in the years before the ex-gay movement and the culture war picked up steam?

The thing that stands out most clearly is that they bring a vision of Jesus:
Jesus, in his saving power. Jesus, who washes us and makes us clean. Jesus, who
brings us into God's family. Jesus, who clothes us in his righteousness. Jesus,

who covers shame and forgives sin. Jesus, who calls us by name. Jesus, who sees us all the way down and still wants to be in relationship with us. Jesus, who suffers with and for us. Jesus, who challenges us to live for his kingdom. Jesus, who gives new life with all its joy. Jesus, who is that treasure in a field for which we sold everything. Jesus, who is that treasure that can never be taken from us.

This is Jesus whose inbreaking kingdom sweeps us up into something he is doing in the cosmos, something larger than ourselves. In Christ we find ourselves in a larger narrative. In him we find our true humanness because we were made for God.

This is not Jesus as a means to an end of heterosexual functioning. This is God himself as the end for which we were made. With this God, the locus of hope is found not in this life but in the coming age, when we shall stand before our Savior and be healed. Without that relationship, there is no point in speaking of a biblical sexual ethic. No gay person is going to embrace such an ethic unless they fall in love with Jesus. A heart smitten by grace is not only willing but eager to follow the one who died for us.

All of these Christian leaders held to the historical understanding of the biblical sexual ethic. This certainly meant committing to life in line with God's creational pattern, his design. Not one supported romantic or sexual unions for believers outside of a monogamous marriage between two people of complementary sexes. But they approached gay people from a posture of humility.

Their vision did not flatten us into our unwanted sexual urges. Instead they recognized that a same-sex-oriented believer's biggest struggle may be not with sexual sin but with the ability to give and receive love. So in their teachings, they emphasized the need for the community of the church, for deep, long-term friendships, for brotherhood, to be known even in celibacy. Stott explained, "At the heart of the human condition is a deep and natural hunger for mutual love, a search for identity and a longing for completeness. If gay people cannot find these things in the local 'church family,' we have no business to go on using that expression."[2]

The significance of Stott's words will become clear as we look at them from the other side of the ex-gay movement. Sadly, the intervening decades of the ex-gay movement have left us in a very different place.

Lewis, Schaeffer, Graham, and Stott viewed the homosexual condition not as a cognitive behavioral challenge to be cured but as an unchosen orientation with no reliable cure in this life. They showed great concern for the emotional and relational needs of gay people. They were sensitive to the ways in which the church has been complicit in marginalizing them. They were wary to engage in political activism targeting gays. Yes, with Schaeffer we realize that churches might have to fight to protect their right to enforce their internal discipline, including with hired ministry staff. But with Graham we see a hesitancy to weaponize politics at the expense of the gospel's reaching gay people.

A PARADIGM OF CARE

What is a paradigm of care?

Not control.

Not fixing people.

Not—as Lewis cautioned—using political power to coerce non-Christians to act like Christians.

Not disgust. Like Schaeffer, save your disgust for homophobic preachers who joke about killing gay people.

Not excluding your fellow believers. Not avoiding. Not blaming. Not rejecting. Not fighting.

Not hammering at them with your theology.

But also not compromising a biblical vision for sex, no matter what our surrounding culture says.

And with Stott, not compromising biblical discipline when it's necessary.

Instead feel empathy toward sexual minorities. Weep with them as Schaeffer wept with them.

Champion their human dignity as image bearers.

Defend gay people when under attack. Like Graham calling the White House, intercede for them when they fall. Remember that Jesus "blocks the rocks that get thrown at vulnerable people."[3]

Be honest about the relative fixity of sexual orientation for most people. False hope doesn't help anyone. Be honest about everyone's sin, your own above all others.

Make the radical grace of the gospel central in everything.

Like Lewis, commend gay people who follow Jesus. Tell their stories. Hold them up as models to follow.

Support them, whether in celibacy or in a biblical marriage. Preach our Lord's calling for all believers—straight ones included—to prayerfully consider celibacy. Pull single believers into the center of your church.

Like Schaeffer, invite them into your home, into your family. Don't let them sit alone at home on Christmas Day. Show them what it means to be family in Christ.

Like Lewis, vacation with your gay best friend.

Love gay people the way Jesus loves gay people.

These authors advocated making the church a haven for gay people who follow Jesus. Despite then-widespread hostility to homosexuality in the surrounding culture, we see a positive theological and pastoral approach toward people attracted to members of the same sex, an approach that placed an emphasis not on cure but on care.

A VISION OF DOUBLE REPENTANCE

Richard Lovelace summarized much of this neo-evangelical ethos in a 1978 book on homosexuality. The book came with hearty endorsements by *Christianity Today*'s Ken Kantzer, by Elisabeth Elliot, by Chuck Colson, and by neo-evangelical founding fathers Harold Ockenga and Carl F. H. Henry. Henry had advocated (against fundamentalist Tim LaHaye) for gay civil and human rights two years earlier in his tome *God, Revelation and Authority*.

Lovelace was professor of church history at Gordon-Conwell Theological Seminary and a Presbyterian churchman. His 1979 *Dynamics of Spiritual Life* would lead countless readers into the beauty of a living orthodoxy of continual renewal. His words in *Homosexuality and the Church* might seem radical in today's climate, but in the 1970s they represented a transatlantic neo-evangelical vision. In words John Stott would later quote, Lovelace laid out the gospel challenge.

> There is another approach to homosexuality which would be healthier both for the church and for gay believers, and which could be a very significant witness to the world. This approach requires a double repentance, a repentance both for the church and for its gay membership. First, it would require professing Christians who are gay to have the courage both to avow [acknowledge] their orientation openly and to obey the Bible's clear injunction to turn away from the active homosexual life-style.... Second, it would require the church to accept, honor, and nurture nonpracticing gay believers in its membership, and ordain these to positions of leadership for ministry.
>
> The church's sponsorship of openly avowed but repentant homosexuals in leadership positions would be a profound witness to the world concerning the power of the Gospel to free the church from homophobia and the homosexual from guilt and bondage.[4]

Only the gospel can open up the humility for a dual repentance. Yet this was the Christian vision of Lovelace and Henry, Ockenga and Elliot, Kantzer and Colson, Lewis and Graham, Schaeffer and Stott, and a young gay evangelical Anglican who felt too afraid to use his own name, even though he was still a virgin.

In this positive gospel vision for gay people and the church, we see a focus not on curing homosexuality but on caring for people. We see that the locus of hope lies in the coming age. This present age is a time not for cure but for care.

But a hard shift from care to cure was approaching. The locus of hope soon would shift to this life. For on the Pacific coast of California, a different kind of evangelicalism was percolating—one that would provide a new approach to homosexuality. The ex-gay movement was being born.

part two

The Paradigm of Cure

five

The Birth of a Movement

When we started Exodus the premise was that God could change you from gay to straight.
—Frank Worthen, Founder, Exodus International

It was May 24, 1973, and all week long, successful businessman Frank Worthen had been thinking about the newest—and arguably the raunchiest—gay bathhouse in San Francisco. Tonight would be his night. Frank knew all too well that gay men over forty, like himself, typically got sex only if they paid for it. Paying for sex was certainly an option for Frank. But at this joint, he could at least look on as some of the younger guys did what they did, even if he didn't get any action himself.

Frank had that quick gay-man-wit that comes from spending entirely too much time alone and needing desperately to make yourself lovable. Tonight Frank was getting ready to head out for a time of desire and, if he was lucky, being desired.

That's when the vision descended.

A voice spoke to Frank: "Today I want you back."

Frank knew it was the voice of God.

Frank's heart sank. It was all true after all. And that put a heavy decision before him. A voice in his heart told him that if he hardened his heart and headed to the bathhouse, this decision would be his final rejection of God as his Father.

Frank panicked.

He turned to one of his employees, who had recently become a Jesus freak. "I've just heard from God," Frank explained. "I don't know what to do." Then he took charge of the situation. "Please take me to your church—right now!" Kneeling on the marble steps up to the altar of that Pentecostal church just minutes later, Frank confessed decades of gay hookups.

Or maybe he confessed everything except the hookups. You see, Frank was an incredible storyteller. The basic arc of his testimony remained fairly constant through the decades, but the details sometimes changed. Sometimes his employee didn't know he was gay. Sometimes his employee had had his entire church praying for his gay boss for two years. Sometimes the employee was a brand-new Christian.

This much we know for certain: Frank asked Jesus to be his Savior. Someone—perhaps his employee or maybe his pastor—suggested he record his story on a cassette tape so others could learn from his newfound Christian experience and hear how God was changing him.

That November, Frank bought advertisements in the smuttiest gay newspaper in the City by the Bay. Nestled among the personal ads offering and soliciting gay sex, alongside the homoerotic images, notes about lesbian Wiccan book clubs, and ads for sex shops and peep shows was a solicitation of a different kind. "Do you want out of homosexuality? Send for a Brother Frank tape on a Christ-centered way out of homosexuality."[1]

With that audiocassette tape, the ex-gay movement was born, with Frank Worthen as its pope and first apostle.

LOVE IN ACTION

Six years before Frank Worthen began recording those cassette tapes, a man named Kent Philpott was driving home from his job at JCPenney when he heard the Holy Spirit say, "Go to the hippies of San Francisco." Then Scott McKenzie's psychedelic pop song "San Francisco (Be Sure to Wear Flowers in Your Hair)" began to play on the radio, which seemed to confirm Kent's call. So to San Francisco he went. There he witnessed demonic spirits at an Anchor Rescue Mission outreach. He found himself speaking in tongues behind the pulpit of Lincoln Park Baptist Church. He began to witness numerous conversions, miraculous healings, and exorcisms. After opening various Christian homes for communal living throughout San Francisco, Philpott in 1972 had founded a collective of five charismatic churches known as Church of the Open Door.

That's where he met Frank.

Frank explained that God had instructed him to tell his pastor at Church of the Open Door about his conversion experience. Frank, Kent, and a man named John Evans—who left Ron, his partner of ten years, in order to join the group—launched a ministry they named Love in Action. The first ex-gay ministry was born, right there at the intersection of the Golden Gate Bridge and the Jesus movement. A brand-new believer was rising to become the global Christian expert on the cure of homosexuality. And even though Frank's sexual orientation had not shifted, at the heart of the movement was his personal testimony that he was no longer gay but had left homosexuality—the ex-gay script.

Within Love in Action's first twelve months, sixty people wrote for copies of Frank's tape. He set up support group meetings to help coach others in the process of change. Within a few years, he had transitioned to full-time ministry to men leaving homosexuality. Already comfortably well off because of his business, Frank never would take a paycheck.

In 1975, Pastor Kent Philpott wrote a book highlighting the stories of three women and three men he knew who had been cured of their homosexuality through Love in Action. A newer publisher of mostly charismatic and neo-Pentecostal books, Logos International, took on the project with some reluctance, but the book, *The Third Sex?*, sold well. People started streaming to San Rafael for treatment.

Sadly, the six individuals highlighted in the book expressed a dimmer view of their transformation than what Philpott's book presented. None of the six had in fact become heterosexual. At least four of the six repudiated their accounts almost immediately. On May 5, 1979, these four sent a notarized letter to Logos International informing the publisher that the claims in the book were false and that "none of us have ever changed and become heterosexual." They demanded that publication of the book cease.[2] But the damage was done. Their stories, albeit false, had helped set the template for ex-gay narratives. And that in turn helped build momentum for the nascent ex-gay ministry. "Once that book hit . . . Wow! The dam burst open," Philpott explained. "We had so many people showing up in the middle of the night with a suitcase . . . from the Midwest someplace. It just expanded."[3]

NEW MINISTRIES EVERYWHERE

Other people throughout the country began taking notice that sexual orientation change was possible. In 1974, at the Melodyland Christian Center in Anaheim, California, a man named Michael Bussee was serving as a volunteer counselor when he felt compelled to confess his homosexuality to his supervisor. The supervisor told him he was no such thing. He should instead take power over it and claim his heterosexuality, and keep praying and be set free. The very next year Bussee cofounded EXIT, the Ex-Gay Intervention Team, to provide individual counseling and support groups for people seeking to leave homosexuality. Bussee had no theological or clinical training, but he managed to grow into his ministry quickly.

Claiming his deliverance in Jesus' name, Bussee, with his ministry partner Jim Kaspar and their friend Gary Cooper, cofounded EXIT in the 1-800 helpline center at Melodyland. Like Frank Worthen, they quickly began giving testimonies of change in churches and at conferences. They wrote booklets on how to help a homosexual change and received referrals from pastors. In no time, they found themselves being interviewed on radio and television shows. Pat Robertson had them on his *700 Club*. Pat wanted to know the specifics and whether these ex-gay leaders had been possessed by gay demons. They said no. But by 1976, they were already considered nationally famous as experts in a new area of Christian ministry.

It may have been Jim Kaspar who, while working the phones at Melodyland, first suggested the term *ex-gay*. At the time, he had been calling himself a celibate Christian homosexual. If it wasn't Kaspar, it was Bussee himself.[4] They had been calling themselves ex-gay only a couple months when they founded EXIT.

Ministries were beginning to pop up outside of California too. Seeing the Love in Action model, Greg Reid founded ex-gay ministry EAGLE in Texas. Standing for Ex Active Gay Liberated Eternally, the name EAGLE was also tongue-in-cheek. In the 1970s, nearly every city had a gay bar named Eagle: the Eagle's Nest in New York, the Pittsburgh Eagle, 501 Eagle in Indianapolis, the DC Eagle, Eagle 562 in Long Beach. They weren't a chain. All had different owners. All were leather bars. Reid was signaling to his audience what kind of person would be welcome at EAGLE.

In 1976, Robbi Kenney founded Outpost in a basement in the Twin Cities, below a telephone hotline ministry known as Love Lines. Conceived as an outpost against the attacks of Satan, her ministry focused on the gospel's power to transform and heal homosexuality. Kenney and ex-gay Ed Hurst would soon write a thirty-seven-page booklet titled *Homosexuality: Laying the Axe to the Roots*. In it, they would explain that "overcoming homosexuality requires more than abstinence; it requires dealing with those root issues that give birth to and sustain the homosexual orientation."

A NEW EXODUS OUT OF HOMOSEXUALITY

In 1976, Michael Bussee got his hands on Kent Philpott's *The Third Sex?* and decided to give the folks at Love in Action a call. That September, Bussee helped arrange for sixty-two ex-gays to gather at Melodyland Christian Center in Anaheim. Together these ministry leaders founded an ex-gay umbrella organization that they named Exodus, in reference to the Israelite exodus from Egypt. Bussee describes the optimism they felt as they looked toward the future. "We thought that, called like Moses and directed by God, we could and would lead many gays and lesbians to the heterosexual 'promised land.'"[5] Frank Worthen, Michael Bussee, and Jim Kaspar soon were joined by Ron Dennis, Greg Reid, Robbi Kenney, and Ed Hurst as the early core of Exodus leadership.

"When we started Exodus the premise was that God could change you from gay to straight," explained Worthen. "Most of the world believes that people are born homosexual and can't change, but we don't believe that at Exodus. . . . We believed that there were conditions that created homosexuality and that conditions could get us out of homosexuality. If we could find the answers to why we became homosexual, we'd also find the answers to how to get out of homosexuality."[6]

The cure from gay to straight.

These early ex-gay ministries set the stage for four decades of ministry across the globe. Decades later, in 2000 and 2001, Tanya Erzen interviewed residents of a treatment center Frank founded—New Hope, which replaced Love in Action shortly after that ministry moved to Memphis in 1994. "All those in attendance believed that through Christian faith, religious conversion, and a daily accountable relationship with one another and with God they could heal their homosexuality."[7]

They had reason for optimism. While at another time or in another place, the ex-gay movement might have flopped, the American evangelicalism of the 1970s provided fertile soil for the movement to take root and start to grow.

THE RISE OF POWER RELIGION

The early ex-gay ministries arose in a spiritual soup of positive religion. Religious Americans had already been thinking about the power of positive thinking when the neo-Pentecostal charismatic movement burst onto the scene in the 1960s. Nowhere did power religion reach the dynamic fervor it reached within nondenominational Protestantism in the 1970s. And with it came a tremendous optimism in the power of supernatural transformation in this life.

E. W. Kenyon had developed his theology of positive confession in the first half of the twentieth century. A Free Will Baptist pastor, Essek William Kenyon in 1898 opened Bethel Bible Institute, an institution that eventually would merge into Gordon College. In books like his *Signposts on the Road to*

Success and *A New Type of Christianity*, Kenyon laid out the power of positive confession. "With that Word we conquer disease. We say, 'Disease, in the Name of Jesus Christ, stop being.'"[8] It was this strand of religion that insisted on believing something even over against the facts as perceived on the ground. "Faith is acting in the face of contrary evidence."[9] Within such a theological construct, nothing would be impossible for the Christian. To acknowledge one's ongoing brokenness was to deny the power of the gospel to change.

Kenyon's disciples drove much of the spiritual fervor within the independent charismatic movement of the 1970s. Preacher Kenneth Hagin Sr., pioneer of the Word of Faith movement, frequently plagiarized Kenyon's work.[10] Radio and television preachers, books, and tracts spread the power of positive confession. By the end of the decade, Oral Roberts University professor Charles Farah lamented how rapidly the teaching had spread throughout charismatic evangelicalism, replacing faith with what he saw as presumption.[11]

The resurgent neo-Pentecostalism of the 1970s placed a very optimistic spin on Christian experience. William Branham and Oral Roberts had popularized the healing revival in the 1940s and 1950s. An Episcopal rector in California had been filled with the Holy Spirit as early as 1960. In 1967, the Charismatic Catholic Renewal broke out among college professors at Duquesne, sweeping up more than a million US Roman Catholics over the next decade. Among Protestants, new networks like the Vineyard movement were forming. Talk of miracles and healings were becoming commonplace.

By 1977, a Christian publication even published an account of a woman's breasts miraculously growing back after a mastectomy. After recognizing it as a hoax, Harold Lindsell complained in the pages of *Christianity Today*. "More and more of these have been appearing in the media in recent months. Radio preachers talk about cures; telecasters introduce people who testify that they experienced healing at the hand of God; and periodicals regularly report physical 'miracles.'" He added, "The miracle business is getting out of hand."[12]

Talk of miracles was everywhere.

Hippie charismatic evangelist Lonnie Frisbee displayed his power evangelism in signs and wonders and visions and miracles. Closeted and gay (the term he used), Lonnie became the driving force, with Chuck Smith, in making Calvary Chapel the epicenter of the Jesus movement beginning in the late 1960s. Lonnie, having been immersed in Laguna Beach's gay scene since he was fifteen, had described himself as a nudist-vegetarian-hippie. After reading the gospel of John to friends while on an acid trip and baptizing them all at Tahquitz Falls, Lonnie had a vision of a vast sea of people crying out for salvation, with him preaching to them. His interest at that point gravitated as much to UFOs as to Jesus. But Lonnie moved to San Francisco, where he became a Christian, and by 1968 he was already leading a major ministry at Calvary.

Lonnie was a featured guest on Kathryn Kuhlman's show *I Believe in Miracles*. He later played a key role, with John Wimber, in the birth of the Vineyard movement, including Wimber's theology of power evangelism. Lonnie had shared his testimony at Calvary Chapel early on. He explained that he had come out of homosexuality, thinking they might hear him more easily with those words. But even then he felt rejected by many. Still, Lonnie claimed to be a "seeing prophet" and founded the House of Miracles commune, which morphed into the largest Christian commune in American history. While he hated his homosexuality, Lonnie also had an out-of-control sexual addiction. And he had few places to be known in either realm. It was not uncommon for him to roll out of bed with a stranger Sunday morning before heading to church. Eventually his churches fired him for sexual sin.

Lonnie died of AIDS in 1993. Hundreds gathered for his funeral in Robert Schuller's Crystal Cathedral. His relatives said that he had died of a brain tumor. Chuck Smith hailed him as a Samson, a miracle worker of God whose worst enemy was his own temptation.[13] Frisbee did more than almost anybody to perpetuate the expectation of miracles and supernatural healing within the budding Jesus movement. But sadly, the prophet of a new era of divine healing could not heal himself.

THE DEVELOPMENTAL MODEL
OF HOMOSEXUALITY

The growing belief in miracles and supernatural healing provided a spiritual context for the birth and growth of ex-gay ministries, but the ex-gay ministries also drew on widespread secular models of sexuality.

The terms *homosexual* and *homosexuality* had been coined in 1869 by Hungarian journalist Károli Mária Kertbeny. German psychologist Richard von Krafft-Ebing disseminated that terminology and the theory that homosexuality was a psychiatric disorder stemming from a partially inborn predisposition. Freud, who viewed all people as innately bisexual, had seen homosexual orientation as an arrested state of development, but one that was not reversible.[14] After Freud's death in 1939, newer theories of the development of homosexuality rose to prominence. Psychoanalyst Sandor Rado, a Hungarian émigré to the United States, rejected Freud's theory of innate bisexuality and located the development of homosexuality as a phobic response to members of the opposite sex, stemming from a breakdown of the same-sex parental relationship. The model was one of mental illness.

The developmental model saw further refinement in the following decade. In the 1960s, Irving Bieber and Charles Socarides published broadly accepted but untested psychoanalytic proposals for the cause and cure of homosexuality.[15] *TIME* magazine ran an article in 1965 titled "Homosexuals Can Be Cured." University of Pennsylvania psychiatrist Samuel Hadden had seen success with a group of men under his care. With psychiatric treatment, the men stopped acting and dressing flamboyantly and started dating women.[16]

At the same time, the American Psychology Association (APA) began facing pressure to remove homosexuality as a clinical diagnosis. Despite the popularity of the developmental model among psychiatrists, the APA was also grappling with research from outside its field. Sexologists such as Alfred Kinsey and Evelyn Hooker were suggesting that homosexuality was more common than realized and that most gay people were not raving lunatics. The APA was also under intense pressure from activists outside the organization.

In December of 1973, the APA decided to delist homosexuality as a mental illness from its *Diagnostic and Statistical Manual of Mental Disorders* (DSM-II). But this didn't mean that deeply held professional beliefs evaporated overnight. Of ten thousand voting members, 42 percent voted against the change. And many psychologists still suspected that a homosexual orientation had its foundations in the childhood dynamic with parents of the same and opposite sex.

The revised DSM-II still listed sexual orientation disturbance as a disorder, meaning that clients could still seek professional help if their homosexuality disturbed them.

THE RISE OF CHRISTIAN PSYCHOLOGY

The 1970s were also a time when evangelicals in America were warming up to psychology. Mainline Protestants and Roman Catholics had been well represented within the field for decades, but up to this point evangelicals had tended to view psychology with suspicion.[17] Beginning in 1954, Clyde Narramore began a radio show, *Psychology for Living*, that played on more than two hundred Christian radio stations. The early 1960s saw translations of the works of Swiss convert and therapist Paul Tournier. In 1964, Fuller Seminary was the first Christian school to offer a doctoral program in clinical psychology. Then Rosemead School of Psychology opened in 1970. Three years later

Rosemead launched their *Journal of Psychology and Theology*. In the words of Eric Johnson and Stanton Jones, "The 1970s were a turning point for evangelicals in psychology."[18]

The increasing acceptance of psychology, and the popularity of self-help resources among evangelicals, further set the stage for the evangelical assimilation of developmental models of homosexuality. Clyde Narramore, in his 1960 Zondervan book *The Psychology of Counseling*, advocated the causation theory of a distant father and a smothering mother.[19] This developmental model of homosexuality would play a major role in the ex-gay narrative. Exodus founder Frank Worthen could repeat, "I have always felt that homosexuality was what I call Father Replacement Search. It was caused by a lack of affirmation by a significant male in your life in early age."[20]

These years were also marked by a conservative resurgence within evangelicalism. The mid-1970s saw moderates pushed out of the Lutheran Church–Missouri Synod. And after a decade of planning, Paige Patterson and Paul Pressler orchestrated the conservative takeover of the Southern Baptist Convention in 1979. That year, the Moral Majority launched, heralding the birth of the Religious Right. Within this cultural and religious milieu combining resurgent conservative evangelicalism, charismatic optimism, and supernatural healings with a newfound trust of psychological theories and approaches, the ex-gay movement found fertile soil.

six

"From Gay to Straight"

*Most evangelical churches are very uptight about homo-
sexuality, relatively very accepting of adultery, and the concomitant problems of desertion and divorce.... There is such a
crusade against homosexuals.*

–Joe Bayly, *Eternity*

At the start of 1917, there had never been a communist nation on the map. That
year, revolution came to Russia. By the end of 1949, a third of humanity lived
under communist rule. It was an explosive growth fueled by the fusion of a
powerful ideology, historical circumstance, and human longing. Circumstance
seemed to destine its rapid growth.

Similarly, the stars seemed to align for the explosive growth of the ex-gay
movement. Such tremendous multiplication could not have happened
anywhere else or at any other time. It took a constellation of social and
religious factors. It also required a certain kind of culture, both outside the
church and within it. And a major public health crisis would further fuel the
movement's growth.

RAPID GROWTH

Ex-gay ministries continued to proliferate in the late 1970s and into the
1980s. A group of Christians "concerned for the issue of homosexualism
in the church" organized Liberation in Jesus Christ—originally Sanctuary
House and Liberation.[1] A ministry of the influential, charismatic Truro
Episcopal Church in Fairfax, Virginia, it was likely the first church-based

ex-gay ministry. An advertisement for the ministry explained, "The results of such ministry has seen [sic] a change in the sexual orientation of men and women of all ages."[2] Aiming for a national and international reach, the organization offered counseling and training, with a mission to help proliferate similar ministries elsewhere. In a radio debate, the group's director, Guy Charles, claimed to have been set free from homosexuality. Charles contributed a chapter on homosexuality to a Gary Collins book, published in 1976, titled *The Secrets of Our Sexuality*.[3] He warned in flagship evangelical magazine *Christianity Today* about the rising tide of gay liberation in American denominations.[4]

Soon it seemed like ministries were popping up everywhere. Alan Medinger started Regeneration in 1979, five years after praying to be miraculously delivered from the desire for gay sex. When in the 1980s he started giving his testimony publicly, his boss told him to stop doing so or resign.

Alan resigned.

Arguably the largest of the ex-gay ministries was Homosexuals Anonymous, a fourteen-step ministry with roots in the Seventh-day Adventist Church. Colin Cook and Douglas McIntyre founded the ministry late in 1976. By 1984, the ministry had grown to nearly twenty chapters. By 1986, the ministry would grow to more than sixty chapters.

Cook was a man with quite a past. A former sex addict with more than one thousand partners, Cook admitted to having had sex with underage boys back home in England. "I could have been in prison today—a molester."[5] He had pastored four years in Britain before migrating to the United States in 1971 to pastor a church in Midtown Manhattan. While not attracting crowds while preaching in Battery Park, he was seeking out anonymous sex "from bathrooms to bathhouses to parks, toilets, to massage parlors and everything— three or four times a week with three or four different men."[6] Cook was finally defrocked by the Adventists in 1974 after sleeping with a man in his church.

That low point was the beginning of a remarkable turnaround.

It was at that time that Cook set about the process of sexual conversion from homosexuality to heterosexuality. He journaled about his healing process along the way.

Two years later, now married to a woman, he started Homosexuals Anonymous to help others find the same freedom he had found. By 1979, Adventist officials were so convinced of his cure that the denomination backed him with a grant of forty-seven thousand dollars to start the Quest Learning Center, a treatment facility. Promising freedom from homosexuality, Cook vaulted to national fame, even scoring two appearances on the *Phil Donahue Show*.[7]

Already by the close of the 1970s, ex-gay ministries had proliferated throughout North America. Thousands of people were being touched by these ministries. But something different, something truly horrible, was also spreading quietly in big cities across North America. It would help fuel the growth of the ex-gay movement through the 1980s and into the 1990s.

THE AIDS EPIDEMIC

In 1981, the British medical journal *Lancet* noted cases of a very rare lung infection in five previously healthy young gay men in the Los Angeles area. About the same time, reports arose of cases of rare cancers in a group of men in Los Angeles and New York. By the end of the year, 270 cases had popped up of severe immunodeficiency among gay men. Once symptoms appeared, the disease spread rapidly. Nearly half of the victims had already died.

By September 1982, the condition had been named acquired immune deficiency syndrome. In Africa the disease was being spread among heterosexuals and was known as slim. But in Europe and North America, everyone was becoming afraid of AIDS. There was no cure. There was no treatment. People were panicking. AIDS was a death sentence. And in America and Europe, it was seen as a gay disease.

The following year, cases were reported in children, and hysteria broke out at the thought that the disease could be spread through casual contact. Though researchers ruled out the possibility—the children caught the disease in utero from their mothers—panicked parents refused to let their children use public toilet seats. Churches reconsidered their use of a common cup at Communion, out of fear of catching the virus through saliva.[8] This paranoia lingered for years, long after information on how AIDS actually spread had become common knowledge. In the 2000s, a family left my church in Saint Louis when we agreed to house an ex-gay ministry. They couldn't have their children use a toilet seat that an ex-gay had sat on.

By 1984, a hundred gay men were dying of AIDS every week in the United States. As a middle schooler realizing that year that I was gay, I looked around and saw young men like me getting sick and dying. Other boys were cracking jokes about how skinny the fags got before they popped off. I was terrified. I resolved right then to try not to become sexually active if I could help myself. The risk of HIV was far too real. I felt lucky to have come of age just in time to know the risks. I felt sorry for the guys just a few years older than me who hadn't realized that HIV was spreading.

I remember watching on the news as Ryan White got kicked out of school after receiving HIV through contaminated blood products. I remember when Rock Hudson died. And Liberace. (Though his publicist tried to deny that it was AIDS, the autopsy told the truth.) And then Robert Mapplethorpe. And Arthur Ashe. By the end of the 1980s, a thousand gay men in America were dying of AIDS every week.

In June of 1983, televangelist and Moral Majority founder Jerry Falwell declared AIDS to be God's judgment. "AIDS is not just God's punishment for homosexuals; it is God's punishment for the society that tolerates homosexuals."[9] It seemed God's prophets were demanding intolerance of gay people as a holy obligation.

With the onset of the AIDS crisis, ex-gay ministries seemed like a lifeline to many as they watched friends, lovers, and partners pass away. Ex-gay leader John Smid, who went on to lead Love in Action for more than two decades, explained that the movement's growth was being supercharged by "a tremendous fear of death through the HIV virus."[10] In a 1993 documentary called *One Nation Under God*, Exodus president Sy Rogers explained, "The impact of AIDS on the work of Exodus has been profound."[11] With HIV as the stick, the ex-gay movement dangled the carrot of hope that we could become straight and live a normal life. One ex-gay participant recalls looking for old friends from high school who were gay. "I couldn't find anyone. Just obituaries or death notices."[12]

There is little wonder that ex-gay ministries multiplied and grew between the early 1980s and the discovery of protease inhibitors in 1996.

But there was another factor driving the growth of the movement.

A HOSTILE CULTURE

On March 7, 1967, *CBS Reports* aired on televisions nationwide a special titled "The Homosexuals," the first-ever discussion of the topic on network television. Mike Wallace, who anchored the hour-long documentary, opened by sharing the results of a CBS News poll: Americans considered homosexuality more damaging to the nation than adultery, abortion, or prostitution. Two-thirds of Americans described their reaction to homosexuality as "disgust, discomfort or fear."[13] The show combined interviews with psychologists Socarides and Bieber about the pathology of gay men with cinema verité footage inside a gay bar. Hustlers worked street corners. A teenager was busted by the police in a sex sting. Wallace spoke:

The average homosexual, if there be such, is promiscuous. He is not interested in nor capable of a lasting relationship like that of a heterosexual marriage.... The dilemma of the homosexual: told by the medical profession he is sick, by the law that he's a criminal, shunned by employers, rejected by heterosexual society. Incapable of a fulfilling relationship with a woman, or for that matter with a man. At the center of his life he remains anonymous. A displaced person. An outsider.[14]

No advertisers purchased commercial time during the episode. No one wanted to be associated with so taboo a subject. To men and women with homosexual orientations—most of whom had never revealed that fact to a soul—this was their first portrayal as a group on network television. It was not a flattering one.

Ironically, most homosexually oriented people at the time were very likely in heterosexual marriages. Social norms demanded it, especially for Protestants. To remain single required a convincing cover story. In the United Kingdom, the convention among obituary writers in the twentieth century was to use the phrase "he never married" as a euphemism to indicate that the deceased was homosexual. By the 1970s, American obituaries were using the phrase "confirmed bachelor" as code for single gay men. But most such people remained closeted and followed social convention by marrying.

Fear of gay people was pervasive in 1960s America. The US Congress in 1965 banned the admission into the United States of "sexual deviates." Sexual orientation had already been, since 1952, a basis for expulsion from America for noncitizens. An estimated three hundred thousand people were arrested from the 1940s through the 1960s for crimes like loitering around a public toilet, oral copulation, or "masquerading"—the criminological term for dressing as a member of the opposite sex. Miami made it illegal to employ or to serve two or more suspected gay people in a bar. The news media regularly associated homosexual orientation with crime and violence.

In 1966, just a year before the *CBS Reports* piece, *Time* magazine had spoken of "homosexuals" as deviate, pitiable, pathetic, and sick. Of the gay man, it explained, "A vast majority of people retain a deep loathing toward him." It continued, "Homosexuality is a pathetic little second-rate substitute for reality, a pitiable flight from life.... It deserves no encouragement ... no pretense that it is anything but a pernicious sickness."[15] If these were the words published in a major magazine circulated nationwide, we can only imagine what words were spoken in private.

VIOLENCE AGAINST GAY PEOPLE

And fear bred violence against gay people. On March 9, 1969, Howard Efland checked into the Dover Hotel in Los Angeles under a pseudonym and was beaten to death by officers of the Los Angeles Police Department because he was gay. In 1973, an arsonist burned to death thirty-two people in a New Orleans gay bar called the UpStairs Lounge. San Francisco Board of Supervisors member Harvey Milk, an openly gay politician, was assassinated in 1978.

About that time, native Saint Louisan and foremost playwright Tennessee Williams and a friend were harmonizing the hymn "In the Garden" outside a Key West gay disco one night when five young men jumped Williams and beat him. In a spate of violence against gay people on the island, Baptist minister Rev. Morris Wright had bought an ad in the *Key West Citizen* calling on a hundred islanders to walk down Duval Street with baseball bats and beat gay residents whenever they found one. He claimed it was how they did it on the key back in his day. Tennessee Williams saw his house broken into and ransacked. His garden was trampled down. His gardener and friend was found stripped naked and dead in a pool of blood at Williams's home, two point-blank shots to the head and the neck. An angry mob gathered outside his home, throwing beer bottles and yelling, "Come on out, faggot."[16] Williams quipped, "I've retired from the field of homosexuality at present. Because of age, I have no desires." It was gallows humor.[17]

The term *homophobia* was not coined until 1972, but it was experienced daily by those who either could not or chose not to hide their sexual orientation.[18]

And then there was the church experience.

UNSAFE CHURCHES

Despite the positive vision that evangelicalism's educated elites cast for gay people who follow Christ, very often church culture was no friendlier than the surrounding culture. Often it was much worse.

In 1979, a popular columnist at *Eternity* magazine, Joe Bayly, offered this observation about churches preaching against homosexuality: "Most evangelical churches are very uptight about homosexuality," but they are "relatively very accepting of adultery, and the concomitant problems of desertion and divorce."

Bayly was an original signer of the 1973 Chicago Declaration of Evangelical Social Concern calling out evangelical failures to confront racism, materialism, injustice, and male domination. In that 1979 article he went on to note, "There is such a crusade against homosexuals."

Then he asked, "Why?"

He answered, "I think it's because homosexual sins are their sins, heterosexual sins are ours."[19]

It was easy for churches to crusade against people as if they weren't in the room. They didn't realize they were silently hiding under a pew. And when they did risk seeking support, a lot of people received abuse.

How many young men and women were told they were demon possessed? How many were told that they couldn't be saved unless their orientation changed? How many were told that God hated them, that they were an abomination, that their sin was the unforgivable sin? How many hid their experience out of fear and shame? How many sat in pews as preachers warned against the homosexuals? How many let themselves be pushed into marriages to people they did not love? How many walked away from the church in despair wondering whether Jesus could ever love someone like them?

The day I realized I was gay was also the day I learned that Christians hated gay people—or so it seemed to me. I was at a Christian cousin's wedding. I was eleven years old. I remember realizing how my eyes seemed stuck to one of the groomsmen. Even without any religious baggage, I felt overcome by shame. But when I realized others were staring at me, I felt afraid. I could feel the palms of my hands sweating. That morning, I had overheard that the groom, who came from a Christian family, had a brother. But that brother had been rejected by the family because he was gay. It was terrible to be an eleven-year-old in a Baptist fellowship hall wondering if all these Christians realized what I was. Knowing that if they did, they would hate me.

I can't imagine what it would have been like to grow up in a church filled with people who were afraid of you. But I've heard stories.

Kids who were told by their youth pastor that the reason they were gay was because they had masturbated and got used to the feeling of a male hand on their sex organ. Young women who were afraid to acknowledge being victims of sexual abuse, because people would tell them that's why they were attracted to other women. A young man I knew was told by his mother to leave home before his father got home, because his father would kill him for being gay. He left and never came back. A few years later he was found murdered outside his apartment.

Just this week, a Christian teenager I know of—a friend of a friend—was disowned and kicked out of his house on account of his sexual orientation. He was sleeping outside in the woods in a cold tent for a week with no food and a dying cell phone. Some believers I know have taken him in and are working now to raise money to get him back into college with a dorm room and a meal plan. "I pray my parents will love me again," he said.

If this still happens in the United States in the 2020s, then one can only imagine what it was like in the 1970s and 1980s. Even today, in a culture that is much less hostile, fully 96 percent of people who realized before age twenty that they were gay admit they have prayed and asked God to make them heterosexual.[20] How much more so decades ago when to be gay was to be subject to so much more abuse.

Ex-gay ministries provided a foil of compassion for such marginalization and abuse. In the face of this hostile culture, ex-gay ministries offered safety and hope.

AN ACCEPTING COMMUNITY

For many, ex-gay ministries provided the first space in which they felt safe enough to be honest about themselves and their human experience. Ex-gay ministries provided them with the community, acceptance, and support they did not find in their churches. In the later years of the movement, it was expected that believers would sometimes fail. That shocked no one. What mattered was your willingness to let others help you get back on your feet. Nobody was shocked to find out you liked other guys or other women. Ex-gay ministries are often depicted as psychologically abusive and manipulative, but a lot of people felt a lot of love within ex-gay ministries, even if they eventually parted ways with the ex-gay approach.

Even Michael Bussee of EXIT, who is now a critic of the movement, acknowledged the good some saw there. "Some had a positive, life-changing experience attending our Bible studies and support groups. They experienced God's love and the welcoming fellowship of others who knew the struggle."[21]

Positive stories are not hard to find, even with all the stories of pain.

As part of an ethnographic study, Jan Gelech asked sixteen homosexually attracted Christian men about their experiences within ex-gay ministries. The responses show that during their time with these ministries, many people found community and forged bonds of kinship that would last throughout their lives. In the face of a hostile culture and unsafe churches, the ex-gay movement provided space for a lot of believers to breathe.

One man named Seth commented, "It opened my eyes [to the fact] that God values . . . a homosexual just as much as a heterosexual." He added, "It helped me see that I am a man because God made me a man . . . [that] the defining characteristics of men isn't [sic] hunting and fishing and drinkin' beer and watching the Superbowl."

Brad noted, "For the first time, it gave me a safe space where I could say 'This is who I am' . . . 'this is what I am feeling.' . . . That ministry probably saved my life . . . having that kind of safe space where people listened . . . without judgment and I felt commonality with other men . . . pulled me back from a pretty scary place." He commented on how he felt reaffirmed in his gender. "What they taught me was the confidence to say, 'Even if I'm not a jock-playing guy, I am still male. And I have something to offer in that.'"

Jordan explained, "It was a safe place to share. You could be open . . . you wouldn't be made fun of or mocked or anything . . . they weren't there to judge."[22]

The Friendships

I spoke with a man who had lost a government contract for downloading gay porn at work. It led to the loss of his job as well as his wife and the respect of his kids. He spent some time in a residential treatment center. The program was six to nine months, and he got two extensions. "God did a work in my heart," he said. He has fond memories of being together with other men who were also seeking sexual integrity. "I made a lot of friends there. It was a fun time in the midst of pain and heartbreak. There was a camaraderie there. That's the thing I miss most." After being discharged, he made it twenty-seven months. After his first failure, though (he masturbated), he broke down, devastated and disgusted with himself. Lacking his family's support, he found his way to a Vineyard church, where a male member seduced him. It was the first time he had been with a man. It led to years of regrets, infection with HIV, and his questioning his faith. He says his time in an ex-gay ministry was the last time he felt like he was truly known and loved.[23]

EXIT's Michael Bussee described the powerful hope instilled by friendships in the ministry. "I met a good, close, Christian friend; he was willing to let me be close to him and love him in a nonsexual way. This completely changed and challenged my ideas on love and sex in general. I had always confused the two. Here was someone loving me with Christ's love in a nonsexual way. I began to see maybe my need to be loved was not bad in itself. Maybe I could express that. Maybe I could get the love I needed without having it turn into a sinful situation."[24]

Richard Holloman had pastored since 1972, a Southern Baptist Theological Seminary–trained pastor, widower, and dad when his double life caught up with him in 1995. "The last thing I wanted anyone to know was my experience of my sexuality." After being exposed and undergoing church discipline, he found his way to Exodus, looking for support and help. "At that time, Exodus was still all about changing orientation. I never bought into that. But there was also an emphasis on discipleship, on intimacy with the Lord. For the past twenty-five years, I've been able to be transparent about my sexual reality, having peace with that." He explained to me, "It was a very powerful experience. Not only Exodus but the relationships. That was new for me in those days. I had been so legalistic." The annual conferences were a lifeline. "There was something about men and women with a kindred spirit. They provided a network of support throughout the year." Exodus brought him to a place where he could say, "I'm loving my life in the way I can be open about my sexuality." Holloman went on to found Sight Ministry—a Nashville-based Exodus affiliate—in 2003.[25]

Nowhere Else to Go

Roger Jones of Denver-based Where Grace Abounds commented, "There was a lot really good about Exodus. There was nowhere else to go if you were gay and Christian. It was encouraging to be at a conference with a thousand other people."[26] Jill Rennick started attending conferences in 1997. "I loved Exodus conferences. I felt known. I no longer felt uniquely twisted, uniquely perverted. And Alan Chambers and Randy Thomas were hilarious. It was the first time I had ever laughed about my same-sex attraction. It was the first time I wasn't so tense."[27]

"Exodus International certainly represented a much safer place than the vast majority of churches for Christians to be transparent about their experience of same-sex attraction," reflected Exodus speaker Nate Collins in 2013. In speaking about the affiliate ministries then-remaining with the organization—those not focused on reorientation—Collins saw that their biggest strength was their people. "Exodus-affiliated ministries, and other independent ministries not formally associated with Exodus International, that exist today continue to represent enormous reservoirs of godly wisdom and decades of valuable experience in coming alongside individuals who struggle with same-sex attraction."[28]

Many ex-gays found in ex-gay ministries the love and support they didn't find in their congregations. More than one ex-gay minister quipped, "If the church were doing its job, we wouldn't be needed." In 2001, when Alan Chambers was being interviewed by the Exodus International hiring committee, they asked him, "What does success look like for you as the Executive Director of Exodus International?" His answer was quick: "Success looks like Exodus going out of business because the Church is doing its job."[29]

The ex-gay movement offered for many a haven where they could bring into the open two seemingly incompatible strands of their lived experience: homosexuality and Christianity. A lot of people experienced grace in the midst of their brokenness.

But even more central to the movement was the conviction that while grace should be given to you as a sinner, grace would not leave you there. Central to the movement's optimism was the motto of Exodus International: "Change is possible." And for many Exodus ministries, one particular change was in view. Explained Worthen, "When we started Exodus the premise was that God could change you from gay to straight."[30]

And the churches were starting to take notice.

By the early years of the 1980s, the ex-gay movement had already begun to step from the fringes of the charismatic movement to gain a place of acceptance within conservative evangelicalism. A February 6, 1981, cover of *Christianity Today* declared, "Homosexuals CAN Change."

The ex-gay movement began with a clearly focused goal of becoming heterosexual. It was called ex-gay for a reason. How were they pulling it off?

seven

Conversion Therapies

There is no such thing as a homosexual. Everyone is heterosexual. Some of you may have a homosexual problem. But you are still a heterosexual.

—Joseph Nicolosi

This would be Josh's eighth stab at conversion therapy. Since his parents caught him looking at gay porn at age ten, he had been taken to therapists and ministries promising to help cure his homosexuality. For Christmas that first year, he asked to be able to stop going to therapy. Through his adolescence and teen years, every time he told a pastor about his problem, the pastor's solution was another counselor, another program, or another Exodus conference.

Altogether he went to eight Exodus conferences.

He had a NARTH counselor and a session with Joseph Nicolosi himself. He tried a residential program. Each program, ministry, or conference held out new hope. "Maybe this time it will work," he would think.[1] His experience was not really a new one.

A HISTORY OF CONVERSION THERAPY

The ex-gay movement was hardly the first attempt to cure homosexuality. Humans have long pondered the causes of the condition. The 1728 treatise *Plain Reasons for the Growth of Sodomy in England* identified the causes of sodomy as drinking tea, "sitting up late on nights, eating meat suppers, drinking wine and other strong liquors," a lack of exercise, and of course "Italy, the Mother and Nurse of Sodomy" and "the pernicious presence of Italian Opera."[2]

Sadly, there is a dearth of peer-reviewed research on whether switching to coffee and Shakespearean tragedy is an effective cure to the problem.

One astrologer in the 1960s explained that homosexuality was caused when "in the natal horoscope, Uranus retrograde in Aries opposes the Sun, Mercury and Mars in Libra, with Mercury being in the critical 30th degree of that sign, or zero degrees of Scorpio."[3] He would have made fourth-century astrologer Firmicus Maternus proud. Other theories have centered on having a clubfoot, being hunchbacked, or masturbating. On the eve of the ex-gay movement, organic farming advocate Bob Rodale suggested in *Prevention* magazine that fluoridated drinking water was the cause. San Francisco had fluoridated water.[4]

The quest for a cure to homosexuality has been just as diverse.

In the nineteenth century, German psychiatrist Albert von Schrenck-Notzing claimed to be able to cure homosexuality with forty-five sessions of hypnosis.

In 1904, doctors sought to eliminate same-sex orientation in a lonely thirty-nine-year-old "gentleman degenerate" in Saint Louis by severing the pudic nerve supplying the testes, effectively making both an erection and orgasm impossible. Dr. Charles H. Hughes—possibly himself the surgeon—afterward concluded, "The case appears to be in the head and not in the genitals."[5]

Other forms of conversion therapy also relied on surgical intervention.

In 1916, Austrian endocrinologist Eugen Steinach pioneered testicle transplantation as a treatment for homosexuality. His first case was during the Great War, when a thirty-one-year-old gunner had to be castrated because of tuberculosis. Since the gunner was homosexual, they proposed transplanting a testicle from a heterosexual soldier who had to have his undescended testicle removed. After the procedure, the soldier claimed to begin experiencing heterosexual longings and later married a woman. What followed in the 1920s was a rush of homosexual men signing up for a procedure that involved castration—removing their homosexual testicles—and replacing them with donated heterosexual testicles. Richard Mühsam in Berlin used the testicles of "hypersexual" men in his practice to improve the odds of success. The brief boom in testicle transplants in an effort to cure homosexuality may not have been strictly voluntary. Men known to law enforcement as homosexuals may have felt they had no alternative.[6]

The desire to cure homosexuality never went away.

THE EXPERIMENTS

During the Second World War, Dachau and Buchenwald were centers for Nazi experiments to cure homosexuality. There Danish endocrinologist Carl

Værnet implanted tubes of testosterone into the groins of subjects, in the belief that testosterone could cure the condition. Some men died of infection from the procedure. At the Flossenbürg camp, homosexual men were forced to have sex with female sex slaves—typically Jewish and Roma women—weekly in an attempt to convert them to heterosexuality. Castration was also used in an attempt to cure homosexuality. A 1943 decree allowed castrated subjects to transfer from the concentration camp to fight in the Dirlewanger penal division on the Eastern Front—itself practically a death sentence. Concentration camp survivor Josef Kohout's experience was chronicled in the 1972 book *Die Männer mit dem Rosa Winkel—The Men with the Pink Triangle*—under the pseudonym Heinz Heger.[7]

After the war, lobotomies were performed on homosexual men and women, in an effort to cure them. In the United States, Walter Freeman promoted the procedure and personally lobotomized as many as sixteen hundred men and women to cure their homosexuality. Freeman would insert a common ice pick into the brain's frontal lobe and sever the prefrontal cortex. It was a brutal procedure with life-altering consequences. Some patients died.[8]

Well into the 1970s, at least one California prison still gave repeat homosexual offenders the grim choice between being castrated or being lobotomized. Freeman in 1971 claimed to have "severed the frontal lobes" of gay inmates at Atascadero, a state prison for the criminally insane—a category that included homosexual men.[9] A 1972 article in the *Advocate* denounced the facility as "Dachau for Queers" for its use of lobotomies, castration, and electroshock therapy on gay men.[10] Inmates could be sentenced to Atascadero indefinitely for having oral sex in a private hotel room while suspicious officers stood atop a stool and peeped in through the transom. That violation of Penal Code 289a is what got Eldridge Rhodes and Thomas Earl sentenced to Atascadero in 1962.[11] Inmates suffered permanent brain damage resulting in the inability to feed and bathe themselves. They experienced bodily mutilation. The psychological scars would last a lifetime.

While Freeman promoted lobotomy, other therapists targeted other portions of the brain. Starting in 1962, seventy-five gay men in Germany received hypothalamotomies—surgical removal of the hypothalamus.

A 1970 scientific study at Tulane University implanted electrodes into the pleasure centers of a gay man's brain and gave him pleasurable stimuli while he looked at pornographic images of women, and then later as he had sex with a New Orleans prostitute—hired with special permission of the Louisiana attorney general. Such research was not controversial at the time.[12]

There were a lot of experiments.

AVERSION THERAPY

The decade of the 1960s had seen significant research into aversion therapy. In one form of aversion therapy, gay men would be shown homoerotic images, and if they showed any physiological response, electrodes would release a shock. The device manufacturer Farrall Instruments included in the box with the shock-emitting device a collection of 35mm slides of heterosexual and homosexual sex acts and male and female nude models.[13] Other doctors used apomorphine, a drug that induced nausea and diarrhea. The goal was to train the psyche to associate homoeroticism with suffering.

Some early Christian practitioners used aversion therapy in their practices, though it never would become an accepted approach in the ex-gay movement. A November 25, 1977, issue of the *Minneapolis Star* ran an article titled "Homosexual Desire Can Be Changed, Counselors Say." The article interviewed William Backus of the Roseville, Minnesota, Center for Christian Psychological Services. Backus was an ordained Lutheran minister and an advisory board member of the American Association of Christian Counselors until his death in 2005. The center "has a treatment program for those wishing to change a homosexual orientation to a heterosexual one." Backus's approach, he explained, "involves pairing thought and/or pictures of the problem object or behavior with a brief, but painful, electric shock, usually administered to the arm."[14]

Jeremy Gavins described what his first appointment at such a program was like. When he was eighteen years old, he was forced to undergo the therapy on threat of expulsion from his Catholic school. "I was met by a male nurse; he took me to some changing rooms and said, 'Take all your clothes off, put them in a locker, and put these on.' He pointed to some slippers and a dressing gown." Gavins added, "I could tell by the way he looked at me that he hated every inch of my body." They strapped Jeremy into a chair and showed him two screens. One would have images of men, the other images of women—some naked, some not. "Before we began he leant forward and opened my dressing gown," explaining he needed to watch this teenager's penis to monitor for signs of an erection. The first shock was excruciating. He tried to explain to the doctor how painful it was. "It's supposed to be," was the doctor's curt reply. "It was a pain I'd never felt before," Gavins said. "What you try to do is lift your arm away from it but you can't because you're strapped down." That first session lasted an hour and twenty minutes.[15]

I remember my sociology teacher explaining to me about aversion therapy in ninth grade. I remember feeling some hope at the possibility of change, though it sounded very violent. My teacher explained that the success rates weren't very good. Of course, therapy of any kind would have required conversations I wasn't emotionally ready to have as a fourteen-year-old.

While early advocates of aversion therapy claimed success rates of 50 percent, most therapists abandoned the practice not because they thought it inhumane but because they found it ineffective. It simply did not work.

THE REPARATIVE THERAPISTS

By the 1990s, nearly all ex-gay ministries were experiencing a powerful influence from the secular world of psychology. Reparative therapy had arisen as a secular model of psychological reorientation therapy. Basing their thinking on the foundational work of Elizabeth Moberly and Joseph Nicolosi, reparative therapists postulated that male homosexuality was an unconscious attempt to self-repair feelings of masculine inadequacy.

Within this model, homoerotic feelings represented an unconscious attempt to meet normal, masculine emotional needs. Attraction to members of the same sex was an effort of self-repair. Reparative approaches, which came to pervade the ex-gay movement by the 1990s, gave an alternative framework to simple iniquity. Within a reparative framework, homosexual temptation became more about Daddy issues and less about the believer's fight against the world, the flesh, and the devil.

In 1983, British research psychologist Elizabeth Moberly published *Homosexuality: A New Christian Ethic* and laid out a psychological treatment plan for male homosexuality. Moberly proposed that, over against the Freudian hypothesis of the domineering mother, male homosexuality was caused by a childhood failure to bond with the father. A boy feeling neglected by his father and ambivalent toward other males unconsciously sought to repair these deficits. His need for male bonding became sexualized. It is likely that Moberly coined the term *reparative therapy*.

I remember sitting in my college apartment in Charlottesville, reading my first reparative therapy book as a young Christian in the early 1990s. I remember reading that my dad made me gay.

I was livid.

If only he had taught me to play football, I wouldn't have wanted that Easy-Bake Oven.

The early 1990s was a time of rapid growth for reparative therapy.

Joseph Nicolosi

No one did more to popularize reparative therapy than American psychologist Joseph Nicolosi. By the late 1980s, Nicolosi had started using Moberly's approach in his private practice. In 1980, he had founded the Thomas Aquinas Psychological Clinic in Encino, California, specializing in the treatment of men wishing to diminish their sexual attraction to men and develop heterosexual potential. Adopting Moberly's model, Nicolosi nevertheless took the credit as the father of reparative therapy, leading to a six-year public feud between him and Moberly that ended when Moberly cut ties with the ex-gay movement in 1996 to focus her effort on AIDS research.

Nicolosi shared one thing with Homosexuals Anonymous. "There is no such thing as a homosexual," he stated. "Everyone is heterosexual. Some of you may have a homosexual problem. But you are still a heterosexual. 'Homosexual' is simply a description of a psychological disorder, prompted by an inner sense of emptiness."[16] Nicolosi was not always consistent in his use of terminology. Elsewhere he spoke of "non-gay homosexuals" as distinct from "gay homosexuals."[17]

During reparative therapy, the client was encouraged to explore what feelings, longings, or desires might underlie their homoerotic attractions. Typically, the therapist would explore for childhood trauma, seeing homosexuality as an unconscious attempt to repair that trauma. Was there sexual or emotional abuse? Was there negative parental messaging about the client or their gender? By identifying and resolving these emotional wounds, the client hoped to lessen or resolve their same-sex attractions.

One client of Nicolosi described his experience. Gabriel Arana was fourteen when he started reparative therapy with Nicolosi, and they had weekly sessions for more than three years. "Nicolosi explained what he meant by 'cure.' Although I might never feel a spark of excitement when I saw a woman walking down the street, as I progressed in therapy, my homosexual attractions would diminish." Typical sessions explored what underlay his attractions. "We mostly talked about how my damaged masculine identity manifested itself in my attractions to other boys," Arana explained. "Nicolosi would ask me about my crushes at school and what I liked about them. Whether the trait was someone's build, good looks, popularity, or confidence, these conversations always ended with a redirect: Did I wish I had these traits? What might it feel like to be hugged by one of these guys? Did I want them to like and accept me?" As he progressed in therapy, Arana did feel he was gaining insight into sources of his attractions. "The problem was, they didn't go away." In Arana's senior year of high school, Nicolosi announced to his parents that therapy had been a success.

"Your son will never enter the gay lifestyle." A few weeks later the housekeeper caught Arana in the backyard with another boy. There had been no change is his sexual orientation.[18]

NARTH

In 1992, Nicolosi, with Benjamin Kaufman and Charles Socarides, founded the National Association for Research and Therapy of Homosexuality (NARTH), based in Nicolosi's clinic. A secular organization, NARTH nevertheless worked closely with faith-based ex-gay ministries. Mike Rosebush, who headed Exodus International's professional counselors network, remembers seeing Joseph Nicolosi's application come across his desk. Nicolosi wanted to get referrals from Exodus. But Rosebush struggled with whether to approve him. Exodus counselors had to have a Christian testimony. Imagine the irony of the largest ex-gay ministry rejecting the application of the founder of NARTH.

Rosebush saw that Nicolosi was Roman Catholic, but he saw nothing to signal an active faith in Jesus. Yet this was the presumed father of reparative therapy. This was Joseph Nicolosi.

So he signed off on it.

Prominent among the self-professed reparative therapists was Richard Cohen. Though his professional credentials were never completely clear, Cohen established the International Healing Foundation in 1990. In its first decade, it had more than twelve thousand clients.[19] At the time, Cohen, who was born Jewish, was a member of the Unification Church. Saying he had been cured of homosexuality through psychotherapy, Cohen in 1982 married Jae Sook, a South Korean woman suggested to him by church leader Sun Myung Moon. The couple later left the Moonies. In 2003, Cohen opened Positive Approaches to Healthy Sexuality (PATH). Frequently in the public eye, Cohen appeared on numerous television shows, including *20/20*, *Rachel Maddow*, *Ricki Lake*, *Larry King Live*, *The O'Reilly Factor*, *Jimmy Kimmel Live*, and *Paula Zahn Now*.

As with faith-based ex-gay ministries, expectations of success could vary. Roman Catholic reparative therapist Richard Fitzgibbons wrote in 1996, "It has been my clinical experience that the recovery rate from the emotional pain and subsequent homosexual behavior approaches 100% in those who are truly committed to the process. . . . As the emotional wounds are healed, homosexual attractions and behaviors diminish and eventually disappear."[20] In a 1997 letter to the *Wall Street Journal*, Fitzgibbons, Nicolosi, Socarides, and two other leaders in reparative therapy were somewhat less optimistic.

"A variety of studies have shown that between 25% and 50% of those seeking treatment experienced significant improvement."[21]

Meanwhile political conservatives were finding the reparative therapists to be useful allies in a rapidly escalating culture war. In 1998, prominent reparative therapist and NARTH board member George Rekers provided expert testimony in Washington, D.C., before the Human Rights Commission on behalf of the Boy Scouts of America, defending their policy of excluding gays. In 2004, he provided expert witness in an Arkansas gay adoption case and did the same in Florida in 2008. His 1982 book *Growing Up Straight: What Every Family Should Know about Homosexuality* explained how to prevent your children from growing up gay.[22]

Masculinity Retreats

Some reparative therapists developed therapeutic retreats as an adjunct to clinical counseling. People Can Change, founded in 2000, offered its Journey into Manhood weekend retreats. Many participants loved the time with other men, with trust-building exercises, visualizations, and role playing. Counselor David Matheson and Rich Wyler—who both claimed to have been cured of homosexuality through reparative therapy—developed Journey into Manhood to help others along in the process.

"You walk into a room with these men and suddenly they know more about you than people your whole life have known about you," said one participant. "It's been life changing. It's been a whole new take on life. It's been absolutely miraculous, for me personally." He added, "I feel some of the feelings or the attractions from time to time, you bet, that can be there. But I don't feel the compulsion anymore to have to pursue that."[23]

People Can Change later rebranded as Brothers on a Road Less Traveled.

Blake Smith participated in retreats, including ones with Journey into Manhood. "My homosexual feelings have nearly vanished," he told the *New York Times* in 2012. "In my 50s, for the first time, I can look at a woman and say 'she's really hot.'"[24] Followed up on eight years later, he said his attractions to other men have diminished further, and his attraction to his wife has increased. He added that his gender dysphoria, which plagued him much of his life, has completely resolved. "I'm comfortable with my masculinity. I'm comfortable in a masculine world." He now leads the men's ministry in his Latter-day Saints congregation. Smith noted that he doesn't like the term *ex-gay* because he never had identified as gay.[25]

One optional yet controversial practice of Journey into Manhood included older participants holding or cuddling younger men to fulfill unmet childhood needs for physical touch. One former participant, though, described everyone being asked to strip naked together, an experience he found traumatic.[26] That practice was subsequently ended, though it continued in the ManKind Project's New Warrior Training program.

The ManKind Project was a favorite of reparative therapists as a means of restoring damaged masculinity in their clients. In a 2010 court case, an Orange County, California, lawyer sued his employer after being fired for refusing to go to the New Warrior Training. Reports included an event that "included 30 to 50 men sitting naked in a circle on the floor of a candlelit room called the smoke hut. A large wooden dildo called 'The Cock' was passed around the room. The man holding 'The Cock' was asked to describe in graphic detail a sexual experience from his life."[27]

To be clear, in my faith tradition, the outward and ordinary means of grace are the Word of God, the sacraments, and prayer.[28]

Professional reparative therapist David Pickup, a senior staff member for the ManKind Project, had been a student of Joseph Nicolosi.[29] Nicolosi, Richard Cohen, Arthur Goldberg, and Paul Miller all recommended the program. In 2020, the program's website still stated, "We welcome men of all sexual orientations . . . including those who identify as having unwanted same-sex attraction."[30]

The demand for reparative therapy was high throughout the 1990s. Exodus functioned as a clearinghouse and referral service for ex-gay affiliate ministries and for reparative therapists. By 1999, director Bob Davies estimated that Exodus had fielded two hundred thousand calls for assistance.[31]

eight

The Ex-Gay Script

Accompanying these erotic and emotional changes is a change in self-perception in which the individual no longer identifies him or herself as homosexual.

—Alan Medinger, Executive Director, Exodus International

"Mr. Johnson, we would like to thank you for your past support of the Lambda Defense Fund. Your generous support has helped us advance the LGBT cause."

I was in seminary at the time. This was back before cell phones displayed phone numbers, back when prank calls to landlines were a thing. I had never donated to such an organization. I was pretty sure I knew what this was. Seminarians aren't always particularly mature. Or kind. But not being certain, I decided to play along.

"Actually, I'm batting for the other team these days. I know they say that doesn't happen. But I'm not gay anymore."

I'm not sure what they expected. But the call was over soon enough.

Obviously, if my fellow students were teasing me about it, I wasn't fooling anyone. Mine was a glass closet. But I was trying to convince myself. I was an ex-gay.

APPROACHES WITHIN THE EX-GAY MOVEMENT

For the most part, the ex-gay movement did not embrace many practices like aversion therapy. But the movement would turn to various other approaches —alongside reparative therapy—to bring about a change in sexual orientation.

Exodus International itself was an umbrella organization involving hundreds of ex-gay ministries. Most focused on sexual orientation change efforts, though others downplayed such expectations, especially in the movement's later years. Some were deliverance ministries. Others were residential treatment centers. Still other Exodus affiliate ministries focused on sexual integrity or on identifying the underlying causes of homosexuality. Homosexuals Anonymous had an approach all its own. And the reparative therapists took a clinical approach to treating individual patients in private offices and counseling centers across North America.

Ex-Gay Deliverance Ministries

Some ex-gay ministries focused on inner-healing prayer for supernatural deliverance from homosexuality. Leanne Payne of Pastoral Care Ministries represents one such advocate for a cure through prayer. Of homosexuality she wrote, "As a condition for God to heal, it is (in spite of the widespread belief to the contrary) remarkably simple."[1] The path of healing was through prayer to Jesus.[2]

EXIT's Michael Bussee approached homosexuality the same way he would approach people struggling with drug addiction, gang membership, and prostitution. "Whatever you claim in Jesus' name, it will happen if you have faith. If you want a physical healing, claim that," Bussee explained. "We believed that by professing it, it had become real on a spiritual level already in heaven, and that if we kept professing it, it would happen here on Earth."[3]

Some ministries would develop a genogram, or spiritual family tree, to identify family curses sent down from previous generations. Then through intense, concerted intercession, they would seek to break the bondage of such curses.

Bill Prickett, who directed Alabama ex-gay ministry Coming Back in the late 1980s, describes his experience with deliverance-based ministry. "I had hands laid on me, I was anointed with oil, I had demons cast out of me, I prayed prayers confessing the sins of generations past—the sins that my fore-parents may have committed. I would try anything because I wanted to overcome these temptations."[4]

In a *Christian Life* magazine article titled "I Was Delivered from Lesbianism," Darlene Bogle, founder of Exodus affiliate ministry Paraklete, explained how she had been "demonically indwelt" by lesbianism but "took authority over the spirits of homosexuality in the name of Jesus and served them their 'vacate-the-premises-immediately' papers and so they had to leave."[5] Still, she admitted that all her struggles didn't leave overnight. Bogle chronicled her ex-gay narrative in two books, *Long Road to Love* in 1985 and *Strangers in a Christian Land* in 1990.

Christian ministries unaffiliated with Exodus were (and in some cases still are) taking deliverance ministry to another level through exorcism. A 1973 deliverance ministry text titled *Pigs in the Parlor* attributed homosexuality to demonic influence. Exorcist Bob Larson purported to have successfully exorcised a demon of homosexuality. A 2009 exorcism on YouTube by the charismatic church Manifested Glory Ministries showed a sixteen-year-old gay boy being forcibly held down, writhing on the floor, and vomiting into a bag as church members berated the "homosexual demon" inside him.[6]

While they were a minority among Exodus affiliates, deliverance ministries were always part of the mix, both within Exodus and beyond it.

Love in Action and the Residential Treatment Centers

The flagship ministry of Exodus International had always been Frank Worthen's Love in Action (LIA), first in California and later in Memphis. In later years clients paid up to three thousand dollars a month to stay at the facility. Some clients remained inpatient for years. Residents received group counseling and instruction as well as weekly individual counseling.

In the beginning, the ministry was strongly focused on orientation change. But in later years LIA had at best an ambiguous relationship to orientation change.

On one hand, it did not promise full conversion from gay to straight. One Love in Action supporter argued that in its later years "Love in Action never portrayed that they were intending on changing someone's sexual orientation, but rather, they offered tools for people who were making the decision to not act upon their homosexual desires."[7] Perhaps on a technical level such an assessment could be valid, at least for some LIA staff and clients.

On the other hand, the idea that LIA wasn't selling orientation change may stretch the realm of plausibility. The suggestion of a cure was powerfully present everywhere. Frank Worthen's recorded testimony was titled *The Brother Frank Testimony: Let Jesus Break the Chains of Homosexuality*. He had spoken of the ministry's foundational promise that "God could change you from gay to straight."[8] Ministry materials sported the motto "Finding Freedom from Homosexuality through Jesus Christ." The application packet for the program read, "If you struggle with these feelings, . . . as [God] draws you out of isolation and takes you through the process of becoming honest about your brokenness, you will find (perhaps to your surprise!) that healing will begin to come through other people."[9]

Participants listened to lectures with titles like *The Essence of Change, Tools for Overcoming Homosexuality*, and *Tracking the Change Process*. Churches supported Love in Action with the expectation that it was curing homosexuality. Men, women, and youth signed up—or were signed up—for the program because of the hope that it would cure their homosexuality.[10] People didn't go to Love in Action because they wanted to masturbate less. They were seeking reorientation, and there was a lot to suggest that's what Love in Action was selling, even in its later years. A desperate teenager, loaded down with shame and facing expulsion from his church or family, would hear in all this talk of change a promise of becoming straight.

Frank Worthen had claimed a 70 percent success rate in a 1988 Associated Press article.[11] A 2008 *Memphis Commercial Appeal* report on LIA stated, "Of 400 people who have gone through the program, more than 300 have been turned straight, the group says." It then quoted Love in Action director Jim Scott: "Our success rate is higher than our dropout rate.... It works for some people, and for some people it doesn't."[12]

Like many Exodus ministries, Love in Action relied on a developmental model of homosexuality. The belief was that homosexuality was a result of an unhealthy dynamic in the family of origin, so they sought to identify those dynamics through counseling. The expectation was that God could heal the experiences of sin- and family-induced hurt they identified. This healing in turn would lead toward sexual fidelity and open the door to heterosexuality.

Classes covered topics such as masculinity and femininity, with the aim of training clients to present themselves in ways that seemed, you know, less gay. Men were taught how to throw a football and how to change the oil in a car. They were taught how to cross their legs so they didn't look gay. The hope was that by reinforcing the masculine or feminine identity, a corresponding internal shift might lead to a change in sexual preference.

High Expectations

Client expectations were high at residential centers. Tanya Erzen, drawing on her immersive ethnographic study of clients at New Hope, a treatment program in California, stated, "All of the New Hope participants . . . believed that through Christian faith, religious conversion, and a daily accountable relationship with one another and with God they could heal their homosexuality. Desires or attractions might linger for years, but . . . God would eventually transform them."[13]

Residential treatment centers were viewed as the best hope for orientation change. One ex-gay man I interviewed told me about his enrollment in Love in Action after its move to Memphis. The ministry representative suggested he had a 50 percent chance of coming out straight if he enrolled and progressed through the program. After years of trying every other alternative, he heard that 50 percent as a virtual certainty of a cure. But between the cost of treatment and his lost wages, this option was expensive.

For those with fewer resources, there were cheap and even free options closer to home.

Nonresidential Exodus Affiliates

Exodus International was composed of hundreds of affiliate ministries with diverse approaches to ministry. Jill Rennick remembers attending her first Exodus conference at Asbury College in 1997. Most participants arrived with a group from their local affiliate ministry, but Jill was alone. She noticed from the start that various ministries had very different models. Participants from Living Hope ministry in Dallas had only their first names on their name tags. They weren't allowed to know each other's last names or have any contact with each other outside the group lest they become emotionally enmeshed or have sex with each other. Other ministries were much less structured and less rule-oriented.

Jill's first days at the conference were eye-opening. "I had never met a gay man before. Within thirty minutes, I realized my own deep homophobia. I climbed up into the balcony and I prayed, 'Lord, I want you to change my heart. Take away my fear. Let me be present.'"

Shortly afterward a group of guys from Where Grace Abounds were playing speed Uno in the campus coffee shop. "Come play with us!" they insisted. Rennick reminisces, "They were real people with real faces with stories just like mine. It was that quick. I have loved gay guys ever since."[14] Where Grace Abounds was the fun group. They had last names on their name tags.

In many Exodus ministries, meetings involved worship, prayer for healing, Bible study, instruction, and accountability. True healing, these programs held, could come only from a vibrant relationship with Christ. Some programs were highly structured, with classes moving through a curriculum together. Others were more relational. Most sought to help the participant identify what he or she was really looking for in sexual experiences with members of the same sex. The love of a father? An injection of masculinity? Safety from the abuse of men?

Jim Venice described his experience with participating in an ex-gay ministry as a new Christian, years before he began leading one himself. Upon his conversion, he explained, "my sins were forgiven and cast as far as the east is from the west. I was a brand-new man, a new creation without a past. I was no longer a homosexual!" He continued, "I have since become involved in an ex-gay ministry (First Stone in Oklahoma City). I have been ministered to by people who have successfully left the gay lifestyle. I have been learning a great deal about how I got into that mess and how to keep from getting back into it." Jim soon reconciled with his ex-wife.[15]

But for every person actively involved in an ex-gay ministry, there were many other people who were never formally involved. They were in their homes and dorm rooms listening to the tapes, reading the books, watching the videos, and eventually scrolling through the websites produced by ex-gay ministries. For every teenager who went to a reparative therapist for counseling, there were many more who went to their pastor, who had probably read a book by a reparative therapist or an ex-gay leader. Other groups met online. The movement's reach extended far beyond the weekly meetings of Exodus affiliate ministries.

Ex-Gay Curricula

Several ex-gay ministries produced structured curricula that found widespread use in the movement.

In Mario Bergner's *Setting Love in Order*, he describes his "trek out of homosexuality and into heterosexuality." Drawing heavily on the approach of Leanne Payne, he sought to help his readers analyze their sexual fantasies. He presented homosexual attractions as an unconscious attempt to integrate one's confused masculinity. The longing for another was seen as a heart cry for "gender identification and personal integration with the same sex." What was it about the man in a sexual fantasy that he was trying to take? What part of his masculinity was he out of touch with, and how does the man in the fantasy symbolize that?[16] He discussed strategies to avoid masturbating, grounding much of the drive to masturbate in personal anxiety. He encouraged praying your loneliness away and repenting of unhealthy attempts to sate it. A chapter laid out healthy same-sex love in contrast to same-sex ambivalence. Another challenged unrealized hatred of women. Yet another discussed opposite-sex love.

Another curriculum was developed by Andrew Comiskey of Desert Stream Ministries. Comiskey founded Desert Stream at the Vineyard Santa Monica in 1981. His approach brought together a strong focus on relationship with Christ, an emphasis on prayer, and Elizabeth Moberly's therapeutic approach to male homosexuality. The ministry later moved to the Vineyard Anaheim and later to suburban Kansas City. Their Living Waters curriculum was used by ex-gay groups everywhere. Comiskey laid out the client's expectations: "What the struggler can reasonably expect is to become *whole enough* in this lifetime to sustain fulfilling heterosexual relationships. By this I mean the capacity to relate intimately, but non-erotically, with the same sex and the freedom to encounter the opposite sex as a desired counterpart—with interest, not fear or distaste. . . . Furthermore, Jesus has granted me enough heterosexual desire and personal maturity to love a woman, take her as my wife, and oversee a household and growing family."[17]

While offering more-realistic expectations than some—for those able to pick up the subtle nuance, the promise was heterosexual functioning, not heterosexuality—marriage to a member of the opposite sex was clearly the desired goal.

Foundational to the process was finding a greater desire in God—a desire strong enough to motivate change. Worship was vital. Chapters addressed submission to Jesus, naming and laying down homosexual practices, and praying through demonic strongholds. Attention was given to developmental causes of homosexuality and dealing with baggage related to the same-sex parent. One chapter dealt with breaking sexual addiction, and another with the need for true intimacy and community, including making peace with others of one's own sex.

Having learned healthy same-sex love and intimacy, Comiskey then stressed the need to press into heterosexuality. "God calls his children to discover who they are through relationship with the opposite sex."[18] After becoming more secure in his masculinity, Comiskey "began to date as a whole, heterosexual person." He described the change. "Through God's healing work in my gender identity, as well as my heeding God's call to be reconciled to the opposite sex, heterosexual desire burst forth in me." While same-sex friendships for Comiskey could still occasion sexual temptation, he presented those temptations as lessening with increased spiritual wholeness.

Individual ministries would adapt these and other curricula to meet their own approach.

As with secular addiction models, it was not uncommon within ex-gay ministries for individuals to work through their sexual past to try to identify specific triggers and develop plans of avoidance. In many ministries, it was expected that homosexual relapses might occur. Training often focused on developing stereotypically masculine mannerisms. One gay friend who went through conversion therapy three times still credits it for helping him learn to act more masculine and fit in with straight men. He's one of the most flamboyant men I know, so I can only image what he was like before.

Behaviorist interventions were relatively rare, as were surgical, hormonal, and drug interventions.[19]

Some techniques were less than conventional. Alan Medinger of Regeneration, also first executive director of Exodus International, had in his 2000 book *Growth into Manhood* an entire section titled "Use of Masturbation to Develop Heterosexual Desire."[20]

Sy Rogers, Exodus president in the late 1980s, emphasized personal cooperation with God. In his widely read booklet *The Man in the Mirror*, published by Last Days Ministries, Sy described his change from gay and transgender to heterosexual as being primarily a work of perseverance. "I did have a lot of struggles in the beginning, but like most worthwhile efforts, perseverance paid off. Today I very much enjoy the opportunity to live beyond my past problems." He added, "My recovery process took time and work and the encouragement and accountability of my supportive friends. More important, my recovery depended on my willingness to cooperate with God. Over the years and around the globe, everyone that I personally know—or know of—that has overcome homosexuality has been enabled to do so as a direct consequence of a life yielded to God and committed to the way of Christ."[21]

Selling a Vision of Heterosexuality

McKrae Game of Hope for Wholeness describes selling an intentional vision, with images of his own family as the carrot to inspire hope for change. Working with children as young as eleven, he describes "billing myself as this example really throughout the organization." He explains, "I would use pictures of my family. I would talk about how in love I was, how happy I was. That wasn't always true." Using photos of his family—with the spouse and the children—was selling to clients a vision of heterosexuality. With so powerful a visual, the counselee couldn't help but get the message that orientation change was attainable, even if in Game's ministry it was never explicitly promised. Game adds, "It was a form of propaganda. We in the ex-gay world are propagandists trying to propagate an ideal."[22]

It was assumed that normal spiritual growth—progressive sanctification— would cause a shift from homosexual temptation to heterosexual temptation over time.

Grace versus Change

Some Exodus affiliates had significantly less focus on sexual orientation change. One such ministry was Where Grace Abounds. "We were always the misfits within Exodus," explains Scott Kingry, who first came to the ministry in the 1980s. "We had more of a grace approach. We had too much fun. We went out for drinks together. Other Exodus people didn't take us seriously at first. At Where Grace Abounds, an agenda of change was not pushed. All these other Exodus ministries were having all these weddings. It took us ten years to have our first one." Kingry notes, "Many of those marriages failed. People left the faith or ended up in the LGBT community." Kingry remained with Where Grace Abounds, which parted ways with Exodus International in 2008.

Though always in the minority, other affiliates also downplayed hopes for orientation change. Richard Holloman founded Sight Ministry in Nashville in 2003 with little focus on such change. And perhaps due partly to their Calvinist views on the continuing presence and power of indwelling sin, Harvest USA in Philadelphia and First Light in Saint Louis did not focus much attention on orientation change. These ministries and others like them focused mainly on trying to overcome lust and sexual "acting out," while providing emotional support within group settings. Most participants would have hoped that moderate modification in sexual orientation might be possible for some people. And with reparative therapy in the air by the 1990s, there would have been exploration of personal roots of homosexuality. But these were examples of Exodus affiliates that did not fit the pattern seen elsewhere in Exodus.[23] One woman I know experienced a significant shift in her sexual orientation, ironically through involvement in one of these ministries that did not focus on orientation change. When people suggest that Exodus International didn't promote orientation change, it's often because their involvement was with ministries like these, and they filtered Exodus conferences through that experience.

Emotional Dependence

Some participants in ex-gay ministries recall a heavy emphasis on not falling into emotionally dependent relationships. Some ministries viewed intense relationships with members of the same sex as potentially sinful in themselves, even when not eroticized. Granted, enmeshment can be a problem whenever we're idolizing a relationship, which can be easy to do when you're lonely. But for some participants, this heavy emphasis left them even lonelier. It left some participants incapacitated in their ability to develop friendships with others.[24]

As I write this, I'm in the midst of the 2020 COVID-19 pandemic. I am single. I live alone. My last hug or handshake was exactly sixty-two days ago. I have it marked on my calendar as "Last Hug." I'm diabetic. I have to be careful. I find it disturbing that we would want anyone to go through their entire life like this.

This wasn't an emphasis in every Exodus affiliate. Exodus affiliates approached reorientation from various angles and with differing approaches and emphases. One very large ministry, however, remained altogether independent of Exodus International.

Homosexuals Anonymous

One of the largest of the individual ex-gay ministries was Homosexuals Anonymous, with headquarters originally in Reading, Pennsylvania, and chapters across North America and around the world. Founded by Colin Cook in 1976—with a first meeting in 1977—the program focused on a fourteen-step program Cook and cofounder Douglas McIntyre developed after reviewing Cook's five-year conversion to heterosexuality.

Homosexuals Anonymous (HA) also ran the Quest Learning Center, an intensive site-based treatment facility in Reading, which closed in 1986. That year, the ministry had more than a thousand active members in sixty chapters in the US, Canada, and New Zealand.[25] The life of the chapters centered on support groups whose members would meet weekly to help one another work through the steps.

The approach was similar at points to Alcoholics Anonymous in that participants were to see themselves as powerless over their problem and to look to a higher power. For HA, that power specifically was Jesus Christ. HA diverged from AA at one very big juncture, however. While Alcoholics Anonymous encouraged people to own their fallen condition, introducing themselves as an alcoholic even after decades of sobriety, Homosexuals Anonymous did just the opposite. Every week, participants recited together from the fourteen steps, confessing that "we had accepted a lie about ourselves, an illusion that had trapped us in a false identity.... We are part of God's heterosexual creation, and ... God calls us to rediscover that identity in him through Jesus Christ."[26]

The rejection of a homosexual self-perception, and its replacement with a heterosexual self-perception, was the heart of the Homosexuals Anonymous process.[27] This was the core conviction of the organization.

Homosexuality did not exist.

Homosexuality was an illusion.

Everyone was really heterosexual. They just didn't know it yet.

"We do not believe that there is something like 'homosexuality,'" states the organization's website. "God has created all of us heterosexual."[28]

Promise of 80–90 Percent Success If You Believe

Cook also saw the heterosexuality of Christ imputed to the gay person who believed, therefore making them heterosexual in Christ. The problem was that their feelings hadn't yet caught up. In a 1981 interview, Cook explained that ministers should be prepared for it to take one to two years for their homosexual members' feelings to catch up to their creational and imputed heterosexuality.[29] But Cook promised, "In time, 80 to 90 percent of the strength of homosexual feelings will pass away."[30]

This was sexual reorientation.

The Homosexuals Anonymous Statement of Philosophy identified the mechanism of change in the power of your confidence that you had already been made and remade heterosexual. "As a trained faith grasps this awareness, there is a breaking of the power of the homosexual inclination.... Homosexual inclination may be healed and ... all who desire it may realize their inborn, though fallen, heterosexuality, thus opening the way to heterosexual marriage and family."[31] The individual's power to believe themselves straight would drive everything. Unbelief about that reality is why some failed to change. In his 1985 booklet *Homosexuality: An Open Door?* Cook says change is achieved through "the power of positive thought."[32] The ministry's website was clear. "Do we believe in freedom from homosexuality? Most certainly so—and the reason some have not found it yet is because they might not really believe it can be done."[33]

In that 1981 interview, Cook described his transformation from gay to straight while following the fourteen steps.

I began to realize that I had been locked for years into a grand illusion about myself—what I call the homosexual lie. Gradually, a new confidence grew as I daily affirmed my heterosexual identity in Christ. I began to claim the right by faith to have girlfriends, though I feared to do so at first.... Then emotional and physical responses began to develop as I went ahead in faith to express affection. I remember the first sexual arousal as I walked with a girlfriend through a summer field. I remember the first kiss....

I was not only righteous in [Jesus], I was also heterosexual in Him, because He was the second Adam restoring all that the first Adam had lost.... I saw myself now not only as heterosexual by creation—though it had been buried by the homosexual condition—but also heterosexual by redemption.[34]

In a 1986 interview with a researcher, Cook emphasized the various parts of the process. The researcher noted the pieces of this puzzle: "to claim Christ's ... heterosexuality by faith, to meet the love need through relationships with Christ (which can include such things as, in fantasy, meeting Christ in a grove while naked) and nonerotic friendships with members of the same sex, and to practice [the] 14 steps."[35]

The HA Experience

Experiences were mixed. Jeff Johnson views his HA experience as the turning point in a life that could have been much darker. It was during his second HA meeting that Jeff "realized homosexuality isn't who I am. My experience with HA was wonderful."[36]

The author of a 1994 HA workbook reflected on his experience with each step. "Step 6 has been, for me, the most difficult of all. It was easier for me to renounce the lie than it was to embrace the truth. It is still easier to say, 'I am not homosexual,' than it is to say, 'I am heterosexual.'"[37]

There was community within these meetings. A 1986 article about an HA chapter in Allentown, Pennsylvania, stressed the relational nature of the group. The chapter coordinator, Earl Miller, explained his experience. "Miller said establishing normal male friendships . . . has been the most important step in his journey so far. He says he has not had a homosexual encounter in four years and now is beginning to feel 'comfortable' around women. Recently, he started to date. He recalls spending a whole evening dancing with women at the recent wedding of a friend as a happy sign of how far he has come."[38]

A news article earlier that year had noted the rapid growth of the HA chapter in Tulsa, Oklahoma. Beginning with just four members only months before, the chapter had grown to two groups with four meetings a week.[39]

A 1995 news article noted a new chapter forming in McAllen, Texas. Like many chapters, they met in a church but declined to identify the church publicly in order to protect the confidentiality of participants. Gary, the chapter's founder, explained, "We believe we were all created heterosexuals." He added, "It's because of Christ we feel we can overcome this." He promoted the group through classified advertisements listing a phone number and post office box. "It can take three to five years of hard work to rid oneself of homosexuality," he said.[40]

One young man described his experience with a Homosexuals Anonymous chapter. Having grown up in the Assemblies of God denomination, Scott loved church and wanted more than anything to please God. But he also knew he was gay. As a freshman in college, he called Exodus International and was referred to an HA chapter in Phoenix. He moved there, got a job as a roofing contractor, and invested his remaining hours in HA. At first he loved the meetings. After opening the meetings in prayer, members would "go through a time of sharing their struggles and pitfalls." He said he loved the closeness of the small group. He was drawn to the openness of the other participants. He described memorizing the fourteen steps, especially step 5, about living "an illusion that had trapped us in a false identity." But his experience began to sour as the hope for change became elusive. "After three months, every guy in there was as gay as the day they walked in." He added, "You begin to view your-self as a continual failure." After seven years of trying to become straight, Scott gave up and eventually ended up in a Metropolitan Community Church.[41]

A 2007 article about a new chapter opening in Marin County, California, quoted the chapter organizer. "It's for people who struggle and don't want to struggle anymore." The chapter met in a Baptist church led by Kent Philpott, who three decades earlier was instrumental in forming Love in Action. Philpott was the author of the dubious 1975 ex-gay testimonial book *The Third Sex?* He explained, "We are here to help people leave their sinful behavior behind, but we are not judging or rejecting them."[42]

Former Focus on the Family vice president and former fighter pilot Mike Rosebush described his experience in his Homosexuals Anonymous chapter. The ministry leader would open the meeting. "Let's begin by saying aloud our fourteen steps." Mike and his fellow group members would respond from memory. "We had accepted a lie about ourselves . . . trapped in a false iden-tity . . . our true reality is that we are part of God's heterosexual creation." His memories are of the chapter leader reinforcing the same points. "Don't look at that attractive man; look down. Don't look back at him; don't look at anything stimulating. Report your sins to us; be accountable. Confess each bad thought. Repent. Join straight men in doing 'masculine' things. Notice women. You will change. God will make you heterosexual."[43]

After seeing no progress, Rosebush eventually left the group.

Courage

The only ex-gay ministry to rival Exodus International and Homosexuals Anonymous in size was formed just four years after Exodus was started. In 1980, with the encouragement of Terence Cardinal Cooke, archbishop of New York, moral theologian Fr. John Harvey began a ministry in New York City to support Roman Catholics seeking to live chaste lives in accordance with the church's teaching on homosexuality. Many Courage chapters follow a twelve-step approach developed by Harvey. Priests lead support groups. In 1994, Courage became an apostolate endorsed by the Holy See. Today Courage has 112 chapters in the United States and 58 in other countries.[44]

TESTIMONY-DRIVEN MINISTRY

If there is one thing that can be said about the ex-gay movement, it's that it was a testimony-driven movement. In 2007, *Christianity Today* observed, "Since its beginnings in the 1970s, the ex-gay movement has engaged gay advocates in a battle of testimonies. Transformed ex-gay leaders are the best argument for their movement."[45] The ex-gay testimony was the life narrative that every ex-gay developed. Usually starting with a wounded childhood, the distant relationship to the same-sex parent, or the stories of abuse, the ex-gay testimony moved to how the ex-gay had always felt different as a child, then progressed to the sexual experimentation and sin, the shame and bondage. The climax of the ex-gay testimony was the ex-gay's turning to God for salvation and healing, often followed by dating, getting married, and having children.

Everyone had their personal exodus story. Just as the Israelites had their story of being led out from slavery in Egypt, we all had our stories of being led out from homosexuality. Our ex-gay testimony told our narrative from gay to not gay.

It was a basic structure repeated thousands of times, a narrative that sought to explain how you became gay—parental dysfunction, peer rejection, and abuse being the big three—and how, because of God, you aren't gay anymore.[46] I know I certainly gave that testimony. This was the ex-gay script. At the heart of the ex-gay movement, the ex-gay script was a driving factor behind efforts at both sexual fidelity and reorientation.

And because the most platformed testimonies ended with marriage and children, the ex-gay testimony created the illusion that the individual's sexual orientation had changed. "These stories of people getting married took on a life of their own," comments Roger Jones. "They added a lot of pressure." Scott Kingry agrees. "As a single person at an Exodus conference, you just felt like a big old failure. I sat listening to these testimonies, praying, 'Please, God, don't let them parade out the wives and kids.' It undercut the whole line about it being about holiness, not heterosexuality."[47]

Kingry adds a qualification. "Once every few years, they would platform Bob Ragan, who would say, 'I'm a single person and I'm thriving.'"[48] His testimony would always release some of the pressure.

The Illusion of the Ex-Gay Script

By saying, "I used to be gay but am not anymore," the ex-gay script fostered the illusion that the individual used to experience sexual attraction to members of the same sex but doesn't anymore, or only very rarely. This effectively made ex-gays more acceptable within the culture of conservative churches. It also left the individual hiding behind an illusion that they had experienced far more change than in fact they had experienced.

By stopping at marriage, the ex-gay testimony didn't mention the ongoing struggle with gay pornography. It didn't mention the difficulty many faced initiating sex with their spouse. It didn't mention the reality of being tempted to fantasize about someone of the same sex while making love with one's spouse. By ending at marriage, the ex-gay testimony hid the infidelities that sometimes occurred and masked the fact that 70 percent of such marriages ended in divorce.[49] Some of the healthiest marriages I have known have involved one spouse's attraction to members of the same sex. The challenges of these couples have only strengthened their resolve to believe the gospel and love one another. But an awful lot more didn't make it. When the ex-gay testimony stopped at marriage, it gave the illusion of a homosexual cure.

There's a reason the movement was called the *ex-gay* movement. "I used to be gay." I have a story to tell. A narrative that moves from homosexual to not homosexual anymore. The name encapsulated the degree to which the ex-gay testimony drove the movement. As real orientation change became elusive as the movement matured, adopting the "ex-gay" identity eventually replaced in much of the movement the desired end point of heterosexuality.[50]

Critics of the movement expressed concern early on about how such testimonies left people with highly unrealistic expectations. In 1982, psychologist Ralph Blair addressed the national convention of the Christian Association for Psychological Studies, cautioning that such narratives were misleading and misunderstood. "Where the 'ex-gays' claim something modest, overly eager evangelical supporters exaggerate the claims and thereby set up expectations on the part of churches and troubled homosexuals and their families to look for changes that never were promised in the first place."[51]

Forsaking Homosexual Self-Perception

Yet the script was enforced. Exodus executive director Alan Medinger insisted that rejecting a homosexual self-perception was key to successful healing. "Accompanying these erotic and emotional changes is a change in self-perception in which the individual no longer identifies him or herself as homosexual."[52] You become a former homosexual. This was part of the sexual conversion process.

So you had Darlene Bogle claiming, "I was delivered from lesbianism."[53] You had Homosexuals Anonymous indoctrinating people with the belief that they weren't really homosexual but heterosexual. Homosexuality was just an illusion. You had Colin Cook telling you to claim by faith your "completed heterosexuality," which already is "your new unseen identity." Still experience homosexual temptation? Cook explains, "Feelings are trying . . . to foist an illusion" on you.[54] You had Joseph Nicolosi telling a crowd that "there is no such thing as a homosexual."[55] You had Michael Bussee saying, "By professing it, it had become real on a spiritual level already in heaven."[56] You had Frank Worthen claiming a 70 percent success rate. You had McKrae Game using photos of his family to sell the vision as reality. They all used different paths to get there, but they were all saying the same thing. The Exodus International motto was "Change is possible."

So you are not homosexual anymore. You are an ex-gay.

Frank Worthen set the script early on. He concluded his testimony with his marriage to a woman. "I struggled with homosexuality for over four decades," he explained, noting his age—forty—at the time of his conversion to Christ. Then he ended it. "But Jesus Christ set me free."[57]

I know of no better way to create the impression of successful orientation change than to convince thousands and thousands of people to say that they used to be homosexual but are not anymore. (We will examine the realities of change in later chapters.)

A New Doctrine

By enforcing this script, the movement created a new theological belief—a doctrine—that you cannot be homosexual and be a Christian.

Step back for a moment and observe the theological shift that took place in evangelicalism's posture toward gay people who come to faith in Jesus.

In 1970, InterVarsity Press could publish a book subtitled *Letters of a Christian Homosexual*.[58] In 1975, Billy Graham could tell the *Atlanta Journal-Constitution* that he supported ordaining homosexuals, provided they're repentant.[59] In 1978, Gordon Conwell's Richard Lovelace could both encourage "professing Christians who are gay to have the courage . . . to avow [acknowledge] their orientation openly" and call the church to "nurture nonpracticing gay believers in its membership, and ordain these to positions of leadership for ministry."[60] C. S. Lewis had spoken fondly of a "pious male homosexual" he had known.[61] Francis Schaeffer in 1968 could describe the "homophile" as "a person who is born so that they have a natural tendency toward affection and sexual practice with their own sex." For Schaeffer, Christian conversion didn't make a person no longer a homophile.[62] Schaeffer's denomination in 1980 could speak affectionately about "our homosexual brothers and sisters."[63] As early as 1978, John Stott spoke of homosexuality being part of a Christian's "identity" and part of their "constitution."[64] There was an openness and honesty here about sexual orientation and the fact that conversion didn't take that sexual orientation away but instead brought a changed *life* orientation.

This ex-gay doctrine is a profound theological shift from the faith of our twentieth-century neo-evangelical fathers.

Certainly, the ex-gay script helped some people break with a past with which they no longer wished to associate, reinforcing their sense of being a new creation in Christ. It helped them center their life not on a narrative supplied by an unbelieving culture but on a narrative of change. But the ex-gay script left others unknown and therefore unloved, living behind a mask that hid the reality that their sexual orientation had not changed. It left them at the mercy of fellow believers who assumed it had changed or insisted that it would. The openness and honesty seen in Lewis and Schaeffer and Graham and Stott seemed to have been swapped out for a positive-confession denial of reality.

These were tensions inherent in the ex-gay identity. And these tensions were being felt within the leadership of the ex-gay movement. They would be among the fissures running the entire length of the movement's history.

nine

Fissures from the Beginning

The leader who'd appeared on national television extolling it one year became, in many cases, the openly gay ex-leader opposing it years later.

—Joe Dallas, Board Chairman, Exodus International

THE POTEMKIN VILLAGE OF ORIENTATION CHANGE

In 1787, Empress Catherine II of Russia traveled with a gathering of foreign ambassadors to the far southern reaches of her domain. She sought to acquaint herself and her companions with her subjects and the conditions in the country. If the stories are to be believed—and nothing in Russian politics has ever been as it seems—the cruise down the Volga was a delightful one. The empress and her posse of hopeful diplomatic supporters passed one beautiful and prosperous village after another.

In reality, the land was quite destitute. The empress's former lover Grigory Potemkin is said to have rushed ahead of her to erect a fake village and plant men dressed up as prosperous villagers. As soon as the empress departed, they disassembled the village and erected it again farther down the river. Repeating this trick over and over offered the illusion of success, when the reality was much more disappointing.

In many ways, the tragedy of the ex-gay movement was that its great early hope—reorientation—was a Potemkin village.

Frank Worthen had started Exodus, according to his own words, on "the premise . . . that God could change you from gay to straight."[1] Worthen claimed that his live-in treatment program Love in Action had a success rate of anywhere from 50 percent to 70 percent. And if you were desperate, those odds sounded pretty good. Yet it soon became evident that the real rate of orientation change was much, much lower than initially promised.

The expectation of orientation change was set early in the movement. And even when many in the movement began backing away from that focus, the ethos and culture of the movement had already been set. Joel and Jane French promised "total sexual reorientation" in their 1979 book *Straight Is the Way*.[2] Teen Challenge had said its program had a 70 percent cure rate, though they mysteriously stopped treating homosexuality by the end of the 1970s.

For decades, ex-gays were propped up in front of church audiences to give their testimony of being converted from gay to straight. But the testimony typically masked a much more complicated reality, a reality churches weren't begging to hear. Roger Grindstaff of the ex-gay ministry Disciples Only had consulted for Teen Challenge, and when asked if he knew of any homosexuals who through ex-gay ministry were becoming heterosexual—including himself—he gave an angry but honest reply: "Of course not, I don't know of any." He explained that the only testimony churches wanted to hear was a testimony of total reversal. So that's what he intended to give them, even if he had never seen one in reality.[3]

He would offer the churches a Potemkin village.

QUESTIONING THE VILLAGE

A lot of Christian leaders were buying the village. Christian psychologist Jeffrey Satinover, in his 1996 book *Homosexuality and the Politics of Truth*, claimed that homosexuality had "at least 50% likelihood of being eliminated" through treatment in ex-gay ministry. And for highly motivated, select individuals, he claimed "a very high success rate, in some instances nearing 100%."[4]

In reality, ex-gay ministry leaders were seeing nothing of the sort.

Michael Bussee of EXIT explained the successes ex-gay ministries were seeing. "Some [participants] . . . experienced God's love and the welcoming fellowship of others who knew the struggle. There were some real 'changes.'" These were significant changes and gave a lot of believers something worth living for. "But," Bussee added, "not one of the hundreds of people we counseled became straight."[5]

This reality was hard to swallow for a movement whose cardinal claim—even if with a dozen caveats—was freedom from homosexuality.

For this reason, the movement received early pushback from evangelical watchdogs. By 1977, the nonprofit Trinity Foundation's *Wittenburg Door* was warning about the unlikelihood of sexual orientation change through ex-gay ministries. The foundation would rise to prominence over the next decades for exposing corrupt televangelists, from Benny Hinn to Robert Tilton to the trashy glitter and gilt of the Word of Faith flagship Trinity Broadcasting Network. But its early sights were set on the expectations being laid out by the newly forming ex-gay ministries.

In "A Christian Sociologist Looks at Homosexuality," Tony Campolo cautioned that there was "no clinical evidence that homosexuals could have their sexual preferences changed." Looking at the evidence, he observed cases in which bisexual men and women could live within a heterosexual marriage. But for believers exclusively attracted to members of the same sex, he wrote, "aside from one dubious case, I found that when homosexuals are converted, they become Christian homosexuals."[6] Even while the ex-gay movement was in its infancy, there were evangelical elites calling it out for spreading false hope.

Christianity Today similarly noted the paucity of evidence for orientation change. When Kenneth Gangel, president of Miami Christian College, advocated for sexual orientation change efforts in his 1978 book *The Gospel and the Gay*, Robert K. Johnston took him to task. The book, complete with an endorsement on the front cover from anti-gay social crusader Anita Bryant, sought to lay out concrete evidence for conversions to heterosexual orientation.[7] In a review, Johnston wrote, "Pastorally, there are sound aspects to Gangel's advice and he seeks to be balanced." He continued, "But his major case study of a 'cure' is of a bisexual, not an exclusive homosexual, hence, his generalizations are suspect."[8]

Christianity Today was being generous. Gangel had cited one instance of a man cured of homosexuality, though the man himself acknowledged that he still masturbated while thinking about men. He subsequently left the ex-gay movement. Gangel also cited an incident of a gay cure involving a young man named Billy, who, though he had never experienced sexual attraction to another man, had experimented some sexually while in prison. Once released from the slammer, Billy still liked girls.

Were these the best examples that ex-gay authors could find of orientation change? I'm sure Billy was a great guy, and it was brave of him to allow his story to be told. But Billy wasn't the first straight guy to go on the down-low while in the clink. A gay-to-straight testimony this was not.

Gangel also devoted a chapter to Greg. Gangel's Greg is described as "A Case Study in Homosexual Regeneration." But Greg's own words were not words of cure. Greg was still attracted to other guys. He was trying to submit his sexuality to Christ, trying to live a life of faithfulness. The Greg Gangel describes is a model of costly obedience. But nothing in Gangel's case study so much as hints at Greg being regenerated from a homosexual orientation to a heterosexual orientation. "I still have a long way to go," Greg explained.[9]

Greg's words reflected the same hope heard in the voice of every cancer victim approaching a faith healer. He spoke a word of faith to claim a hoped-for cure. "I believe that the Lord is going to cure me," Greg said. "I claim that promise."[10]

To present Greg's story as a cure of homosexuality was to build yet another Potemkin village.

Michael Bussee of EXIT had a sense that their carefully crafted facade was collapsing around him and his fellow ministry leaders. "In the midst of all of this, my own faith in the Exodus movement was crumbling. No one was really becoming 'ex-gay.' Who were we fooling? As one current EXODUS leader admitted, we were just 'Christians with homosexual tendencies who would rather not have those tendencies.'" Bussee added, "By calling ourselves 'ex-gay' we were lying to ourselves and to others. We were hurting people."[11]

By the mid-1980s, ex-gay leader Jeff Ford of Outpost admitted that he still wrestled with his own homosexual urges, admitting he was not "cured." He added that he doubted "anyone has shed their homosexual orientation" through ex-gay approaches.[12]

Were there no shifts in sexual orientation? Did no one experience any change in their attractions at all? Of course some did. But most did not. And the minority who did didn't experience change to the degree that anyone wanted.

One young man who frequented Exodus conferences described his struggle to cope with his sense of duplicity. "Most of the ex-gays I met at the conference were working off a life sentence. They still had homosexual cravings but managed them, the way an alcoholic manages their disease. Their future, my future, would be one day at a time and involve endless books, tapes, Bibles, and temptation." He continued, "Unless there was a divine miracle, I would never feel about women the way a heterosexual man felt about women. To me the 'ex-gay' label felt more and more like a deception, a lie both to myself and any woman I would be involved with."[13]

A Potemkin village.

LAPSED LEADERS EARLY ON

Some ex-gay ministries in those early years had a tremendously short shelf life. Programs, treatment centers, and ministries crashed and burned as quickly as they started. Untrained leaders set about a trailblazing mission with little support from churches. Leaders burned out. The ministries experienced incredibly high turnover. Already by 1980, Sharon Kuhn observed, "Most ministries to Christian homosexuals soon die out."[14]

A major contributing factor: in its early years, the ex-gay movement was beset by profound leadership failures. Frequently, within the movement there was a lack of connection to either the organized church or the mental health profession. Early on, leaders developed entire theologies and clinical approaches on the fly. Few leaders at that time had any formal training. Usually all they had was a personal testimony, a new believer's zeal for God, and a sincere desire to help others.

One issue, according to Alan Medinger, Exodus executive director in those years, was that some of the ministry leaders returned to their old lifestyle.[15] So many men—and they were typically men—had traveled the circuit from church to church, telling their testimony of being delivered from homosexuality. With each big fall, the ex-gay narrative took a hit.

In 1977, trouble came to Guy Charles, leader of the oldest church-based ex-gay ministry, Liberation in Jesus Christ, a ministry of the charismatic Truro Episcopal Church. As it happened, Guy, who had claimed to be cured of his homosexuality, had been having gay affairs with a number of the young men who had come to the ministry for help. The parish shuttered the ministry. Charles spent his last twenty-one years living with his gay partner, Mike.

Nineteen seventy-nine was a rough year for John Evans, who had been with Love in Action when it launched with Frank Worthen and Kent Philpott. John had left his lover to help lead Love in Action. Through the ministry, he had developed a close friendship with Jack McIntyre, a client in the ministry.

Within a couple years, Evans quit Love in Action and renounced the ex-gay movement. He would spend his last twenty-five years with his life partner, Danny.

In 1979, Exit founder and Exodus cofounder Michael Bussee and one of his volunteers, Gary Cooper, were sharing a flight to speak at a church in Virginia. While on that flight, the two realized they were in love with each other. They quickly scrapped their testimonies and wrote a speech arguing that the church should affirm the experiences of gay men. The church, expecting to hear two former homosexuals describe how they became straight, was suitably shocked. Checking into their hotel that night, Bussee and Cooper noted the room had only a single bed and took that as a sign from God.[16] Bussee left his wife and exchanged rings with Cooper in a commitment ceremony in a Metropolitan Community Church.

Other leaders left because their vision or beliefs began to deviate from the ministry's focus.

At some point, Greg Reid shut down EAGLE and disappeared from public view. There were reports that he had walked away from his ex-gay beliefs. But before abandoning the ministry, he admitted a sense of failed priorities that put people up front who had no business being there. "There have been many [ex-gay] failures," he explained. "Ex-gay testimonies are touted before they are ready." He complained about the impossible expectations he felt while driving the ministry. "Evangelicals and gay Christians alike are looking for a 'perfect record'—and heterosexuality to boot. Ex-gays play right into that destructive game. The scriptural standard is NOT 'are they reoriented.'"[17] It was another leader lost to the ex-gay movement.

Joe Dallas explained, "Exodus branches represented many denominations and practices. Some were Baptist, some liturgical, some charismatic. Some offered counseling, others preferred deliverance prayer, others held support groups." But such diversity carried risk. "This lack of uniformity allowed room for both individuality and error." And that individuality left room for something more. "It also allowed, at times, the raising up of leaders who were gifted but not yet seasoned enough to sustain moral integrity while operating their gifts." That added a degree of spectacle and delight for the movement's opponents. "The leader who'd appeared on national television extolling it one year became, in many cases, the openly gay ex-leader opposing it years later."[18]

"We had a terrible time the first few years," said Frank Worthen, one of the Love in Action founders. "Most of the people were in it for their own needs. They were lonely, they felt guilty and stayed on the fence and started ministries that should never have been started.[19] So many leaders were spiritually immature. Too often that meant the blind were leading the blind.

LEADERS LOSING FAITH IN THE EX-GAY NARRATIVE

Often the biggest threat to the grand narrative of leaving homosexuality— the gay-to-straight script—were the ex-gay leaders themselves. They saw a lot. Sometimes leaders of ministries would spend years or decades selling a change process, only to come to the conclusion that it didn't work.

John Smid led Exodus flagship Love in Action for twenty years after taking over from Frank Worthen. In 2008, Smid left the organization and later explained, "Yes, there are homosexuals that make dramatic changes in their lives as they walk through the transformation process with Jesus. I have heard story after story of changes that have occurred as men and women find the grace of God in their lives as homosexual people. But, I'm sorry, this transformation process may not meet the expectations of many Christians. I also want to reiterate here that the transformation for the vast majority of homosexuals will not include a change of sexual orientation." He added, "Actually I've never met a man who experienced a change from homosexual to heterosexual.[20]

By 2007, former Exodus president Sy Rogers had also rejected orientation change as a goal. Sy quietly refocused his ministry on grace for the sexually broken, without reference to sexual orientation.[21] He removed from his website all references to his being ex-gay or formerly transgender. He removed all references to homosexuality, replacing them with comments that reflected his shift.[22]

This was a huge shift for the Man in the Mirror.

The chorus of ex-gay leaders calling out their Potemkin cure has not ceased. In 2019, McKrae Game, founder of the Hope for Wholeness Network, then one of the nation's largest ex-gay organizations, announced that he was still gay. Soon thereafter he left his wife and began looking for a relationship with a man. The ministry, founded by Game twenty years earlier, had affiliates in fifteen states. Game renounced change therapy in no uncertain terms. "Please forgive me!" he begged.[23]

Love in Action's Smid said that when parents asked about the ministry's success rate, "I would say, 'Well, our real goal is to lead people to have a better relationship with God. And everyone that goes through LIA, they have a better relationship with God. So I would say that's a pretty good success rate.'" He now admits, "Underneath it, I was afraid to say, we haven't seen anyone change. . . . Like any nonprofit, we needed their funds."[24]

The expectation that everyone's sexual orientation can change—whether within a faith-based ex-gay ministry or with a professional reparative therapist or after meeting with a pastor who has read all the books—set up a huge number of people for failure. As with the faith healer who keeps telling the cancer patient that God will heal her, this ever-elusive expectation of change kept believers feeling constantly like failures. Why am I not cured yet? Am I not repenting deeply enough? Not praying hard enough? Too often such expectations took the deep shame that gay people already felt and added layer upon layer of blame, dejection, and despair.

FOR SOME PARTICIPANTS,
A SLIDE INTO DESPAIR

In 2007, Stanton Jones and Mark Yarhouse analyzed the experience of participants in Exodus-affiliated ministries. Given many such ministries' relatively benign practices—Bible studies, worship, prayer, and accountability—they found that on average these ministries did not generally harm their participants. The added presence of personal support and the community these ministries fostered offset their limited effectiveness at orientation change. On average, psychological distress did not increase among the group of participants they followed.[25] This was solid research that gave us the very best hard data on the movement.

There are several things to note about the subjects of study, though. This was a study during the 2000s, the ex-gay movement's mature later years, when expectations of orientation change had already lowered a great deal. This was a very different ex-gay ministry than what we saw in the 1970s through the 1990s. These subjects also were mature adults who chose a ministry of their own volition. This was not a study of teenagers being forced into ex-gay programs by disapproving parents. These were also Exodus International ministries, which by the 2000s had more accountability than independent ex-gay ministries, and far more accountability than a pastor in a small church somewhere who had read *Man in the Mirror* and was determined to straighten out a kid in his youth group. This was a study of the ex-gay movement at its very best.

And this was a study that found that psychological distress did not elevate on average.

Of course, not everyone's experience even in these ministries was average.

The impact of false hope—and its strenuous chasing after the wind—could be devastating for some in the movement. With Exodus's slogan "Change is possible," many of the ministry's participants bore deep wounds. "A lot of people were hurt because they had unrealistic expectations," said Richard Holloman of Sight Ministry.[26]

My friend Josh's eighth attempt at changing his attractions was at a small residential program in Florida. There were no doors in the bedrooms of the house, and the internet was monitored. When Josh was caught looking at porn, he was forced to print up a list of everything he looked at and, in front of the leaders of the program, go over why he looked at each one. When he concluded he wasn't open to marrying a woman, he was expelled. "So many of my friends lost their faith because of what we went through. When someone suggests, 'It wasn't that bad,' I say, 'You never lived through it. It was awful. Drugs and alcohol are an issue for many of my friends now. It's hard because of the shame and things you deal with. Pastors need to see that this is what happened to us.'"[27]

The Cost of False Hope

Like leukemia patients sitting under faith healers, there was a cost to the movement's early overconfidence. Jack McIntyre, close friend to Love in Action cofounder John Evans, is a sad, albeit perhaps extreme, example of this reality. Jack had spent four years in Love in Action and found himself crippled by his inability to convert to heterosexuality. The failure left him feeling God's continual disappointment.[28] With so deep a burden of having failed God, Jack walked into his hotel room and swallowed a bottle of pills. Jack survived but was committed to a mental hospital outside San Francisco. There he saved up pills over several days. After praying and serving himself Communion, he took an overdose of Valium and Dalmane. This time his attempt was successful. In a letter he left behind, he explained,

> I must confess that there were things in my life that I could not gain control, no matter how much I prayed and tried to avoid the temptation, I continually failed. It is this constant failure that has made me make the decision to terminate my life here on earth. I do this with the complete understanding that life is not mine to take. I know that it is against the teachings of our Creator. No man is without sin, this I realize. I will cleanse myself of all sin as taught to me by His word. Yet, I must face my Lord with the sin of murder. I believe that Jesus died and paid the price for that sin too. I know that I shall have everlasting life with Him by departing this world now, no matter how much I love it, my friends, my family. If I remain it could possibly allow the devil the opportunity to lead me away from the Lord. I love life, but my love for the Lord is so much greater, the choice is simple. . . . To continually go before God and ask forgiveness and make promises you know you can't keep is more than I can take. I feel it is making a mockery of God and all He stands for in my life.[29]

Were suicides like this common? Less so than the movement's critics would suggest. But especially early in the movement, when expectations of change were very high, the sense of failure proved very distressing for some.

EXIT's Bussee described what he saw in the movement's early years of overconfidence. "Many of our clients began to fall apart—sinking deeper into patterns of guilt, anxiety and self-loathing." He continued, "Why weren't they *changing*? The answers from church leaders made the pain even worse:

You might not be a real Christian. You don't have enough faith. You aren't praying and reading the Bible enough. Maybe you have a demon. The message always seemed to be: You're not enough. You're not trying hard enough. You don't have enough faith."[30]

Jeanette Howard's experience was more subtle. In the 1980s, she had traveled from the United Kingdom to participate in Frank Worthen's residential program Love in Action. She had become a Christian in January 1985 and knew she had to leave behind the life she had previously embraced. During her first Exodus conference that year, she was encouraged by Frank Worthen's confident assertion that the average length of time for someone to change from being homosexual to being heterosexual was five years.[31] Howard's heart jumped at the thought that if she stayed faithful, she would gradually gain heterosexual attractions. Howard went on to run an ex-gay ministry and publish a book with a foreword by Andrew Comiskey. But in March 1999, Jeanette came to the realization that after eleven years of ex-gay ministry and fourteen years as a Christian, her orientation had not changed. She came to terms with the fact that left to her own devices, she would still pursue a relationship with a woman. Her attempt to pile Scripture and right living on top of her attractions did not make them go away. It had left her isolated from her internal reality. In 1994, she had begun to struggle with depression. The next year, she would spend time in a psychiatric hospital. Her ex-gay expectation was killing her.

Realizing that fourteen years of effort at orientation change had failed was disappointing. But the realization also left her feeling surprisingly relieved. She explained, "I felt unburdened by expectation and fully free to be myself!"[32] She remained celibate and centered her life on Christ. But she felt a freedom she never knew she could have.

McKrae Game has admitted the damage he saw because of unrealistic expectations. "I certainly regret where I caused harm. I know that creating the organization . . . was in a large way causing harm." He continued, "People reported to attempt suicide because of me."[33] He described a young man who worked for him as his assistant who would come to him and admit he had bought porn. "Finally, he attempted suicide. That really had a serious impact on me. But I fired him. I regret telling him that he was going to hell." Game described another young man who succeeded at killing himself. "He just wanted friends. But for whatever reason, he did kill himself. That deeply impacted me."[34]

Drain Cleaner

Bussee described one young man so traumatized by his ex-gay experience that he got himself drunk and deliberately drove his car into a tree.

He described another fellow leader early in the ex-gay movement who left Exodus and started going to straight bars, looking for someone to beat him up. "The beatings make me feel less guilty," he had explained. They were his atonement for his sin.[35]

Another man, named Mark, went even farther. "After six months of celibacy, [he] went to a bookstore and had a sexual encounter, and felt so guilty about it that he repeatedly slashed his genitals with a razor blade."

He then poured drain cleaner over the wounds.[36]

After months of sexual purity, he had failed. So great was his sense of despair.

These most dramatic examples of harm speak to the spiritual and emotional impact of a false hope with an overfocus on sexual purity as personal accomplishment, which itself at times was wedded to a toxic level of shame.

One wonders if there couldn't have been room to breathe, room to fail. There certainly was in many other ex-gay ministries. Why not here? Does the cross of Jesus Christ not open up a space to accept the deeply rooted effects of the fall? God doesn't always heal in this life. While Joni Eareckson Tada's injury is of a different quality than mine—I claim no moral neutrality to my sexual propensities of my fallen nature—surely, she speaks wisdom in accepting the reality of our human condition. Frequently asked whether she wants God to heal her, she can say with peace, "He has chosen not to heal me, but to hold me. The more intense the pain, the closer His embrace."[37]

But I'm getting ahead of myself.

These stories are among the most shocking. They were not daily occurrences and are not representative of the average Joe's daily experience in the ex-gay movement. Many ministries saw nothing of this sort. At the same time, there was tremendous personal support within many ex-gay ministries. Participants formed lasting friendships. They prayed together and worshiped together. The American Psychological Association's 2009 Task Force on Appropriate Therapeutic Responses to Sexual Orientation, while concluding that sexual orientation change efforts did not work, nevertheless refrained from concluding that noninvasive forms were necessarily harmful. "Recent research reports indicate that there are individuals who perceive they have been harmed and others who perceive they have benefited."[38]

Self-Hatred

One man I interviewed shared with me his nearly twenty years of experience in ex-gay ministry. John is a Christian and he's still a virgin.

Such a species does exist.

While John had never been sexually active, he invested two decades of his life, from 1988 to 2007, with various ex-gay ministries in the United States and Canada. These included New Directions, Living Waters, Jubilee, and the residential treatment program at Love in Action in Memphis. John described himself as a same-sex-attracted man who has never acted on his attractions. Yet he described his time in ex-gay support groups as mostly unhelpful. He told me folks sitting around in support groups "would say, 'Yeah, I jerked off this week,' and people would nod. We all just cried because none of us was changing. We were all in two groups plus in therapy and in counseling."

He explained his journey: "If there was a book written in the 1980s and 1990s for Christians who wanted to overcome unwanted same-sex attractions, I owned it. These books were supposed to fix me. For the next two decades, I went to prayer and healing ministries. I saw a Christian counselor for seventeen years. I went to support groups. I participated in the Living Waters program. Twice, in fact. I attended several Exodus International conferences for many years. These were supposed to fix me. But when all was said and done, there was no change in my attractions. And it left me defeated."

He went to Love in Action's yearlong live-in program in Memphis. "This was supposed to fix me. In fact, that's pretty much what that live-in program 'promised' to do. It didn't." Realize that nonstraight believers in conservative spaces frequently already suffer spiritual trauma. John continued, "In 2005, the . . . congregation I had attended for more than a decade got a new pastor. I was very forthcoming about my life journey. He said, 'So you've been in reparative conversion therapy for fifteen years, and you aren't healed yet?' My answer was no. My attractions had not changed. Less than two weeks later, I got an email from this pastor—not a letter, not a face-to-face conversation, an email. He deemed that I was (direct verbatim quote) 'too needy and too broken' to be allowed to come to church."

His seventeen-year attempt to find a cure for his homosexual orientation had only led to his expulsion from his own church.

John's most positive experience with ex-gay ministry happened two years later in the summer of 2007. John had been meeting every week with a counselor through an ex-gay ministry in Canada when his counselor asked him a diagnostic question. "John, you've been at this twenty years. If God doesn't heal you—if he doesn't take away your same-sex attraction—will you still follow him?"

There was silence, followed by an honest answer.

"No. No way. Absolutely not."

John explained, "I wanted to be fixed. I wanted to be married with kids and a house with a white picket fence, like normal people. How could I possibly continue to trust in God if I'm never going to be healed of this? It didn't matter that I had never once acted on my attractions; I just wanted to be fixed. I wanted them gone. I wanted change."

The counselor listened and then summarized what he was hearing.

"John, the issue isn't that you're same-sex attracted. The issue is that you hate yourself because of it."

At that, John curled up in a ball and sobbed on his counselor's office floor. But it was the truth he needed to confront. "From that day, all my self-loathing disappeared. I accepted the fact that this was me. And I let God love me." That October, John opened up about his story on *Live Journal* and emailed two hundred friends.

His counselor introduced him to a network of Side B Christians—believers who, while gay in sexual orientation, were more fundamentally oriented toward Jesus and committed to celibacy. "For the first time in my life, I found self-worth and community that I trusted." Well more than a decade later, he continues to walk with Jesus faithfully in celibacy and in service to a church very different from the one that kicked him out.[39]

CONFLATING ADDICTION
AND ORIENTATION

John's story demonstrates a fatal flaw that in hindsight is glaringly obvious from the ex-gay movement's earliest years. Ex-gay ministries frequently conflated two distinct pastoral issues. One issue involves breaking cycles of sexually addictive thoughts and actions. An entirely different issue involves changing one's sexual orientation. When ex-gay ministries promised that "change is possible" and spoke about "coming out of homosexuality," which change were they referencing? Were they promising that I could become straight? Or were they promising I could become faithful to Jesus?

And too often the answer was yes.

That was the problem.

It would be a fissure running the full length and breadth of the ex-gay movement. Is this a ministry of sexual integrity? Or is this an effort at sexual orientation change—to change what type of person tempts me?

Many clients entered programs struggling with sexual addictions as well as unwanted homosexual orientations, and few ministries had the clinical discernment to distinguish between these two issues. While sex addicts could hope to gain help in breaking free of destructive patterns of risky sexual behaviors, the promise of becoming straight remained elusive. Ex-gay ministries had some success in treating sexual addiction, and there are thousands of believers who benefited greatly on that front. With God's grace, hard work, perseverance, and the support of friends, church, and family, a ministry could help a same-sex-oriented sex addict who needed help breaking his addictive cycle, whether that be pornography or weekly hookups with strangers. We have God-given gospel resources to help believers grow in faithfulness to Christ.

But for a sexually inactive and exclusively homosexual man filled with self-loathing, like John, the ex-gay model had little to offer. It took an ex-gay counselor going off script after twenty years to pinpoint the real issue. John added, "After that, my counselor said to me, 'John, you don't need me anymore.' For the first time in my life, I felt like a whole person. Coming out of the closet was the most soul-nourishing thing I ever did." John now walks with God joyfully in celibacy.[40]

ten

The Movement Matures

Old school Exodus folks might have still identified as ex-gay,
but not newer folks who came in during Alan's tenure. There
was an intentional shift from ex-gay to same-sex attracted.
—Richard Holloman, Sight Ministry

Those familiar with the mature Exodus of the 2000s are often surprised to hear how gung ho was the movement's early emphasis on curing homosexuality. They recall the later emphasis that it was "not about becoming heterosexual but about becoming holy."[1] They remember having to lower the unrealistic expectations of unknowing newbies who figured a few months of ministry would make them straight.[2] By the 2000s, Exodus was becoming more realistic, more honest, and less strident. For a younger generation, this was a welcome change. But for an old ex-gay guard, the change was troubling.

INCREASING ACCEPTANCE OF CELIBACY

From its earliest days, the ex-gay movement had privileged the testimonies of ex-gay believers who married a spouse of the opposite sex. These were the role models, the successes, the heroes. Marriages were celebrated in ex-gay ministries as the ultimate success. These were the testimonies churches wanted to hear—testimonies whose narrative arc moved from a life of anonymous gay hookups in public restrooms and parks through a spiritual and sexual conversion that ended happily ever after with a wife and children.

The leading ex-gay ministries promoted this view. Alan Medinger defined homosexual healing as culminating in marriage.[3] Within such a marriage-centric system, celibacy would seem like a failure. To be married seemed almost de rigueur for any ex-gay wishing to rise among the ranks of leadership in the movement. The spouse was the outward proof of successful conversion to heterosexuality.

The alternative route—celibacy—was largely neglected, if not even feared. Andy Comiskey told *Christianity Today*, "We must renounce the unbelief prevalent in certain evangelical circles that resigns homosexual strugglers to little if any release from their tendencies. That perception of God is too small!"[4] As late as 2012, Comiskey was still warning about celibacy being "a concession" to same-sex attraction.[5]

Yet there had always been dissenters within the movement. Early on, Robbi Kenney advised other leaders in the movement to lower their expectations. As early as 1981, she pleaded, "Know what you are offering.... You are NOT offering heterosexuality ... [but] the power to come into celibacy." She also added that it might be wiser to "avoid calling them ex-gays."[6]

But such voices had been rare and were about to become even rarer.

Some of those earliest ministries affiliated with Exodus were quite skeptical of claims of orientation change. Such ministries saw celibacy as a positive calling from God. In 1978, during the third Exodus conference in Saint Paul, Minnesota, one guest speaker explained to those in attendance that change wasn't possible for most gay people. He pointed instead to God's power to enable believers to be faithful in celibacy. There was, he stated, no "next level" of change.

To the horror of Worthen and other core Exodus leaders, the message seemed to resonate with most people at the conference. Despite later revelations that none of the Exodus leaders had become straight, these leaders nevertheless doubled down on their conviction that becoming heterosexual was the proper goal.[7] This resulted in a split in Exodus that year. Ministries that downplayed reorientation and emphasized celibacy left the organization.

A decade later, though, with orientation change still elusive, we started to notice slight shifts in emphasis at Exodus. Then, twenty-one years after the split over celibacy, something unthinkable happened at Exodus.

Roughly twelve hundred delegates were gathered at Wheaton College for the July 1999 Exodus conference. It was the largest crowd of ex-gays ever. The announcement was made, and the change it declared was a big one. For the first time in its history, Exodus International publicly declared that some believers cannot change their sexual orientation. They declared that God calls such believers to celibacy.[8]

Exodus was twenty-three years old before it publicly acknowledged that people cannot always expect orientation change. This was a huge shift. Exodus had just demoted the *expectation* of orientation change to a *mere hope* for orientation change. It was clear evidence of a shift in the movement away from the exaggerated expectations of previous decades. The cracks in the wall of orientation change were growing wider.

In 2008, Focus on the Family for the first time endorsed celibacy for gays who became Christians. In a new position statement that year, Focus said, "While we do not believe an individual typically 'chooses' his or her same-sex attractions, we do believe that those who struggle with unwanted same-sex sexual temptation can choose to steward their impulses in a way that aligns with their faith convictions."[9] While the statement still promoted efforts toward sexual orientation change, it signaled quite a shift, leaving the door open for celibacy when sexual orientation did not change.

By 2014, the fifty-thousand-member American Association of Christian Counselors (AACC) would revise its code of ethics, replacing support for reparative therapy with encouragement of celibacy. "Counselors . . . will encourage sexual celibacy or biblically prescribed sexual behavior while such issues are being addressed."[10] By then the *Washington Post* had already spotted the trend, noting how the ex-gay narrative was being eclipsed by the stories of Christians who were gay and celibate.[11]

THE INCREASINGLY PROBLEMATIC EX-GAY IDENTITY

As the ex-gay movement matured in the late 1990s, it became increasingly evident that conversion from gay to straight was far more rare than ex-gays had previously assumed and taught. Yet the growing acceptance of celibacy was only one consequence of this realization. Another consequence was seen in the terminology of the ex-gay movement. Adopting the ex-gay identity was becoming more and more problematic. I certainly felt the tension during my ex-gay days. I recall filling out a medical questionnaire for a new doctor in 1997. I got to the question about my sexual orientation. There were three boxes. Heterosexual. Homosexual. Bisexual. I struggled with how to answer the question. After staring at the boxes for thirty minutes, I checked the heterosexual box.

I was being a good ex-gay. I was claiming my new reality.

But it didn't sit well with me. Who was I kidding? Had I just lied to my doctor? Did Jesus really want me lying to my doctor? Was that how Jesus would make me straight? Was this faith, or was it deception? Was I living a lie?

I remember how awkward I felt during those years whenever I used the term *ex-gay*. What did *gay* even mean? And how was I an *ex*? Did *gay* speak of a promiscuous lifestyle of gay sex? I was a virgin. Did *gay* speak to my sexual orientation? Because that had never changed after I began following Jesus. I was still a six on the Kinsey scale. Even though I wasn't lying by the standards of the movement, I know I felt like a liar whenever I described myself as ex-gay.

But I didn't want to call myself gay, because that's what I was earnestly trying not to be. Besides, these were the years of purity culture. Joshua Harris had kissed dating goodbye, raising the bar of holiness for all of us. So *gay* was definitely out. *Ex-gay* seemed dishonest.

But *homosexual* was no better. Its use as a noun was already considered offensive by the 1990s on account of its clinical nature and its past association with mental illness and criminology. Without even realizing it, I—like many ex-gays—was looking for a new term. A term that would enable me to talk about my ongoing homosexual orientation without calling myself either *gay* or *ex-gay*.

CONSTRUCTING SAME-SEX ATTRACTION

Little did I know it at the time, but a Roman Catholic reparative therapist had already been promoting an alternative. In a 1998 interview with *Our Sunday Visitor*, Dr. Richard Fitzgibbons explained how the term "Same-Sex Attraction Disorder," or SSAD, was first suggested to him. "It was coined by a mother whose son was lost in the lifestyle," he said. "SSAD fits, because we're talking about a lifestyle that calls itself 'gay' but is characterized by overwhelming sadness."[12] At a 1999 Parents and Friends of Ex-Gays and Gays conference in Washington, DC, Fitzgibbons again explained why he had renamed homosexuality Same-Sex Attraction Disorder after twenty years of treating the condition. That year, he published a chapter on the disorder.[13] That same year, *Our Sunday Visitor* published David Morrison's *Beyond Gay*, which used the phrase "same-sex attraction."[14]

Fitzgibbons intended the term to supplant "gay" or "homosexual," though, not to supplant "ex-gay."

The term "same-sex attraction" had been used by sex researchers since the early 1980s in clinical literature to describe the momentary experience of finding oneself drawn to an individual of the same sex.[15] There is no evidence of "same-sex attraction" ever being capitalized before Fitzgibbons. The phrase was always used to describe a clinical observation, not to describe a condition or as a euphemism for homosexual orientation.

In print, the phrase first showed up in a nonscientific context within ex-gay ministries associated with Mormonism. Erin Eldridge introduced the term to a nonclinical audience in a 1994 book titled *Born That Way? A True Story of Overcoming Same-Sex Attraction.*[16] This was the book that first put together the later ubiquitous phrase "struggle with same-sex attraction," using that construction at least eighteen times. Another Mormon ex-gay book three years later would use the same verbiage at least nine times.[17]

Yes, it was the Mormons who taught us to "struggle" with same-sex attraction.

Besides publications within Mormonism, Google Books lists only one twentieth-century book that spoke of "struggling with same-sex attraction"—a 1994 InterVarsity Press commentary on Song of Songs that mentioned it once.[18] Otherwise, pretty much all books from the nineties used "same-sex attraction" only in its earlier, clinical sense. Nicolosi used the term twice in his 1997 text—again, though, in its older, clinical sense.[19]

In 2000, reparative therapist Richard Cohen picked up the "Same-Sex Attraction Disorder" terminology and joined Fitzgibbons in promoting it. Cohen's book *Coming Out Straight* outlined the causes and healing of the disorder. Going through three editions, the book helped define how "ex-gay" Christians started becoming "same-sex attracted," or—as a disorder—"Same-Sex Attracted." The language was beginning to disseminate beyond the offices of reparative therapists.

Christianity Today signaled its adoption of the phrase "same-sex attraction" in a September 4, 2000, editorial that used the language.[20]

But it would be ex-gays Anne Paulk and Joe Dallas who would really popularize the language of "struggling with" same-sex attraction. It previously had been a "struggle" only for Mormons and British commentary authors, until Anne Paulk's 2003 book *Restoring Sexual Identity: Hope for Women Who Struggle with Same-Sex Attraction.*[21] The next year, Joe Dallas published a book that also spoke of "struggling with same-sex attraction."[22]

Après ça, le déluge.

In 2005, author and psychology professor Mark Yarhouse recommended that in working with clients, therapists adopt a three-tier distinction between same-sex attraction, homosexual orientation, and gay identity.[23] In the following years, scores of books hit the presses about same-sex attraction and its struggle. Richard Holloman observed, "Nobody at Exodus identified as gay. There was a wall up against that. But the term *homosexual* was offensive as a noun. Old school Exodus folks might have still identified as ex-gay, but not newer folks who came in during [Alan Chambers'] tenure. There was an intentional shift from *ex-gay* to *same-sex attracted.* It seemed less offensive and more understanding. Ex-gay suggested you no longer were same-sex attracted."[24]

DITCHING THE EX-GAY LABEL

By the late 2000s, the shift from "ex-gay" to "struggling with same-sex attraction" was nearly complete. This restructuring of how conservative Christians spoke about homosexual orientation took less than a decade.

After another decade of this, a lot of folks I know now cringe at the word "struggle."

By the mid-2000s, some top leaders in the ex-gay movement were lobbying to ditch the ex-gay label permanently. In an August 2006 conversation with Michael Bussee, Alan Chambers gave permission to be quoted on the matter. Bussee wrote, "I just got off the phone with Alan Chambers of EXODUS. . . . Regarding the term 'ex-gay,' he gave me permission to quote him: 'We need to do away with the term entirely and make sure it's never used again.'"[25] Chambers by then was making no secret of his disdain for a label that suggested a result the movement was realizing it could not deliver.

The adoption of the language of same-sex attraction in the 2000s made it more tenable to continue maintaining the ex-gay script, however. I no longer had to say, "I used to be gay" and thus imply that I'm now straight. That was the old ex-gay script. Now I could say, "I used to be gay, but I don't think of myself as gay anymore. Now I'm just same-sex attracted."

Now, I acknowledge that to anyone outside the narrow halls of conservative Christianity, the new statement sounds sillier than the old one. But after all those years I spent being an ex-gay, there was still that emotional need to renounce a homosexual self-perception. Even if it sounded silly to a lot of people.

REPENTING OF GAY IDENTITY?

Remember, the ex-gay movement had spent decades creating a narrative in which the gay person stopped being gay or homosexual and changed to become something else: ex-gay or heterosexual or on the healing path toward heterosexual functioning. That expectation of change did not go away. There remained an expectation that you repent of a homosexual self-perception and think of yourself as having been changed. With the language of same-sex attraction, Christians could still speak of having repented of a gay identity or gay self-perception without having to pretend that their orientation had changed.

Within the confines of highly conservative religious spaces during a raging culture war between the gays and the Christians, this new language opened up a way to speak about our experience while signaling our commitment to biblical sexuality. This was a great help for a lot of us. I jumped ship from "ex-gay" to "same-sex attracted" at my earliest opportunity.

But the new terminology raised a question. What does it mean to stop being gay, when you're openly admitting that you're exclusively same-sex attracted? Is the expectation of possible sexual orientation change the only difference between perceiving of yourself as homosexual and perceiving of yourself as same-sex attracted? If so, what happens if that expectation of orientation change drastically diminishes? At that point does the ex-gay script just become semantics? As a relic of reparative therapy, does repenting of a homosexual self-perception still have any real meaning?

We will pick up that question in later chapters. As the shift in terminology continued, troubling reports were reaching Exodus leadership.

TROUBLING REPORTS FROM AFFILIATES

By 2007, the ex-gay movement had in many ways been humbled by the failure of its early overconfidence in a homosexual cure. One *Christianity Today* reporter was struck by the change at the Exodus conference that year. He observed, "No hype. Limited faith in techniques. No gay bashing. No detectable triumphalism."[26] The movement had matured.

At least that's what it looked like on the outside. Insiders were feeling increasingly troubled about what they were seeing within some ministries. Randy Thomas stepped into the vice president position at Exodus in 2002. What he saw from that vantage point surprised him. "I was part of an Exodus affiliated ministry in Texas that believed being in relationship with Jesus alone was our goal. I never felt pressured to change my same-sex orientation. . . . I assumed this was what happened at every Exodus group," he explained. But in his role as vice president, "I was confronted with the reality that some methods used by some of our local ministries ended up bringing hurt and pain to the very people they were trying to comfort." Over the course of eleven years, he and other Exodus staff tried to address these concerns privately. But to protect the larger Exodus ministry, he never addressed concerns publicly in a way that might have forced systemic change. He kept quiet, "not even letting our own leaders know the depths of what concerned us."[27]

By the 2010s, concerns within the ministry were growing. Exodus president Alan Chambers commented, "Love in Action . . . had an increasing number of former clients of their live-in program making ugly disclosures of their negative experiences at the ministry."[28]

Love in Action had been investigated by the state of Tennessee in 2005 for dispensing psychotropic medicine and treating minors without a license. That same year, the ministry drew international attention after a teenage client was forced into the program against his will and wrote about it. His words spread across the internet as the words of a gay teenager being held against his will.[29] In 2003, a report had surfaced in which one client of LIA, Tom Otteson, explained that LIA director John Smid had told him that "it would be better if I were to commit suicide than go back into the world and become a homosexual again."[30]

Love in Action had become noticeably more structured and rule oriented under John Smid's leadership after Frank Worthen stepped down. A 374-page *Love in Action Handbook* governed life in the facility. The ministry routinely confiscated as contraband items like Calvin Klein underwear and muscle shirts. A young man named KC described how he was forbidden to play the piano at Love in Action because piano playing contributed to his being gay.[31] They had egg timers to time their showers so they wouldn't have time to masturbate. They were not allowed to call their families. They were told to drive only to work and back and not to talk with strangers.[32] There were a lot of rules, and they penalized teens who broke the rules. Garrard Conley, who detailed his experience in *Boy Erased*, described the account of one teenage boy who was forced to undergo his own mock funeral after he had "defected." Other teens read aloud his obituary, detailing his slow death because of HIV.[33] These were hardly the sorts of clinical interventions Exodus leadership wanted to promote. But Love in Action had always been the Exodus flagship.

How common were stories of trauma coming out of ex-gay ministries? It's an incredibly difficult question to answer. If you gather a roomful of people who aren't straight, particularly if they were Christians in the 1980s or 1990s, you will hear stories.

While the average adult participant in an Exodus-affiliated ministry in the 2000s did not consider his experience at the time psychologically harmful, the picture is much more troubling with youth.[34] A 2018 study of 245 LGBT young adults found that having undergone sexual orientation change efforts during adolescence was associated with poor mental health outcomes. Young adults whose parents had attempted to change their sexual orientation between age thirteen and age nineteen were three times more likely to have attempted suicide than those whose parents had not attempted to do so. Those teens whose parents took them to an ex-gay ministry or reparative therapist were five times more likely to have attempted suicide.[35]

Realize that nonstraight youth already have a much higher suicide rate than youth who are straight. A 2019 study surveying thirty-four thousand LGBT youth in the United States found that 39 percent of nonstraight youth had seriously considered suicide over the previous twelve months. This study found that students who had undergone sexual orientation change efforts were more than twice as likely to have attempted suicide.[36]

Mark Yarhouse reflected on the many Christians he has known with experience in ex-gay ministries. "Some of the people I have met who are celibate and gay may have benefited from religiously affiliated support groups primarily because of the opportunity to be honest and to receive support as they were navigating sexual identity questions or concerns." He added, "But they, too, often say that the promise of change or healing was overstated and that the emphasis on achieving heterosexuality was unhelpful to them psychologically and spiritually."[37]

Concerns continued to arise throughout the 2000s.

The fissures were there all along. Leaders claiming to have become heterosexual falling badly. Orientation change proving more elusive than ever imagined. Some clients spiraling into despair. Addiction getting conflated with orientation. Shifting perspectives on celibacy. Reports of trouble in member ministries.

Yet another fissure had started to appear in the final years of the twentieth century. At first it looked like a godsend to the movement. But it would backfire badly in the 2000s.

POSTER CHILD IN A CULTURE WAR

Early on, Exodus ministries shunned the spotlight. They were too gay for traditional churches and not gay enough for the secular gay community. But in the late 1990s, the ex-gay movement became a valued political pawn in a culture war pitting Christians against gays on the battlefields of gay rights and gay marriage. Political conservatives saw the tide of secular media and popular opinion shifting away from them in the public sphere. They needed a way to turn the tide again in their favor.

By 1998, a group of twenty-five conservative Christian groups had been strategizing for more than two years as they watched the culture around them change. Gay people were now adopting children. Cities and states were enacting laws prohibiting discrimination on the basis of sexual orientation. Gay characters were coming out of the closet and into our televisions.

In a June 4, 1998, conference call with the twenty-five conservative leaders, Janet L. Folger of the Center for Reclaiming America proposed a strategy to turn the tide. They would take out full-page ads in America's largest newspapers, highlighting "former homosexuals" who had overcome their sexual orientation through ex-gay ministries. The ads cost as much as six hundred thousand dollars and reached eight million subscribers in papers like *USA Today*, the *Wall Street Journal*, and the *Los Angeles Times*. Anne Paulk's image ran in the *New York Times* with the words "wife, mother and former lesbian." The Family Research Council's Robert Knight called it "the Normandy landing in the culture war."[38]

Overnight the ex-gay movement had become the poster child (literally) for the Religious Right. The ex-gay narrative had just been weaponized toward a political end. Why legalize gay marriage if gays can change and become straight if they really want to?

In 2003, the first annual Ex-Gay Lobby Days sent ex-gays traversing the halls of the US Congress. Ex-gay organizations as diverse as Parents and Friends of Ex-Gays and Gays, Exodus International, and NARTH filled the US Capitol and congressional office buildings to educate members of Congress on the "adverse effect of sexual orientation legislation on former homosexuals."[39] They lobbied against hate crime laws and against same-sex civil unions. Through the early 2000s, Exodus president Alan Chambers was numbered among the powerful Arlington Group, a politically conservative coalition of prominent religious and political leaders with close connections to White House political adviser Karl Rove and President George W. Bush. "We went to D.C. at least every other month, sometimes more," recalls Exodus vice president Randy Thomas. "It was a rush to have all these high-profile people wanting us to join them in public policy pushes."[40]

With their newfound political usefulness came new sources of funding. After 2001, Exodus doubled its financial support base.[41]

And the political usefulness brought welcome visibility. *Christianity Today* in 2007 observed, "Perhaps nothing has brought Exodus into the mainstream of evangelicalism more than its embrace by James Dobson's Focus on the Family."[42] As Focus shifted more resources toward conservative political activism, ex-gays gained their national platform. That same year, Exodus president Alan Chambers received phone calls from Mike Huckabee's campaign, from Mitt Romney's campaign, and from John McCain's campaign—all seeking his backing in the Republican presidential primary.[43]

"STILL NOTHING BUT A FAGGOT TO THEM"

There was a cost to the political activism of Exodus International. In 2008, Where Grace Abounds, one of the movement's oldest affiliate ministries, pulled out. The ministry's director, Roger Jones, explained, "WGA has chosen to remain silent on issues of public policy, as we see this as a distraction from the ministry to which God has called us."[44] Scott Kingry commented, "Exodus had a combative posture toward the LGBT community. . . . Then you had the Change campaign with the billboards, the *Time* magazine piece. They became politically aligned with Focus. They were pushing away the people we want to work with. We did not take the decision to leave lightly. But LGBT people get vilified so easily."[45]

In 2008, Exodus International gave its support to California's Proposition 8 to change the state constitution to ban same-sex marriage. Chambers spoke in favor of the amendment. Proposition 8 passed. But his heart sank as the results rolled in. He explained, "The night Prop 8 passed in California, I watched the coverage on a Fox News split screen. On the right was a ballroom full of celebrating supporters, and on the left was a ballroom full of devastated opponents. Watching shattered families on the left trying to regroup after being told their relationships were less than and not equal to those on the right changed me."[46]

Chambers knew they were being used by the political right. "Too often we were listened to only when it was convenient and when we could help promote an agenda."[47] It was not an uncommon sentiment. One ex-gay minister reminisced about something John Paulk, chairman of Exodus International, had uttered years earlier at a dinner party when they worked together at Focus on the Family. They were in the kitchen together, preparing the meal for a group of colleagues from Focus. In a mocking tone, John whispered to him, "They love you to your face. But you know behind your back, you are still nothing but a faggot to them."[48]

After Proposition 8, Exodus pulled out of politics to refocus on its core ministry of helping people navigate their sexuality and their faith. Becoming the poster child in a culture war had brought with it collateral damage. By letting itself become a political pawn in battles over gay rights, they had further alienated the very community many Exodus leaders had hoped to reach.

Becoming the poster child in a culture war also cost Exodus International supporters. As the North American cultural climate became more affirming of gay people, politicization of ex-gay ministries made it harder for some organizations to publicly support them. Exodus saw numerous ministries leave, and in 2009 it lost a longtime supporter, Willow Creek Community Church—then one of the country's largest churches.[49]

The ex-gay movement's alliance with the political right had backfired. The culture war had been lost. And in the aftermath, many churches trying to reach a population that increasingly supported gay political rights could no longer afford to be associated with the poster children who had been used to oppose such rights, regardless of the churches' own unchanged convictions.

eleven

Questioning the Paradigm

We have been distracted by the politics around homosexuality....
We have been distracted by a focus on orientation change....
We have been distracted by the question of causation.
—Wendy Gritter, New Direction Ministry, 2008

In many ways, the decline and death of Exodus International and the ex-gay movement remind me of watching, as a young adult, the Soviet Union collapse. The Union of Soviet Socialist Republics had seemed remarkably strong. It had a defining narrative of working-class struggle and socialist revolution leading from the slavery of capitalist oppression to a future socialist utopia. Many early Soviets sacrificed everything, so great was their faith in that narrative. But there were repeated failures along the way. Famines. Sluggish industrial production. Stalin's purges. Chernobyl. By the 1980s, few Soviets deeply believed that communism worked. Ultimately, Soviet leaders ushered in a season of *glasnost* and *perestroika*, openness and restructuring, to try to right the ship. But it was too late. By then the Soviet leaders no longer believed their own grand narrative. That's what led to the Soviet Union's dissolution in 1991.

While the ex-gay movement was spiritually and morally very different from godless Soviet dictatorship, the parallels between the two are remarkable. Early ex-gay leaders sacrificed everything for their grand narrative of a reorientation from gay to straight. But there were failures along the way. A lot of people lost faith in the movement. New leaders brought a refreshing openness and restructuring. But it was too late. The leaders themselves no longer believed their own grand narrative.

They had their reasons.

ONGOING LEADERSHIP TROUBLES

Leadership had always been an issue for the ex-gay movement, as we explored in chapter 9. Leaders lacking formal training. Leaders engaging in gay affairs, despite their claims of having been cured of homosexuality. Leaders becoming increasingly skeptical of the ex-gay narrative. Leaders growing alarmed at the stories they were hearing about some affiliated ministries. But the leadership troubles didn't end there.

In 1986, a researcher interviewing twenty clients at Homosexuals Anonymous–affiliated Quest Learning Center discovered that HA founder Colin Cook had sexually molested sixteen of the twenty boys and men he interviewed. Cook's victims described in graphic detail disturbing experiences of sexual abuse masquerading as professional therapy. From his position of authority, Cook had attempted to sexually coerce boys as young as sixteen who were under his care. The researcher blew the whistle and alerted church authorities, who pulled their funding from Quest Learning Center. Cook was fired from Homosexuals Anonymous, and the Quest Learning Center was shut down. With the departure of the founder who developed the fourteen-step program whereby his homosexuality had been "cured," Homosexuals Anonymous sought new leadership to continue implementing that same fourteen-step program with others.

And there was hypocrisy. In 1990, Darlene Bogle of Paraklete, who had so vividly described her deliverance from the demon of lesbianism, was outed for being in a lesbian relationship with another woman. Her publisher dropped her. Her church fired her, and her denomination took away her ministerial credentials. It was another hit to the ex-gay movement, but not the hardest.

In 1993, a minister founded his counseling center, FaithQuest Colorado, and quickly grew to prominence. He received client referrals from Focus on the Family. Colorado for Family Values brought him on as a speaker at their Time to Stand Seminars.[1]

Two years later, on October 27, 1995, the front page of the *Denver Post* broke the story that this ex-gay minister was sexually abusing male clients.[2] Who was this minister? Homosexuals Anonymous founder Colin Cook. The same Cook who had been fired by the Adventists in 1974 for having sex with a man in his church. The same Cook who had been fired by Homosexuals Anonymous in 1986 for raping men and boys under his care—a national story that had been covered in the pages of *Christianity Today*. Colorado for Family Values was now unknowingly platforming a sexual predator. Focus on the Family was unwittingly referring clients to a sexual predator. The organization tried to vet counselors for clinical expertise and for biblical convictions, but this was before Google and the modern internet, and he slipped through.

According to a UPI news report, "Cook insists he has not had homosexual sex since his 1986 admissions, but two young Colorado men he counseled in the past two years reported he engaged in hours of phone sex with them." The article included interviews with victims. It explained, "The *Post* quoted one man Cook counseled as saying, 'He thinks if he's having erotic phone conversations it's okay because he's not having sex.' Other men who had face-to-face sessions with Cook said the meetings consisted of similar discussions, mutual masturbation, removal of clothes and naked massages."[3] He instructed his patients to bring gay porn with them for desensitization sessions.

And the response from his supporters?

"Colorado for Family Values spokesman Kevin Tebedo defended Cook, saying the group believes 'Colin's message is valuable and the response to Colin has been tremendous. All the people [at the seminars] thought he was top-notch.'"[4] Two months later Cook bragged to the news media that the number of men coming to him for ex-gay therapy had doubled since the *Denver Post* investigation.

Cook again insisted on his innocence and again claimed to have been cured of his homosexuality. But by the 1990s, his clients had better technology. They had recorded Cook sexually abusing them during their therapy sessions.[5]

Colorado for Family Values quietly let Kevin Tebedo resign but took no public responsibility for promoting a known abuser. They dropped Colin Cook from their list of recommended resources and discontinued future collaboration. Focus on the Family did the same, announcing they would no longer send clients to him.[6]

Three years later, in 1998, Focus on the Family launched a ministry called Love Won Out, for families and church leaders. Later renamed True Stories, the ministry sought to equip Christians to love gay people without abandoning the biblical sexual ethic or accepting a gay political and social agenda. Under the leadership of Exodus chairman John Paulk, the ministry promised that "same-sex attractions can be overcome."[7] John told his story of freedom in a book titled *Not Afraid to Change: The Remarkable Story of How One Man Overcame Homosexuality*.[8] The back cover provocatively asked, "Can a homosexual become straight? Leading psychologists say no, popular media figures say no, national gay activists say no. Today, a chorus of authoritative voices all agree: gays can't change. But it's not true. An increasing number of men and women around the world are living proof that those authorities are wrong."[9] That year, the former homosexual Paulk and his former lesbian wife, Anne, wrote a book titled *Love Won Out: How God's Love Helped Two People Leave*

Homosexuality and Find Each Other.[10] That August, their faces were on the cover of *Newsweek* magazine.[11]

In September 2000, however, John Paulk was photographed in a gay bar named Mr. P's in Washington, D.C. Founded in 1978, Mr. P's had been the first gay bar in Dupont Circle, the gayborhood long a center of gay cruising in the District. A hot spot for drag queens as well as gay white men, it had a confederate flag above the bar that was intended to signal that not all forms of diversity were welcome there. It was a strange spot to find the head of Focus on the Family's Homosexuality and Gender Division, let alone for the then–chairman of the board of Exodus International.

Paulk's story shifted several times. First, he denied that he was John Paulk, insisting he was instead a "John Clint." He claimed he didn't know that Mr. P's was a gay bar. He was just there to use the restroom. But clients insisted he had been there more than an hour, flirting with other men and telling them he was gay. He later confessed he was there to seek the comfort of gay men. John left both Focus on the Family and Exodus. He again began frequenting gay bars and divorced Anne.

In 2003, trouble came to Michael Johnston. Johnston was founder of Americans for Truth and of National Coming out of Homosexuality Day and was director of ex-gay Kerusso Ministries. Johnston had been a literal poster boy for sexual conversion, appearing in ad campaigns as a model of change. In 1999, pastor and activist Jerry Falwell had held Johnston up as living proof that homosexuals can be cured. Johnston supposedly helped write the Assemblies of God position paper on homosexuality. He traveled to speak in churches and schools about the gospel's power to change sexual orientation.

What Michael didn't tell them was that he also held an online profile wherein he went by the name Sean. As Sean, he continued cruising for sex with young gay men and organized gay sex parties.

And he had not even practiced safe sex.

Nor had he disclosed to his partners that he was HIV positive.[12]

In 2007, Exodus officially distanced itself from self-reputed reparative therapist Richard Cohen after media attention shed a spotlight on some of his unorthodox counseling techniques. His approach included nonsexual cuddling of clients to repair the emotional bond to the same-sex parent. He had even demonstrated such therapeutic cuddling live on Comedy Central's *The Daily Show.* Exodus posted a statement to its website: "Exodus International does not endorse the work of Richard Cohen or the methods utilized in his practice. Some of the techniques Mr. Cohen employs could be detrimental to an individual's understanding of healthy relational boundaries and disruptive to the psychological and emotional development of men and women seeking clinical counsel and aid."[13] Both NARTH and Parents and Friends of Ex-Gays and Gays—of which Cohen had been president—scrubbed their websites of any positive mention of Cohen.[14]

If the scandals had slowed down as the ex-gay movement matured, they certainly didn't go away. In 2010, prominent Southern Baptist reparative therapist George Alan Rekers scandalized his supporters. Rekers had been a founding board member of the Family Research Council in 1983 and was a board member and officer in NARTH.

On May 4, 2010, the *Miami New Times* reported that Rekers had been photographed in Miami International Airport with a twenty-year-old male prostitute he had arranged via male escort website rentboy.com. News media around the globe picked up the story. Rekers acknowledged having hired Jo-Vanni Roman as a "travel assistant" for his ten-day European vacation. But Roman acknowledged that his services included more than carting around luggage. Soon another individual stepped forward with a similar story involving Rekers, from 1992.

This was the same Rekers who wrote *Growing Up Straight*. This was the expert witness in court cases arguing against gay people adopting children, and defending the Boy Scouts of America's ban on gay youth.

In resigning from NARTH, Rekers insisted, "I am not gay and never have been."[15]

John Smid of Love in Action had caused a stir back in 2005 when reports surfaced that he was telling clients suicide was preferable to homosexuality. In November 2014, Smid caused another stir when he—a speaker platformed by Focus on the Family's Love Won Out tour for his powerful testimony of healing from homosexuality—married his husband, Larry.

In fairness, it wasn't only ex-gay leaders who were falling. In 2018, the *Houston Chronicle* reported that multiple men had made accusations of rape and sexual abuse against Paul Pressler, the hero of the 1979 Southern Baptist conservative takeover. A 2017 lawsuit had claimed Pressler raped a teenage boy at his home two to three times a month. Pressler had paid out $450,000 in 2004 over another assault. He had been fired as youth minister from a church in 1978 for grabbing a boy's penis in a sauna. Paige Patterson was also named in the suit for helping cover up the abuse in 2004.[16]

Evidently, Patterson learned how to cover up abuse early on.

The claim against Patterson was dismissed because of the statute of limitations. But he was fired from Southwestern Baptist Theological Seminary for more recent attempts to cover up sexual abuse.

It wasn't just the evangelicals. In 2018, news surfaced that in the early 1990s, John Harvey, founder of Courage, had pressured bishops to return pedophile priests to the ministry.[17] According to the same account, the reparative therapist influencing Harvey in this direction was Richard Fitzgibbons, creator of the term "Same-Sex Attraction Disorder" and the initial figure behind the push to popularize the language of "same-sex attraction." It cites a 2011 case in which Fitzgibbons was shown hundreds of images of child pornography found by a computer repairman on a priest's laptop, including photos of children's genitalia. Fitzgibbons denied that the images were pornographic. His advice to the bishop was that the priest was suffering from loneliness and depression. The courts disagreed and sentenced the priest to fifty years in the slammer for production of child pornography. As bishops looked to him for his expert evaluation, Fitzgibbons was responsible for returning a significant number of abusive priests to the ministry.[18]

The Mormons had their cases too. In 2019, prominent Mormon conversion therapist David Matheson, who developed and led the ex-gay retreats Journey into Manhood, announced he was gay, was divorcing his wife, and would pursue a relationship with another man.[19] That was the same year that purity culture icon Joshua Harris renounced his faith, left his wife, apologized to the LGBTQ community, and went to his first PrideFest, wearing rainbow colors and eating a rainbow donut.

I'm not judging anyone. Nor am I celebrating these leaders' falls. Each of these situations left spiritual siblings bruised and bleeding, spouses betrayed, followers feeling duped, and the vulnerable injured. I am just pointing out that there was a pattern of leadership failures in the ex-gay movement over the course of forty years. There were so many leaders who ended up hurting people or walking down a very different path than the one they'd once endorsed.

MANY GODLY LEADERS PERSEVERED

Realize there were also countless examples of faithful leadership. Frank Worthen was one of those. He remained faithful to his wife and to God the rest of his life. Even Frank's enemies loved him and acknowledged the ways he had been a father to so many men during an often-turbulent period in their lives. He lived a life that was above reproach.

Men like Bob Davies of Exodus, Andy Comiskey of Desert Stream, the late Alan Medinger and Bob Ragan, Jason Thompson of Portland Fellowship, Joe Dallas, and countless other leaders remained faithful to Jesus and faithful to their ex-gay cause. Anne Paulk has remained faithful even after her husband John crossed the Rubicon. Christine Sneeringer has walked with God faithfully for thirty years now and continues to inspire those seeking change. Individuals like these were models of self-sacrificial obedience in faithfulness to Christ.

Still for me, who once had high hopes for the ex-gay movement, learning about one leadership failure after another was like watching a line of dominos fall.

WHY SO MANY METEORIC FALLS?

What was it about the ex-gay movement that set so many prominent leaders up to fall, and fall badly?

These were (almost exclusively) men who were trying to serve Jesus. But they were leaders within a system that said that becoming heterosexual is what success looks like. They would have faced incredible internal pressure to convince themselves and their followers that they were farther along than they were. Their donors wanted to know that the ministry model they were selling had worked for them. The pressure to hide their ongoing homosexual orientation—from themselves and others—created an incredibly lonely space in which no one knew the real them. The real them was a secret and therefore unreached by grace. The psychology seemed designed to breed moral failure in leaders.

Contrast this psychology of denial with Alex Davidson's pseudonymous 1970 IVP book *Returns of Love: Letters of a Christian Homosexual*. Alex explained, "[God] calls me by name: 'Alex—sinful, hypocritical, embarrassed, homosexual Alex,' He calls; and in doing so He demonstrates both that He knows all about me and that He still loves me in spite of it."[20]

You see, it's the homosexual Alex who needs to be known and embraced by the love and mercy of Jesus. It's the homosexual Alex who needs to know that God sees him all the way down and still wants to be in relationship with him.

Anyone who is hiding or in denial about the one area where they most need the gospel's warmth to flood in has set themselves up to fall. No one sees the real them. No one loves the real them. Others love the mask they wear. Such isolation will only compound the loneliness they feel. Eventually the longing to be known and accepted is bound to succumb to the pull of indwelling sin.

I feel great sympathy for each of these ex-gay leaders. They were undone by the unrealistic expectations of the movement they served. And that movement was only trying to give the church the gay cure it wanted and demanded. They bowed down to that expectation, and it devoured them.

INTERNAL QUESTIONING WITHIN THE MOVEMENT

By the time Mikhail Gorbachev took the reins of the Soviet Union, Soviet leaders were quietly questioning the system's sustainability. The cracks and fissures within the ex-gay movement by the last half of the 2000s similarly left leaders and promoters at the very highest levels questioning their most basic assumptions. Quiet conversations were happening among colleagues. Doubts were being voiced. Prominent leaders and churches were distancing themselves from the movement. Exodus itself was becoming more open about the rarity of orientation change.

By the mid-2000s, Grove City College psychology professor Warren Throckmorton was questioning reparative therapy. Throckmorton had been a champion of the ex-gay movement. He had spoken at NARTH conferences and in 2002 received the reparative therapists organization's Sigmund Freud Award. It was Throckmorton who had produced the 2004 ex-gay documentary *I Do Exist*, highlighting the stories of five "former homosexuals."[21] But 2004 was the last year Throckmorton spoke at NARTH. He cancelled a planned appearance there in 2006.

That year, Noe Gutierrez, one of the principal voices who testified in the documentary *I Do Exist*, informed Throckmorton that he was still gay. Throckmorton explained, "In our conversations it became clear to me that he had felt a social pressure to say he had completely changed. So had the rest of the people in the video. And so that's what really pushed me back to reexamine the studies I had used to convince me that change is possible."[22] On February 1, 2007, Throckmorton retired the documentary, and soon afterward he voiced his skepticism about the work. "The stories of the people involved were freely offered and reflected their experience at that time," he explained in the FAQ section of his website. "Since then, more changes have taken place. It is not appropriate to see the film as a testament to change of sexual orientation. . . . *I Do Exist* is not a current depiction of what I believe to be accurate about sexual orientation."[23] Throckmorton now concluded that the research that had led him toward reparative therapy had little merit.

That year, he and fellow psychologist Mark Yarhouse of Regent University presented the sexual identity therapy (SIT) framework as an alternative to reparative therapy. Sexual identity therapy helps clients identify their core beliefs and helps them live according to those beliefs.[24] Throckmorton and Yarhouse recall having been at a conference of the American Association of Christian Counselors right as Richard Cohen was blowing up all over the media because of his unorthodox and potentially harmful therapeutic interventions. Yarhouse looked at Throckmorton and asked, "What have we gotten ourselves into?" They wanted an alternative to reparative therapy, but one that wasn't crazy.[25]

Because of what happened in 2007, Throckmorton lobbied Focus on the Family and NARTH to adjust their approaches.

Exodus International was also shifting.

Alan Chambers had begun rethinking the question of orientation change as early as 2006. "As I heard more stories and evaluated my own realities," he explained, "I realized change in orientation was not possible or happening."[26] The following year he told *Christianity Today* that he wondered whether change is ever 100 percent in this life.[27] In an appearance on *The Montel Williams Show*, Chambers insisted that Exodus could not change people. When Montel noted that the wording on the Exodus website suggested just the opposite, Chambers agreed the website needed to change.[28]

On other occasions, Chambers continued to defend orientation change, albeit with an important caveat. In 2009, Chambers told *Christianity Today* that it's wrong to say sexual orientation can't change as a result of therapy. "That flies in the face of the testimonies of tens of thousands of people just like me," he explained, pointing to his wife and two children. But then came the caveat: "That's not to say that you can flip a switch and go from gay to straight."[29]

This was a shift from Frank Worthen's original vision.

Chambers had gained media attention in 2007 when he personally disavowed the label ex-gay, saying he had come to resent the term for implying a neat, clean break from gay to straight—a kind of change he himself had not experienced. That year's Exodus conference did not spotlight a single successful ex-gay testimony. Chambers said he wasn't sure he had ever even met an ex-gay whose testimony of change panned out to be genuine. By then he and other Exodus leaders were speaking openly about possible biological bases for homosexuality.[30] Jill Rennick, who leads Grace Place in Milwaukee—formerly Exodus affiliate Broken Yoke—and was volunteer coordinator for the last four Exodus conferences, remembers it well. "It was such a relief when everyone at Exodus started admitting that their attractions hadn't changed. Alan was the first one I heard say it."[31]

By the late 2000s, Richard Holloman, director of Sight Ministry, stated that "everyone I knew at Exodus, including leadership, was open about that. I never knew anyone who had been 'delivered.'" Leaders within Exodus were questioning its motto "Change is possible." Holloman wondered what "change" meant. "Many of us came to the view that change meant choosing to follow Christ in a traditional biblical view of sexuality," he explained. Under Chambers' leadership, Exodus was steadily becoming more focused on grace and discipleship and less focused on lists of rules and orientation change. Holloman said, "I could identify the people in leadership who still focused on change, on rules. I could see how damaging it was." He then quipped, "Some of those leaders now have gay partners or a gay marriage."[32]

At a January 2008 Exodus leadership conference, Wendy Gritter of Canadian Exodus–affiliate New Direction Ministry threw down the gauntlet. She called for Exodus ministries to stop political lobbying, stop emphasizing change, show genuine respect for those who came to different conclusions about sexual ethics, and repent of the tone suggesting that those who abandoned the movement just hadn't tried hard enough. In a follow-up article, she explained, "We have been distracted by the politics around homosexuality.... We have been distracted by a focus on orientation change.... We have been distracted by the question of causation." Her ministry, she explained, sought to be "pastorally focused, not politically driven ... relationally focused, not program driven ... discipleship-focused, not change driven ... partnership-focused, not empire driven." Critics of Exodus saw her words as a much-needed breath of fresh Canadian air.[33]

Wendy Gritter was not alone in her criticism of Exodus's focus.

Roger Jones of Where Grace Abounds reflected, "What change meant varied from ministry to ministry. At core, everyone wanted people to have a relationship with Christ. But that got sidetracked with all the talk about change.... Change seemed to be what Exodus was all about."[34]

Mike Rosebush was Exodus International's director of professional counseling and a clinical member of NARTH. Previously a vice president at Focus on the Family, Rosebush became the central connection between Exodus, its network of professional counselors, and the potential clients seeking help. In an interview, he explained that nearly all counselors in the Exodus counseling network—a significant majority of them straight—provided reparative therapy and that nearly all of the counselors who were heterosexual believed homosexual orientation to be a mental disorder. Rosebush recalled one disagreement he had with a straight Exodus reparative therapist who was lamenting the American Psychiatric Association's 1973 ruling that homosexuality was not a mental illness. As director of the Exodus network of counselors, Rosebush responded, "I am a homosexual. And I do not consider myself to be mentally ill simply because I have this attraction." The reparative therapist responded with incredulity.

In the fall of 2008, Rosebush presented at the annual NARTH conference. He began by explaining that we don't really know the exact cause of homosexuality in males, and we most certainly cannot predict it.

Realize he was speaking to a crowded room of professional reparative therapists.

That's like dropping a Ming vase on a concrete patio next to a swimming pool filled with sinologists and antiquities dealers.

Rosebush then explained, "I have counseled hundreds of homosexual clients, and I have talked with hundreds more, and I have never met a single man who could honestly tell me his same-sex attraction had been extinguished."

Having acknowledged the failure to cure sexual orientation, the director of the Exodus counseling network then laid out his approach to therapy, an approach he named sanctification coaching, which centered not on cure but on care. "The goal of therapy is to focus on shame reduction," he explained, "and such therapy can be successful in perhaps as little as six weeks." This was in stark contrast to reparative therapy, which typically lasted two to seven years. Rosebush told the therapists that he considered such lengthy counseling with so little success to be—in his words—"professional malpractice."

Even in the season of Exodus International's *glasnost* and *perestroika*, this went too far. "After my NARTH presentation," Rosebush explained, "I was asked to resign as the director of professional counselors for Exodus. I was told that I would no longer receive any referrals from either NARTH or my own Focus on the Family." He added, "It was at that point that I ceased my counseling practice."[35]

But other key leaders within Exodus were not far behind Rosebush in thinking that a more radical openness and restructuring was needed.

In October 2010, Exodus canceled its yearlong sponsorship of the annual Day of Truth, a day on which high school students wore T-shirts advocating for "an honest conversation about the biblical truth for sexuality."[36] One homemade shirt was black with masking tape across it with large letters in all caps, stating, "HOMOSEXUALITY IS SHAMEFUL. ROMANS 1:27."[37] The event had been conceived in 2005 as a response to the annual Day of Silence, an effort to bring attention to name-calling, threats, and abuse against LGBT students. Alan Chambers told *Christianity Today*, "Day of Truth was always perceived in an adversarial manner, and became more about policy than people. That is in conflict with the mission we have chosen to embrace as an organization. . . . We want to continue to promote dialogue and to equip Christian kids to reach out with compassion, grace and truth."[38]

twelve

The Death of Cure

In our experience, Exodus has been filled with vulnerable, well-meaning men and women who took up an impossible task without adequate support and were then shamed by their own kin for failing.

—Christianity Today

In December 2011, *WORLD* magazine named Alan Chambers its Daniel of the Year. "Part of Chambers' work involves treading into the lion's den of mainstream media outlets that scorn the notion that homosexuality is wrong," it wrote. "Critics have called him a bigot, a homophobe, and a spiritual terrorist." The praise continued: "In a year that has brought the legalization of gay marriage in New York, the repeal of the U.S. military's 'Don't Ask, Don't Tell' policy, and a decision by the Presbyterian Church USA to allow the ordination of [practicing] homosexuals, Chambers has continued to champion publicly a historic Christian teaching: Christ can change the life of anyone who seeks Him—including a homosexual."[1]

ALAN'S SHOCKING ADMISSION

The following month, January 2012, Alan Chambers walked into a packed ballroom to address the evening session of the annual meeting of the Gay Christian Network (GCN) in Orlando. In this room, Chambers was not a hero. Most of the four hundred people in attendance viewed him as the seventh incarnation of Beelzebub. They disagreed not only with the ex-gay approaches he represented but also with the traditional Christian sexual ethic.

As Chambers took the podium, he joked that he wished he had a martini and a cigarette to get through the evening.[2]

During his remarks, the president of Exodus International came clean about the numbers. He said, "The majority of people whom I have met, and I would say the majority meaning 99.9 percent of them, have not experienced a change in their orientation or have gotten to a place where they can say that they could never be tempted or are not tempted in some way, or experience some level of same-sex attraction. The vast majority of people that I know do still experience some level of same-sex attraction."[3]

Chambers would later clarify that the 0.1 percent was a particular woman he had in mind. She later said that she was still bisexual.[4]

Though Chambers had been saying something similar for the previous five years, he hadn't said it quite so succinctly. Or so publicly. The fact that he said it to a meeting of the enemy appeared to be an admission that the ex-gay movement had failed.

If anyone doubted whether the president of Exodus International had finally rejected the paradigm of curing homosexuality, Chambers left little doubt at the thirty-seventh annual conference of Exodus International that June. At the "Made for More" Exodus Freedom Conference in Saint Paul, Minnesota, Chambers stated, "I do not believe that *cure* is a word that is applicable to really any struggle, homosexuality included. For someone to put out a shingle and say, 'I can cure homosexuality'—that to me is as bizarre as someone saying they can cure any other common temptation or struggle that anyone faces on Planet Earth."[5]

The collapse of Exodus may very well have been inevitable. Mark Yarhouse explained, "One reason for the decline of the ex-gay narrative is the emerging stories of 'ex-ex-gays'—people who once claimed to have experienced sexual orientation change but who later recanted."[6] *Christianity Today* noted in 2007, "Those who've left the ex-gay movement in despair and disgust are the best counterargument" to the movement.[7] Misty Irons described going to the first Ex-Gay Survivor Conference in Irvine, California, in 2007 and hearing all these voices who had left the movement without seeing orientation change and often with deep emotional wounds. "Being at this conference showed me that ministries like Exodus International were simply churning out a growing army of credible witnesses against its claims of orientation change." At some point, there would be so many ex-ex-gays that the ex-gay movement would have to either radically change or die. "It would only be a matter of time before that number would reach a critical mass."[8]

From 2012 on, Exodus International would no longer endorse reparative therapy.

DOES ORIENTATION CHANGE . . . *EVER?*

By the 2000s, most ex-gay ministries had finally learned to add the qualification that "orientation doesn't *always* change." In a 2003 interview with the *Orlando Weekly*, Alan Chambers estimated that 30 percent of those who seek to change their sexual orientation succeed in doing so.[9] His estimates would continue to shrink over the next decade. Ex-gay leaders were beginning to stress more clearly that heterosexuality was not the goal. Holiness was. Celibacy was now an acceptable alternative to marriage. Within a decade, though, the larger question had become somewhat different.

Does sexual orientation change . . . *ever?*

Exodus International's first president, Frank Worthen, had never become straight. He was unsure whether he would even be able to consummate his marriage. He and his wife, Anita, taught a seminar titled "Making Your Marriage Work" in which he advised ex-gay couples to consider waiting a year before attempting to consummate their marriage.[10] It took the final Exodus president, Alan Chambers, eight months and twenty-three days to consummate his marriage.[11]

John Smid of Love in Action has stated that he "never met a man who experienced a change from homosexual to heterosexual."[12] He described a sense of denial within the organization at not seeing anyone experience orientation change. "Along with our board and staff, we'd most often attribute a lack of personal success in a client's life to a lack of application of the tools, or a lack of obedience to God. We certainly didn't accept the limitations of our programs." This went on for years. "We did not do a thorough evaluation of the program's effectiveness. We did not consider that a *very* high number of men and women ended up right back where they started before the program and oftentimes even more wounded."[13]

Alan Chambers, Mike Rosebush, and other ex-gay leaders with whom I have spoken have said much the same.

In 2013, John Paulk apologized for his role in Love Won Out. "Please allow me to be clear: I do not believe that reparative therapy changes sexual orientation." He continued, "I know that countless people were harmed by things I said and did in the past. Parents, families, and their loved ones were negatively impacted by the notion of reparative therapy and the message of change. I am truly, truly sorry for the pain I have caused."[14]

There were some individuals who experienced profound shifts in their sexual preference. Jill Rennick recalls several cases that could be deemed orientation change. She counts eight women and one man whose stories she is confident pan out.[15] I spoke with one woman, named Debra, who has experienced a significant shift in her sexual orientation.[16] So it's not impossible in some instances, but the rarity of these cases is striking.

Jan Gelech, who conducted a study in which she asked sixteen homosexually attracted Christian men about their experience within ex-gay ministries, noted that in most cases, the positive benefits people described as a result of their involvement in ex-gay ministries "were unrelated to any changes in sexual desire." If anything, what she found was frustration. One subject, Todd, said, "It didn't work. It absolutely would not work. None. Zilch. So it just made me all the more frustrated, you know?" Explained Brad, "I'd been working through the system. And I was getting healthier and better and saner, but I wasn't getting any 'straighter.'" Another man commented, "I was still attracted to men—they . . . were doing nothing to change it." In time, these men started to accept that their basic patterns of desire were more or less unmalleable. Matt explained, "It became clearer that, well, there really wasn't going to be change . . . it's just something I'd have to struggle with for the rest of my life." Todd confessed, "I was very self-loathing . . . like, 'How come this isn't working?' . . . I felt so cotton-pickin' defeated that the only time I actually fell and had sex with a guy was during the time I was going to those sessions."[17]

JONES AND YARHOUSE

A 2011 study by Stanton Jones and Mark Yarhouse followed ninety-eight homosexual and bisexual men and women over a period of up to seven years. While study subjects were highly committed participants in Exodus-affiliated ministries, more than a third dropped out of the study during that time. Jones and Yarhouse found that some participants did experience a clinically significant shift in their sexual attractions, with an average shift of 0.78 on the seven-point Kinsey scale, seven being exclusively homosexual and zero being exclusively heterosexual. (While much of Alfred Kinsey's research has been called into question, his scale is still used.)

Their data is open to interpretation, depending on how optimistic or pessimistic you are. The authors state that 9–26 percent of participants experienced a larger change in their sexual functioning or in their orientation, such that they now thought of themselves as heterosexuals. Some also experienced a smaller increase in heterosexual attraction. Most shifted from one end of the bisexual scale to the other. As Warren Throckmorton observed, "On average, the group rating indicated both heterosexual and homosexual attractions at the beginning, middle and end of the study."[18] Of the fifteen individuals who described themselves as heterosexual at the end of the study, five were highlighted in the study. Two of these simply said they were heterosexual, with no additional explanation of what that meant. Two others made it clear that they were still attracted to members of the same sex. And the other one recanted his story and said he was still gay.

Jones and Yarhouse were quite clear about the implication of their research. "These results do not prove that categorical change in sexual orientation is possible for everyone or anyone, but rather that meaningful shifts along a continuum that constitute real changes appear possible for some."[19] Nevertheless, this study continues to be selectively quoted and misrepresented to suggest that a quarter of participants went from gay to straight, further implying that such a thing is attainable for many who want it. Robert Reilly, in his 2014 book, is just one example.[20] Earlier the American Family Association cited the study as proof that gays can change. A Focus on the Family affiliate stated that "23 percent reported a complete change in orientation after six years."[21]

Since no one in the current cultural climate is likely to fund clinical research on sexual orientation change efforts, the Jones and Yarhouse data is the most reliable we have. But it's also open to interpretation. The researchers noted that their data may indicate some change in sexual orientation. Alternately, they noted that it could instead indicate more a change in sexual identity and sexual behavior.

Psychology professor Warren Throckmorton leaned more toward that alternate explanation of the data.[22] He also questioned the significance of the high dropout rate. If most of those dropouts gave up on orientation change, then the actual success rate is much lower. Throckmorton also noted that the study combined data from men and women. "Given the low number of people involved, I understand why this was done," he explained. "But the practice may inflate the assessments of change for the group. It has become well accepted that the sexuality of women is more fluid than for men. A few women experiencing large shifts could influence the group averages."[23]

SEXUAL FLUIDITY

Human sexuality does have a level of fluidity. In parts of the world, there are more bisexual people than there are gays or lesbians, even if they think of themselves as straight. A 2015 YouGov poll found that only 46 percent of British eighteen- to twenty-four-year-olds described themselves as "completely heterosexual"—that being a zero on the Kinsey scale. Another 6 percent described themselves as "completely homosexual." A surprising 43 percent put themselves somewhere in the middle, though most much closer to heterosexual. Sexual attraction aside, 83 percent self-identified as heterosexual, even if their attractions were more complex.[24]

And it's certainly possible, particularly among women, for some individuals to shift from one end of the bisexual range to the other. Recent surveys of American high school students have documented a significant increase in female teenagers identifying as bisexual. A nationwide federal study of American high school students in 2017 found that 13.1 percent of female students identified as bisexual, compared with only 2.8 percent of male students. More than one in five female teens identified as lesbian, bisexual, or "not sure," compared with one in twelve male teenagers.[25] And lest you assume such trends are because of pinko leftist school systems in Boston or San Francisco, let me note that the two states with the highest percentage of teenagers identifying as gay or lesbian were Arkansas and South Carolina—the buckle and first hole in the Bible Belt.

In her 2008 book *Sexual Fluidity: Understanding Women's Love and Desire*, Lisa Diamond noted this fluidity in female sexuality. She concluded, based on a study of one hundred nonstraight women over a decade, that sexual orientation, while unchosen, can shift involuntarily in some women.[26]

Throckmorton noted within ex-gay marriages an additional dynamic which to those on the outside could mistakenly appear to be orientation change. "Some men and women . . . can develop attractions for specific opposite sex attachments without altering their essential orientation." He observed, "Some people in mixed orientation marriages report that they remain generally attracted to the same sex but have fallen in love with a person of the opposite sex. The sexual relationship is legitimate and intense, but the attraction to the opposite sex partner does not generalize to other members of the opposite sex."[27]

Such a description fits quite a few of my friends.

My own story is that God's grace has taught me to remain chaste. My attractions are somewhat more emotional today, slightly less sexual than when Christ called me thirty years ago. Is that progressive sanctification, or is it just aging? I don't know. But when I do experience sexual attraction—I call it same-sex distraction—it has only ever been toward another man.

A UCLA study in 2018 estimated that 698,000 Americans then between the ages of eighteen and fifty-nine had been through some form of conversion therapy or other sexual orientation change effort.[28] If even just 1 percent of those men and women had been cured of homosexuality, we'd have thousands and thousands of living testimonies just in the US.

Our struggle to confirm *even a couple of handfuls* of cases of true gay-to-straight orientation change is telling. God has power to do anything. It appears this is something he has chosen to do only very rarely in this era. The reason ex-gay leaders lost hope in their grand narrative is because they could see that it had failed.

THE FINAL YEAR

Exodus International had been started in 1977 under the premise that "God could change you from gay to straight."[29] After Exodus president Alan Chambers announced in 2012 that 99.9 percent of Exodus clients had never seen their attraction to members of the same sex go away, Exodus leadership had to face a hard decision.

Almost immediately after Alan's public admission about orientation change, Exodus drew sharp criticism from some leaders within the ex-gay movement. "There was strong division over whether it was possible to change orientation, or instead to focus on walking with people to help them come to terms with their sexuality without compromise," recalled Richard Holloman, founder of Sight Ministry. "It was ugly. On one side, you had ex-gay, reparative therapy, and orientation change. On the other, you had same-sex attraction, grace, and discipleship."[30]

Chambers reminded ministry leaders of the conversations about change. He mentioned the unrealistic expectations he and Exodus leaders had allowed to continue. He mentioned the abusive patterns in local affiliate ministries.

The division was apparent at a March 2012 discussion among Exodus affiliates. On one hand, Exodus founder Frank Worthen called for a renewed focus on sexual orientation change efforts. In an online forum of Exodus leaders, he insisted, "Exodus was founded on change. Somewhere along the way the understanding about change was lost. God works on the whole person. . . . He begins with the root causes of homosexuality rather than the homosexuality itself."[31] Stephen Black of Oklahoma City–based First Stone Ministries concurred with Worthen.

On the other hand, another ministry leader defended the direction Exodus was heading. In the same discussion, he emphasized the need to contextualize for a post-Christian world immersed in radically different cultural assumptions about sexuality. "We must find ways to communicate the eternal truths of Scripture clearly, without compromise, and yet with an awareness of current culture as it really is, including the underlying changes in paradigms, concepts, and language." He added, "If we choose *not* to contextualize for the world as it really now is, we shouldn't really complain when everyday people are repulsed by our presence and/or presentation. We can't blame their responses totally on their spiritual blindness when we prove ourselves to be culturally blind."[32]

Anne Paulk demanded that Alan Chambers explain exactly where he intended to steer Exodus. In an April 3, 2012, letter to Exodus ministry leaders, Chambers delivered. He mapped out a direction for Exodus, one that emphasized "discipleship over therapy, holiness over sexual reorientation, and honesty over ambiguity."[33]

By that point, six former and current leaders critical of Chambers had asked him to resign. They and twenty others were already strategizing for an alternative trajectory.

Chambers was not going to resign.

The Ex-Gay Old Guard's Exodus from Exodus

For affiliates who were still deeply committed to sexual orientation change, the path forward was to leave. Some Exodus affiliates jumped ship right away, including Andy Comiskey's Desert Stream, Exodus's then-largest ministry affiliate. In an open letter, Comiskey wrote about a young woman who, after an eight-year attempt at orientation change, had seen no lessening of her attraction to other women. He complained, "Many of you seemed quite alright with the idea that our ministries should do little more than support celibate Christians who after 8 years of pursuing help (this woman's example) are as passionately attracted to their own gender as ever." He continued, "We have a problem with that." Comiskey criticized what he saw as Exodus leaders' lack of "vision for her progression onto whole relating." He criticized their "new emphasis on 'discipleship over therapy, holiness over sexual reorientation.'" And he doubled down on his ministry's support for reparative therapy. "Regarding sexual orientation change, we at DSM will continue to uphold change as a reasonable goal for Christians. . . . The new creation involves reconciling with one's true heterosexual self."[34]

On April 20, Stephen Black notified Exodus that his First Stone Ministries had withdrawn its membership in Exodus after thirty-six years.[35]

"Defining change was a challenge within Exodus from the beginning," said Exodus board chairman Joe Dallas. "Figuring out the best way to articulate the process, and the best ministry approaches for people who wanted it, would always be problematic."[36]

Now the many fractures that had riddled the ex-gay movement from its inception were finally coming together: The lack of promised results. The ongoing problem of leadership failure. The psychological, spiritual, and physical harm done by the false hope of orientation change. The conflation of orientation and addiction. The reports of abuse concerning Exodus ministries. The injury done to youth subjected to therapy. The politicization of ex-gays and the subsequent backlash. The distancing of prominent Christian psychologists and churches.

And to these were added the financial strain experienced when angry donors pulled back. Exodus had already been struggling financially for several years. They had laid off staff and cut benefits in 2010. It was a very uncertain time for Exodus International.

But there was one additional factor that left even those most-loyal Exodus folks unsettled.

Alan's Theological Shift

Complicating the situation further were theological shifts happening within Exodus president Alan Chambers. In a televised interview with Lisa Ling, Chambers seemed to indicate that homosexual practice was not as serious a sin as once believed. He said, "There are people out there who are living a gay Christian life—an active gay Christian life. God is the one who called them and has their heart, and they are in relationship with him. And do I believe that they'll be in heaven with me? I do."[37] In another interview, with the *Atlantic*, when Chambers was asked about professing Christians sexually active within a gay marriage, he answered, "Some of us choose very different lives than others. But whatever we choose, it doesn't remove our relationship with God."[38]

Such statements demonstrated a tectonic shift in historical Christian teaching about repentance. While Christians had always believed that a sincere follower of Jesus could be so deceived as to engage in ongoing unrepentant sexual sin for a season, Christians had never thought to give such individuals an assurance of salvation. Rather, apostolic instruction seemed to do just the opposite. "Do not be deceived," Saint Paul had written. "Neither the sexually immoral nor idolaters nor adulterers nor men who have sex with men nor thieves nor the greedy nor drunkards nor slanderers nor swindlers will inherit the kingdom of God" (1 Cor. 6:9–10).

Chambers was echoing the theology of his pastor, Clark Whitten of Grace Church Orlando, who in 2012 published a book arguing that Protestantism had gotten it wrong about Christian growth. Christians are not sinners saved by grace, he argued. Grace makes us no longer sinners but saints alone, and a transformed life is therefore not a necessary outcome of the new birth and saving faith in Jesus. "My bad works don't move God any more than my good works move him," he wrote. While understandably trying to help Christians off their legalistic performance treadmills, he seemed at times to play fast and loose with biblical instruction about confessing sin. "Christians are not required to confess their sins to God in order to be forgiven, we already are forgiven.... How much time will that free up!"[39] That Alan's mentor was teaching this was already setting off alarm bells. To be clear, I am very much a radical grace kind of guy. But understand that the radical grace that gave me saving faith and united me to Christ is the same radical grace that regenerated my heart and gave me a love for God that makes me want to do what he says, even if sometimes in fits and starts. Whitten's theology struck many of us as bordering on antinomian, to say the least.

That the head of Exodus International was espousing a theological view shared by few if any Exodus ministries was surprising. The tradition within Exodus was to avoid controversial theological pronouncements—even about questions like whether salvation could be lost—in order to maintain the inter-denominational nature of the organization. Such comments left even Alan's closest supporters wondering where Alan's theological trajectory would lead him. At this point, it became clear that Chambers was speaking for himself and not for his supporters.

The Vote to Kill Exodus International

By the end of 2012, two board members and a vice president had resigned, and many staff members had quit. A string of Exodus affiliate ministries had departed. The cat was out of the bag about the paucity of examples of genuine sexual orientation change. Those who still chased that dream had left Exodus. Now the ministry faced a serious question: Should Exodus even continue as an organization? If so, toward what end?

That final year, a group of Exodus leaders—leaders of affiliate ministries, network counselors, and church network contacts—identified four possible paths forward for the ministry. First, they could stay the course, though that was never a real option. Second, they could rebrand, but that was not a real option either. Alan explained, "I had lost faith in too much of what we were trying to sell." A third option was to modify the organization in a more radical way, with the gospel rewriting the DNA of Exodus International. The early changes in 2012 were certainly steps toward that potential outcome. A fourth and final option was for Exodus, the face of the ex-gay movement since 1976, to close.[40] "There were those who wanted to sink the ship," explained one participant, Nate Collins, "and there were those who countered, 'No, there's some good in here.'"[41]

The group presented its recommendation to the board. They recommended closure.

The board accepted the recommendation to shut down Exodus International. The vote was unanimous.

While some critics saw the closure of Exodus as a conspiracy, the deed was done.[42]

Explained Exodus board chairman Richard Holloman, "Exodus had been moving in the right direction. Because of where I was, I saw where leadership was trying to correct itself. Exodus was becoming more loving, more understanding, more compassionate. It was helping parents understand what their gay children were experiencing. I hated to see it go.... But," he added, "there was so much damage done—and being done—in the name of Exodus. That damage could not be undone."[43]

Whether by accident or by design, Exodus would close.

True Story: The Ugly Duckling

The final Exodus International conference gathered in Irvine, California, in June 2013 and drew fewer than three hundred participants—many less than in previous years. It was a fraction of the attendance from the ministry's heyday, though large numbers of others joined in by livestream.

In his keynote address on opening night, June 19, Chambers spoke of the scandal of the previous eighteen months and reflected on the need to be honest about temptation. And he spoke in words that were clear, direct, and powerful.

> Exodus International has become something that it wasn't intended to be. I believe the major failure of Exodus is that it promised to be completely different from the religious system that forced its creation and yet became a religious institution of rules and regulations focused on behavior management and short on grace. It's time our message changes to be one of hope and love and grace. It is for these reasons and other reasons that we, the board of directors of Exodus International and many within our leadership, believe it's time for Exodus to close.[44]

As he stepped down from the podium, the room was frozen. No one offered applause. No one got up. "There were a few sniffles," Alan has written, "but it was eerily still like a village that had just been bombed and was still too shell-shocked to move or to look to others for consolation."[45]

The conference continued for the next few days as Exodus staff and volunteers sought to offer whatever support they could. The theme of the conference was True Story, and the first keynote after Chambers was a former Southern Baptist missionary named Chip and his gay son, a young Southern Baptist Theological Seminary doctoral student in New Testament with a wife and family, named Nate Collins.

Nate Collins closed his speech with the much-loved tale "The Ugly Duckling." After enduring years of ridicule, shame, and humiliation because he was different from the other ducks, the unsuspecting creature, now fully grown, catches sight of his reflection in the water. Through all that suffering, he had become a beautiful swan.

As Hans Christian Andersen narrates, "The swan now felt glad at having suffered sorrow and trouble, because it enabled him to enjoy so much better all the pleasure and happiness around him." The point was clear to everyone in the room. There is suffering that comes to people like us, who experience ridicule, shame, and humiliation as we try fitfully to offer our lives to Jesus. God will not waste that suffering, even if it lasts a lifetime. What God will do will be beautiful.

In the weeks following the conference, Collins reflected on the closure of Exodus. "Exodus International certainly represented a much safer place than the vast majority of churches for Christians to be transparent about their experience of same-sex attraction. But it nonetheless did so within the context of a triumphalist church subculture that often preferred 'finished product' Christians to 'in-process' Christians."[46]

Christianity Today offered its own eulogy upon the demise of Exodus.

It is noteworthy to us that Chambers did not accuse the church as mutually culpable for the demise of his ministry, though he clearly could have. The men and women who looked to Exodus International and other such organizations for help did so because much of the church refused to talk openly about sexuality and gender or offer genuine support to those who were conflicted about it.

For this reason, it seems malicious how both the churched and unchurched have ganged up on Exodus and other similar ministries in recent years. In our experience, Exodus has been filled with vulnerable, well-meaning men and women who took up an impossible task without adequate support and were then shamed by their own kin for failing. Despised and rejected by both the church and the gay community, it's no wonder Exodus succumbed to this auto-immune attack.[47]

At its peak, Exodus International (including its Global Alliance) had served as an umbrella organization for more than four hundred local ministries across seventeen countries, rallying ex-gays under the banner "Change is possible."

Now it had closed.

After four decades, the path to cure was a dead end.

The ex-gay movement had died.

thirteen

Postmortem

If a biological cause or genetic link explaining same-sex attraction is ever discovered, Christians should be among the least surprised.

—Al Mohler, President, Southern Baptist
Theological Seminary

There is a large wood buffet table in the auditorium of my church. Wedding celebrations, luncheons, baby showers, and birthday parties happen around that table. It's the perfect height for a buffet, has sturdy old wheels on it, and can hold up any weight. And it's huge. A towering wedding cake looks delightful upon it.

It is, of course, an autopsy table.

Our church picked it up from the coroner's office in the 1950s during a remodel down at the lab. Grab your bone saw and scalpel, forceps and rib shears. I'll roll up the autopsy table. It's time for a postmortem.

The church's great experiment failed. The ex-gay movement died. A forty-year experiment to cure homosexuality—using thousands of human test subjects—came to naught.

As we contemplate this cadaver, we have a question to face.

Why did it die?

In subsequent chapters, we'll consider whether we simply got the biblical sexual ethic wrong—that and other questions increasingly asked in a post-Christian context. In this chapter, though, I want to do a theological postmortem. Obviously, the ex-gay movement failed to deliver on its namesake hope of orientation change. What were the theological blind spots that set us up for such a colossal failure? And one that impacted so many lives? What can we learn from the death of the ex-gay movement?

A FAILURE OF THEOLOGY

Ultimately, the ex-gay movement died because it was theologically shallow. From its earliest days, the movement was led by anyone with a story to tell. Bubbling up first within independent charismatic circles in the 1970s, its early leaders invented things on the fly. Often these leaders were brand-new believers, and most lacked any theological or pastoral training. By and large, their only qualification was that they were gay, became a Christian, and knew how to give an ex-gay testimony that suggested they were no longer homosexual.

The result was a movement with a vastly underdeveloped theology of sin, coupled with a vastly overrealized eschatology. The theological union of these two failures set the movement and its untold thousands of clients up for failure.

Failure 1: An Underdeveloped Theology of Sin

From the beginning, ex-gay approaches assumed that homosexuality could be cured. While different ministries had nuanced beliefs, they overall perceived the experience of homoerotic longing as a psychological disorder in response to bad parenting or abuse. They assumed that addressing family baggage and focusing on personal spiritual growth would bring about a gradual conversion of sexual longing from being toward members of the same sex to being toward members of the opposite sex.

For most that never happened.

The movement grossly underestimated how deeply rooted indwelling sin is in the human person. Consider Paul's description of his experience of indwelling sin, in Romans 7:15–21.

> I do not understand what I do. For what I want to do I do not do, but what I hate I do. . . . As it is, it is no longer I myself who do it, but it is sin living in me. For I know that good itself does not dwell in me, that is, in my sinful nature. For I have the desire to do what is good, but I cannot carry it out. For I do not do the good I want to do, but the evil I do not want to do—this I keep on doing. Now if I do what I do not want to do, it is no longer I who do it, but it is sin living in me that does it.
>
> So I find this law at work: Although I want to do good, evil is right there with me.

Though commentators don't always agree, there's good reason to believe Paul is giving voice to his present experience as a believer. In this passage, he speaks of how he delights in God's law in his inmost being. That seems to suggest a spiritually regenerated Christian—alive to God. Yet even as an apostle, having penned biblical books under divine inspiration, having walked with Jesus for decades, Paul still has sin living in him—indwelling sin. Evil is right there with him. Temptation doesn't always go away.

This deeply rooted sin is what theologians have variously called concupiscence, the sinful nature and its motions, indwelling sin, or internal corruption.

The Protestant reformer John Calvin explained the relative permanence of indwelling sin in his discussion of Romans 6. "So long as you live, sin must needs be in your members," he wrote. It must be. There is no cure. He continued, "At least let it be deprived of mastery."[1] The 1647 Westminster Confession of Faith expressed this reality succinctly: "This corruption of nature, during this life, doth remain in those that are regenerated."[2] The 1689 Baptist Confession of Faith quoted Westminster verbatim at this point. The Baptists saw nothing to improve upon.

There is no cure for corrupted nature in this life. We remain inescapably children of Adam. There is only a charge to fight our corrupted nature's temptations to sin.

So distorted is our fallen human nature, and so deeply rooted our sin, that a believer can never really be rid of it in this life. The seventeenth-century Anglican bishop William Beveridge lamented, "I cannot pray but I sin. I cannot hear or preach a sermon but I sin. I cannot give an alms or receive the sacrament but I sin. Nay, I cannot so much as confess my sins, but my very confessions are still aggravations of them. My repentance needs to be repented of, my tears need washing, and the very washing of my tears needs still to be washed over again with the blood of my Redeemer."[3]

Seventeenth-century scholar and divine Samuel Bolton wrote, "It was said of Carthage that Rome was more troubled with it when half destroyed than when whole. So a godly man may be more troubled with sin when it is conquered than when it reigned. Sin will still work."[4] Princeton Seminary's legendary Charles Hodge called it a "universal and incurable corruption of our nature" which reveals redemption to be no small matter, but the work of God.[5]

Incurable.

A Deeply Loved Mess

We can't fake it 'til we make it.

For me, the sexualized pull toward people of the same sex is not likely to go away. This is a lifetime calling not to let it rule over me.

Twentieth-century theologian John Murray was a lifelong celibate until, shockingly, he married at the age of sixty-nine. Murray said this of sin: "There is a total difference between surviving sin and reigning sin, the regenerate in conflict with sin and the unregenerate complacent with sin. . . . It is one thing for sin to live in us; it is another for us to live in sin."[6]

The sinful nature, internal corruption, concupiscence, indwelling sin. Whatever you call it, this is a larger category than just the internal pull of sexual sin. In his *Confessions*, Augustine described his nighttime theft of pears from a pear tree as concupiscence. It wasn't the sensual appeal of the pears that drew him in. Rather it was the allure of companionship—doing the deed with the other boys. Indwelling sin was always operating in the background to entice him.

I, personally, have not struggled with the temptation to steal pears. But I am not judging Augustine. We all have our struggles.

The erotic pull of homosexuality is deeply rooted.

Some prominent conservative evangelical leaders have realized the reality of homosexual orientation. In a 2014 address, Al Mohler, president of Southern Baptist Theological Seminary, stated, "Early in this controversy, I felt it quite necessary, in order to make clear the gospel, to deny anything like a sexual orientation." He continued, "I repent of that. I believe that . . . a robust biblical theology would point out to us that human sexual, affective profiles—who we are sexually—is far more deeply rooted than just the will. If only it were that easy."[7] He followed up, "The concept of sexual orientation is not only helpful, it is in some sense essential. Even those who argue against its existence have to describe and affirm something tantamount to it."[8]

There is a deep-rootedness here. Lest we flatten this into mere internal corruption, though, let's realize there's also a complexity to sexual longings.

Sin, Augustine argued, is always a privation of the good. There is no such thing as pure evil, he explained, only good things that have been bent and therefore have lost their goodness or had some of it distorted. What is bent when I experience that internal pull toward homoeroticism? Well, actually, quite a lot about me is bent. My sexuality may be the least of my issues. But when considering homoerotic temptation, what else is going on? Certainly, this is not less than the temptation of indwelling sin; it is more than that. That's always how sin works.

What good thing has been bent? What else is going on?

For one thing, we're dealing with a legitimate God-given human longing for community. Yes, this longing has become sexualized in ways that distort God's creational design. But it is a legitimate longing nonetheless. It might be a longing for healthy intimacy—to know and be known. It might be a longing for acceptance, a need to feel wanted. Our longings for intimacy, community, and friendship, our longings to be loved and accepted, our recognition of human beauty—these are not evils. The longing for nurture, inclusion, and affirmation are not evils. The longing to matter to someone, to be unique and special to them, the longing for family—don't you dare call these sin. They are core human needs we all share as image bearers of God. We all long to be delighted in. We all long for companionship. We all long to be seen inside and out. These longings are good longings placed there by God.[9]

God does not call us to put these to death. These are not sin. They are part of how he created us as humans designed for relationship. These are good longings that inborn sin bends in spiritually unhealthy directions. Sin overdesires the good, to our own damage. That's how sin works—by bending the good. That's true for all of us.

Thankfully, a cured internal corruption is not required for us to be adopted into God's family. Only Jesus is required. Being a sinner—not a former sinner or sinner emeritus but a real sinner—points us to our ground of hope. Sinners are the only class of people Jesus came to save (1 Tim. 1:15). Only those who are spiritually bankrupt—poor in spirit—will be blessed (Matt. 5:3). The middle class in spirit cannot be saved. Jesus didn't come to call the righteous, only sinners (Matt. 9:13). Indeed, he developed quite a reputation as a friend of sinners (Luke 7:34).

Knowing you're the biggest sinner in the room is a great position to be in. It was certainly a self-understanding Saint Paul adopted. He declared, "Christ Jesus came into the world to save sinners—of whom I am the worst" (1 Tim. 1:15). It's like taking the worst seat at the banquet. Those are the folks the master likes to move up.

We're all a mess—a deeply loved mess. God delights to meet us in our mess.

Reformed pastor and theologian John Piper stated, "All our disorders—all our brokenness—is rooted in sin—original sin and our sinful nature. It would be right to say that same-sex [sexual] desires are sinful in the sense that they are disordered by sin and exist contrary to God's revealed will." Then Piper offered a huge and helpful qualification: "But to be caused by sin and rooted in sin does not make a sinful desire equal to sinning. Sinning is what happens when rebellion against God expresses itself through our disorders."[10]

We're not sinners because we sin. We sin because we are sinners.[11] It's deeply rooted in our fallen nature, our internal corruption. Being a sinner and choosing to sin are different things.

This biblical honesty about our sinful nature ought to have added a hefty dose of skepticism to ex-gay hopes. Sin is deeply rooted. Behavior modification cannot rewire the longings of the human heart. It would be naive to think that something so deeply rooted as the inward pull of sexual temptation could be eliminated in this life. Internal corruption remains this side of glory. A biblically and historically developed theology of sin might have shifted the paradigm from cure to care.

The Sinfulness of Heterosexuality This Side of the Fall

This same theology applies to straight Christians too. I was once on a podcast with some church leaders who seemed to be of the opinion that a gay person who becomes a Christian can choose not to be attracted to members of the same sex anymore. I questioned them about their own sexual attraction to women other than their wives. Can you choose to turn that off? They scoffed.

"For one, heterosexual men don't need to repent of being attracted to another woman," one panelist said.

Another added, "Because that's natural."

A third agreed. "That's the way God planned it."

The first one then jumped in again. "What we need to repent of is being lustful."

They seemed to have a very shallow view of their indwelling sin—their own internal corruption. Did God design Adam to feel an internal sexual pull toward his neighbor's wife? To see another man's wife and have sexual feelings for her? Was that our Father's good design for sexuality? Or is that not—like sexual attraction to a member of the same-sex—also an effect of the fall? Is that not internal corruption? Is that not overdesire? Is that not a natural longing for beauty or approval or intimacy that has been bent by the fall?

Saint Paul instructs us to see "older women as mothers, and younger women as sisters, with absolute purity" (1 Tim. 5:2). You don't feel an internal sexual pull toward your mother or your sister. Think of Adam. Eve was created, and the two conceived and bore a son. But all other women from then on would have been Adam's daughters and granddaughters. He likely would not have felt a sexual pull toward them. And almost certainly not had there been no fall and expulsion from the garden. Sexual longing was designed to exist within marriage. Since the desire for sin involves a motion of the sinful nature, I wonder how a sexual longing for someone other than your spouse is "the way God planned it."

Let me expand upon the scope of the problem. We all know that heterosexuality is being drawn to people of the opposite sex. People—as in plural, more than one.

And that's the problem. It seems to me that the polygamy of heterosexual sexual desire—or more technically, a polyamory or polyeroticism—is also disordered.

Heterosexuality as experienced this side of the fall is drenched in sin. As Al

Mohler writes, "Every single human being who has experienced puberty has a sexual orientation that, in some way, falls short of the glory of God."[12] Nate Collins argues that God's design was not heterosexuality but uni-heterosexuality: "The biblical pattern for ordered sexuality portrayed for us in Genesis 2 is not a generic desire for the opposite sex (heterosexuality) but a specific love and desire for one particular member of the opposite sex (uni-heterosexuality). In the moral exam of life, straight people don't get partial credit simply for being straight." He adds, "Every one of us, gay and straight alike, experiences intrinsically disordered sexual desires."[13] I'm willing to be corrected here if I'm wrong. But somebody tell me: how else can we look at this if the Scriptures are shaping our norm?

Heterosexuality as experienced this side of the fall is also a fallen orientation on account of its failure to remain exclusive to one spouse at the attractional level. A man's sexual longing for his neighbor's wife is a sinful temptation to be resisted, not a natural desire put there by God. Like all temptation, it's a good thing that's been bent. Whether we speak of a sexual pull to a neighbor's wife or to a neighbor's brother, we're not dealing with something that's morally neutral. As Saint Paul explains, wherever I go, "evil is right there with me" (Rom. 7:21).

Again, all the straight people I know are bent.

Only Jesus had a nonsinful, nonshameful sexual orientation.

There is no reason to believe that the ordinary progress of spiritual growth would involve the replacement of sinful homosexual temptation with sinful heterosexual temptation. That's aiming too low. Coveting your neighbor's wife is not a step in the right direction. Neither should we assume that spiritual growth makes us asexual. The reality we have to face is that we will all feel sexual attraction to people other than our spouse. It does not magically disappear as we walk with Jesus. However our sexual attractions happen to be bent, God calls us to holiness, not to heterosexuality.

Now, I'm not trying to elevate homosexuality to say that it's not that bad. No. I want to bring the rest of you down to the level I inhabit. Because the basement is where Jesus is hanging out. He's a friend of sinners. And I want to help you.

Our pastoral response to believers with fallen heterosexual orientations should be grounded in grace. We don't need to set up a bunch of exstraight ministries to help you sisters and brothers be cured of your unwanted attractions to other people's spouses. That approach has been tried for forty years with a very similar fallen sexual orientation, and we found that internal corruption didn't go away. I don't tell straight men they're not real Christians for identifying as straight, even though that typically means attractional polygamy. So long as they're not bragging about it and they recognize that it's disordered, I don't get too worried.

If my internal sexual pull is disordered 100 percent of the time, perhaps theirs might be disordered 90 percent of the time? I don't think that gives anyone room to boast. There is no one righteous. Not even one. Saint Paul says there is no difference. The ground is level at the foot of the cross.

Is There a Pedophilia Connection?

"The ground is level at the foot of the cross?" you query. "Now, Greg, that's not fair. Sexual attractions to members of the same sex are unnatural. How's that any different from pedophilia?" If I had a dollar for every time I've heard someone jump from same-sex orientation to pedophilia, I'd be driving a nicer car. This accusation is bantered about youth ministries and family ministries. It is weaponized in an effort to bar believers from ministry at every level. Critics point to the child sexual abuse scandal rocking the Roman Catholic Church and blame it on the ordination of men who experience unwanted attraction to members of the same sex.

It's a seemingly easy connection to make.

But someone with a same-sex orientation is not the same thing as a sexual predator. And for decades, the Roman Catholic Church's psychological profile for potential priests looked a lot like the psychological profile of a sexual predator.

Is there no similarity between the two? Granted, the apostle Paul did say homosexual acts violate the creation order—nature—in Romans 1. And pedophilia also violates the creation order. So on that point there is similarity. But there is a huge power differential with pedophilia. Children by definition cannot give consent. Every act of pedophilia is raping a child. I hope when your college student tells you she thinks she might be bisexual that you don't immediately compare her to a child rapist.

Besides, the only study that ever looked at the adult sexual attractions of child molesters found that none of them was homosexual. In an analysis of 175 convicts convicted of sex crimes against children, 13 percent were bisexual. Forty percent were heterosexual. Forty-seven percent were classified as "fixated," meaning they were sexually attracted only to children and not at all to adults. Among the bisexual cases, none was attracted more to members of the same sex than to members of the opposite sex.[14]

An expert panel convened by the National Academy of Sciences concluded, "The distinction between homosexual and heterosexual child molesters relies on the [mistaken] premise that male molesters of male victims are homosexual in orientation. Most molesters of boys do not report sexual interest in adult men, however."[15] There is no statistical link between pedophilia and homosexuality.

A good child protective policy doesn't require knowledge of one's sexual orientation. A good child protective policy says that a man is never to be alone with a child not his own. Two adults are always present, and at least one of them has to be a woman. A good child protective policy background checks everyone or uses licensed, bonded professionals.[16] Child sexual abuse is real and incredibly destructive to its victims. Scapegoating gays and lesbians will not prevent this tragedy.

A Pastoral Response to Sinful Heterosexuality

My point here is Paul's point in Romans 1–3. Heterosexuality as experienced this side of the fall is also a fallen sexual orientation in need of grace. Let's be realistic. We're all really committing the greatest sin all the time, loving God with 67 percent of our heart, three-eighths of our mind, and a little more than half of our strength. By implication, Jesus called that the greatest sin. I haven't loved God with *all* my strength for five seconds. There is no difference, for all have sinned and fall short.

Your concupiscence doesn't smell much better than mine.

But please don't feel like I'm judging you, heterosexual reader, for your sinful heterosexuality.

Our pastoral response to sinful heterosexuality should focus on the gospel. Your Father forgives you for your shamefully polygamous attractions. He clothes you with the righteousness of Jesus. That means Jesus' resume has your name on it. That means that you fed the five thousand. You raised Lazarus from the dead. You always did what pleased the Father.

Sound familiar?

And then when you're feeling released from the shame, we can help you learn to do battle with the lusts of the heart out of blood-bought loyalty to our Rescuer, who loves us.

The gospel is for straight people too.

As Christians, we are the family of God. We are all in this together. The Bible reveals a God who is glorious in holiness, fearful in praises, working wonders . . . and who stoops down to gently embrace shamefully defective people like you and me. Shamefully defective straight people. Shamefully defective gay people. Sinners loved by Jesus.

Failure 2: An Overrealized Eschatology

If the ex-gay movement by and large functioned with an underdeveloped theology of sin, it coupled this theological failure with another related one. Michael Bussee of Exodus talks about how confident they were in those early days in the Jesus movement with people being healed of drug addictions and healed of diseases. Everyone was naming and claiming deliverance from one form of bondage or another. They felt that if they could believe it to be true, then their new reality was already awaiting them.

Frank Worthen spoke about the confidence that if they knew what caused homosexuality, they could find out how to cure homosexuality. Almost everyone who participated in an ex-gay ministry did so at some point because—on one level or another—they were hopeful of freedom from homosexuality in this life. Those who worked these ministries wanted deeply to help their gay siblings walk with Jesus. If there were hope for a cure, it would have been cruel to withhold it.

The history of the ex-gay movement is a history of a movement coming to terms with a huge disappointment.

The ex-gay movement fostered an overrealized, triumphalistic eschatology which lined up neither with Scripture nor experience. An overrealized eschatology transfers the Christian's hope from the coming age to this present life, placing expectations on God that he does not place on himself. The Christian Scriptures are much more measured about what we should expect during this brief lifetime.

If any church in the apostolic age had an overrealized eschatology, it was the church at Corinth. So in writing to them, Paul zeroed in on the error. Paul told them, "Now we see only a reflection as in a mirror" (1 Cor. 13:12). He continued, "Now I know in part" (v. 12). He wrote, "If only for this life we have hope in Christ, we are of all people most to be pitied" (1 Cor. 15:19). While the kingdom of God has broken into the world, we do not yet see its fullness.

God does promise to strengthen us as we put to death the misdeeds of our bodies. He does not promise to translate us into a realm in which we no longer experience temptation. God does promise to hear our prayers. He does not promise to always give us what we want. God does promise grace to help us break free from addictive cycles of sin. He does not promise to make us sinlessly perfect. God does promise to walk with us through suffering. He does not promise to shield us from suffering. Indeed, Jesus promised that you will suffer in this life.

Paul wrote to the Corinthians to stress just how limited our transformation is in this life. Yet many well-meaning believers, having drunk the ex-gay Kool-Aid, continue to twist Paul's letter to say something very different.

Twisting 1 Corinthians 6

How many times have I watched someone abuse my spiritual siblings by twisting 1 Corinthians 6:9–11 to say something it does not?

Do you not know that wrongdoers will not inherit the kingdom of God? Do not be deceived: Neither the sexually immoral nor idolaters nor adulterers nor men who have sex with men nor thieves nor the greedy nor drunkards nor slanderers nor swindlers will inherit the kingdom of God. And that is what some of you were. But you were washed, you were sanctified, you were justified in the name of the Lord Jesus Christ and by the Spirit of our God.

Some older translations substituted the word "homosexuals" for "men who have sex with men." The effect of such a mistranslation was to suggest that Paul was stating that anyone with a homosexual orientation was damned. If they were "washed"—if they were truly saved by Jesus—then their sexual orientation would have changed. "And that is what some of you were."

It was a very cruel thing to do to a child of God who desperately wanted to walk with Jesus. God was not promising orientation change. He was promising the grace to forsake an unrepentant pattern of sex with other members of the same sex.

Such an overrealized eschatology caused a lot of believers to be disappointed with God when he didn't come through and make us straight. (Why did we even assume that God's goal was sinful heterosexuality? At the resurrection we will be like the angels.) It caused a lot of believers to doubt God. Or to question our salvation. Or to miss realizing all the ways God was in fact changing us—helping us entertain fewer lustful thoughts, breaking us free from a pornography addiction, growing our love for Jesus and our love of his church, not to mention developing in someone like me the fruit of gentleness that I had long doubted I would ever see.

If recent research is accurate, there is an added factor as well.

God does not promise to always grant us physical healing in this life. And more and more studies are suggesting that homosexuality might be more of a physical thing than we've thought.

Be warned: this is about to get scientific and more than a little controversial.

ARE PEOPLE BORN GAY?

Few areas have been more controversial than the question of homosexuality's physiological component. In North America, about half of the population believes that some people are born gay. As we have seen, in antiquity this was not an uncommon belief. And as we saw in the early chapters, it was a belief espoused by Francis Schaeffer and Billy Graham, among others. Research suggests that the reality is rather more complicated and requires more nuance.

Before you get your defenses up, realize that a genetic or inborn component shouldn't surprise us. As Al Mohler reflected, "If a biological cause or genetic link explaining same-sex attraction is ever discovered, Christians should be among the least surprised. Such a finding would certainly inform our pastoral understanding and approach to persons with a same-sex orientation because we recognize that sin even affects our biology."[17] Our biology is fallen.

With the extensive research we do have, we still don't know the exact underlying causal nexus of homosexuality. As with research on alcoholism, research on homosexuality points strongly to a mixture of inborn and other factors.[18]

Research has shown that several structural differences exist between the brains of heterosexual and homosexual people. Gay men have symmetrical brain hemispheres with functional connections derived from the left amygdala, just like straight women. Lesbians have larger right hemispheres with functional connections derived from the right amygdala, just like straight men.[19] Gay men have a larger anterior commissure, just like straight women.[20] We can't always assess causality. Theoretically, given the plasticity of the brain, it could go either way. But there is correlation. A meta-analysis of studies involving seven thousand gay people and sixteen thousand straight people found that gay men are 34 percent more likely to be left-handed than straight men. Lesbians are 91 percent more likely to be left-handed than straight women. And we don't know why.[21]

But no, forcing your elementary school lefty to use his right hand will not improve his chances of growing up straight.

An extensive 2019 study of 492,000 participants identified five genetic loci associated with same-sex sexual behavior, with genome-wide significance. The study estimated the family-based heritability of same-sex behavior at 32.4 percent. The role of these five genetic loci accounted for 8–25 percent. The study concluded that the genetic component to homosexuality involves the additive interplay of multiple loci spread throughout the human genome. Some of these genes help regulate the olfactory system.[22] Think pheromones. Research had previously identified differences, between gay and straight people, in the regions of the brain associated with smell.

I know it's weird. But our sense of smell seems to play a big role in shaping sexual orientation.

Another locus relates to sex hormone sensitivity and is close to genes involved downstream with the gene that triggers initiation of male sex determination, causing an XY embryo to develop into a male.

This research aligns with studies of identical twins.

TWIN STUDIES

If one twin is gay, is the other twin more likely to be gay?

The most helpful such study was a 2010 analysis of the entire population of twins in Sweden. Using data from the Swedish Twin Registry, it looked at twenty-six thousand male and female twins. The results for men identified a 34–39 percent genetic component for their homosexuality. Growing up in a shared environment (same womb and family) was not a causal factor. Women had less of a genetic component (18–19 percent) and a much greater influence of their shared environment. This could account for the greater sexual fluidity observed in women.[23]

Women have always been more open-minded.

These conclusions were similar to those of a 2000 US study that included fraternal twins and nontwin siblings for comparison. That study found that the identical twin of a nonstraight twin had a 31.6 percent chance of also being nonstraight. This number was much higher than with fraternal twins of the same sex (13.3 percent), who still shared the same environment both in utero and in childhood. And that number was higher than with opposite-sex fraternal twins (8.3 percent).[24]

This does not prove that people are born gay. Were there a simple "gay gene," the concordance among identical twins would be closer to 100 percent. It's not.

But it is really, really high.

Epigenetics may provide additional insight into the development of homosexuality. Epigenetics is the study of chemical modifications of genes that change a gene's activity without changing the actual DNA sequence itself. A 2015 study examined sets of identical twins—sixteen pairs where both twins were gay and twenty-one where one was gay and the other straight. Researchers identified five areas on the genome where specific methylation patterns were very closely linked to sexual orientation. Their model predicted orientation with 70 percent accuracy within their sample, though one cannot extrapolate that level of predictability to the general population.[25]

HORMONAL, IMMUNOLOGICAL, AND DEVELOPMENTAL FACTORS

Other inborn factors may be neither genetic nor epigenetic, but hormonal. Heated debate has focused on the influence of intrauterine factors like fluctuations in androgens in the womb. Some research suggests that atypical hormone levels during the sensitive perinatal period before and after birth modulate sexual orientation.[26] Women with congenital adrenal hyperplasia—an inherited disorder that exposes the fetus to high levels of testosterone—are much more likely than other women to be more attracted to women than to men (15–30 percent).[27]

One of the best-documented correlations involves birth order of male sons. Boys with more older brothers are more likely to be gay, a statistic that increases with the number of older brothers. Each older brother may increase the likelihood of developing a homosexual orientation by 21–33 percent. One proposed explanation is the maternal immune hypothesis. With this model, each additional male fetus triggers a stronger maternal immune response targeting the key proteins in the brains of subsequent male fetuses. Such an immune attack would affect sexual differentiation in the fetal brain and therefore sexual orientation.[28]

This would be a nongenetic but inborn factor.

And one study was able to isolate abuse as a developmental factor. This research estimated that childhood sexual abuse accounted for 9 percent of attraction to members of the same sex (whether exclusively or bisexual) and 21 percent of lifetime same-sex sexual partnering.[29] Of course, we do not know whether that means it accounts for the whole story in 9 percent of cases, or—for example—it accounts for half the story in 18 percent of cases. There are many unanswered questions.

Yes, this is quite a lot of data. Where does all this research leave us?

Genetics alone appears to get us a third of the way to Oz with Dorothy and her friends.

Present research indicates that homosexual orientation is about one-third genetic. Epigenetic effects appear to further shape the development of sexual orientation. Additionally, intrauterine, hormonal, and immunological factors may play a significant causal role. Similarly, childhood sexual abuse is a factor in some people. Other environmental factors may play a somewhat larger role in women than in men.

WHAT ARE THE THEOLOGICAL AND MORAL IMPLICATIONS?

None of this means that homosexual practice must be okay. Alcoholism is about 50 percent genetic, but we don't encourage drunkenness. Overeating is a sin in the Bible, yet its temptation has everything to do with a hormone named ghrelin. We are not mere brains on a stick. Body and soul are intimately interconnected. And our biology is fallen. But if this research is correct and it becomes clear that a homosexual orientation contains a significant physiological component, then we have a theological reality to deal with. Fallen biology does nothing to shift the moral vision of Christian Scripture. But here our theology does draw out a life-altering reality.

God does not promise to always heal our bodies in this life.

He does not promise to repair our DNA in this life.

He does not promise to alter the epigenetic effects on our methylation pattern.

He does not promise to rework the structures of our fallen brains in this life.

He does not promise to undo the physiological effects of immune attacks that affected our brains in utero.

Our fallen flesh will tempt us in this life. Should it be any surprise that Saint Paul refers to our fallen nature as flesh? God does not promise to cure our damaged bodies. He promises to embrace us in our brokenness. He promises to wash us, to clothe us, and to sing over us in song. He promises us rest from our weariness. He promises to deliver us from our need to perform. And he promises to teach us—step by faltering step—to believe his gospel enough to become willing to sacrifice daily in order to obey him. And he promises to use even our areas of greatest weakness to help us see the riches of his amazing grace. Whatever Paul's thorn in the flesh, we know Jesus refused to heal it so that God's power might be made perfect in weakness.

THE DEATH OF A MOVEMENT

The ex-gay movement died because it began on theologically weak foundations. An underdeveloped theology of sin. An overrealized eschatology. We are all far more corrupted than we care to admit. Sin is deeply rooted in our internal corruption. Indwelling sin is always at work within us. And it has a lot to work with, since even our physiology is deeply affected by the fall, in ways that God does not promise to cure in this life. The expectations of a movement that called itself ex-gay set up a lot of women and men to fail.

And so Exodus International closed its doors. Many of its affiliates had already been shifting away from orientation change toward sexual integrity.

And so we bid our farewell to the ex-gay movement. Having exhumed its corpse for a postmortem, let us bury the remains.

This thing really is a thing of the past, right?

part three

The Rising Challenge to a Historical Ethic

fourteen

Did We Get the Biblical Sexual Ethic Wrong?

*We can appreciate the way the ancient writer is seeking to pre-
serve the integrity of Israelite life in Leviticus without assuming
that the same concerns are relevant to life today.*
—James Brownson, *Bible, Gender, Sexuality*, 2013

Among adults age eighteen to thirty-three who left their conservative faith, nearly one-third told Public Religion Research Institute in a 2014 survey that it was because of their church's negative treatment of sexual minorities.[1] That trend has only intensified.

Over the past decades, our post-Christian culture in the secular West has seen a profound shift in how people view gay, lesbian, and bisexual people. And that shift is international. Gay marriage has been legalized in much of the world. Same-sex couples around the globe raise children together.[2] The shift has been experienced at every level of Western civilization.

One *Sesame Street* writer even claims he wrote Bert and Ernie as gay characters in the 1980s, based on a same-sex couple he knew at the time. The Sesame Workshop quashed the rumor in 2018. The organization took to Twitter, clarifying that "Bert and Ernie are best friends. . . . They remain puppets and do not have a sexual orientation."[3] It was good of them to clear that up. But it still points to the startling degree to which the world has changed.

Granted, we had all wondered about Ernie.

What's at stake in this question about gay people and homosexuality, though, is not just the future of gay people. What's at stake is the next generation. They have watched their parents' adversarial and self-righteous posture toward gay people, and it has left a very bad taste in their mouths. They find themselves feeling an empathy that an earlier generation was too fearful, too defensive, and too politicized to feel. They hear fearmongering about the gay agenda and roll their eyes. They understand we're talking about real people and not just issues.

Many younger people in our churches consider the thought of mandatory celibacy, and it feels unfair that gay people who become Christians can't have someone special in their lives. And then they hear of a new biblical hermeneutic that carves out space for monogamous same-sex sexual unions in the church, and they are ready to bite.

There is a rising challenge. All of this begs the question.

Have Christians historically misunderstood the sexual ethic revealed in the Hebrew and Greek Scriptures? Does the Bible even speak into the modern experience of committed, mutual same-sex unions?

This is the question being asked in our churches right now, even in very conservative churches. A younger generation of evangelicals is coming to conclusions very different from those of their parents and grandparents.

Yet this question is not exclusively a recent one. In the 1970s, educated evangelical elites like Schaeffer and Stott grappled with this question as they proposed their paradigm of care. The ex-gay movement in the following decades developed a paradigm of cure. A third paradigm also arose, offering a radically different understanding of the biblical teaching on homosexuality.

Now more than ever, it is challenging the historical Christian ethic on sexuality.

RALPH BLAIR AND EVANGELICALS CONCERNED

In the early 1960s, Ralph Blair began arguing that biblical teaching did not necessarily rule out committed, monogamous homosexual relationships.[4] In 1971, Blair—by then a psychotherapist in private practice in New York City—started the Homosexual Community Counseling Center to help gay and lesbian clients sort through their issues from having grown up gay. Four years later he founded Evangelicals Concerned to help professing evangelical Christians wrestle through these same issues including whether what they thought the Bible taught about homosexuality was really what it taught.[5]

Fuller Seminary's Robert K. Johnston noted how questions about homosexuality and the church were in the air. "In its first issue for the year 1978," he wrote, "*Christianity Today* asked a variety of evangelical leaders to assess what was the most noteworthy religious development of the previous year and to predict what would be most important in the upcoming one." He noted that Wheaton president Hudson Armerding answered, "I personally feel that the issue of homosexuals in the church was one of the most significant religious developments of the year." *Eternity* magazine editor Stephen Board offered a similar response, as did *Los Angeles Times* evangelical religion correspondent Russell Chandler. "Homosexuals will dominate religious news for several years," Chandler added.[6]

Blair charted the way for what would become known as the affirming evangelical paradigm. Blair argued that none of the classic biblical "clobber passages" like the account of Sodom, Leviticus 18 and 20, Deuteronomy 23, Romans 1, 1 Corinthians 6, and 1 Timothy 1 addressed the question of monogamous homosexual relationships. "There are no homosexuals in the Bible," he wrote, "[not] the men of Sodom, cult prostitutes, slave boys and their masters, nor call boys and their customers. The Bible is an empty closet."[7] In Blair's view, the Bible does not address the modern gay partnership, because the passages we assumed addressed them were in fact condemning other forms of abusive or idolatrous same-sex activity like male prostitution, pedophilia, and temple sex.

Note that from Blair's perspective, he was not intending to eliminate biblical sexual ethics. He taught against promiscuity long before the AIDS crisis arose. Rather he sought to carve out space within evangelicalism for committed monogamous same-sex unions.[8]

The year after Blair formed Evangelicals Concerned, the National Association of Evangelicals publicly denounced the organization. In a 1977 article in *Christianity Today*, NAE executive director Billy Melvin declared, "NAE wants to disavow any connection with Evangelicals Concerned. The basic error in the teachings of such a group has been well documented."[9]

Yet Evangelicals Concerned grew and within a decade had twenty chapters across the country. A 1987 *New York Times* article described a meeting. "It is no one's image of what homosexuals do in New York City on a Friday night. Every week, 30 men, most of them in their 20's and 30's, meet in a therapist's office on Manhattan's Upper East Side where, for an hour and a half, they study the Bible."[10]

What became known as the gay-affirming paradigm had its exegetical roots in mainline Protestant scholarship. Derrick Sherwin Bailey's 1955 *Homosexuality and the Western Christian Tradition* was the first modern book-length theological treatment of the subject.[11] Bailey, an Anglican theologian, developed the exegetical paradigm that set the stage for most theologically liberal scholarship on the topic.[12] It was with Bailey that John Stott interacted as early as the 1970s.

Bailey also set out to distinguish "inverts"—people with a genuine homosexual orientation—from "perverts"—heterosexuals who engaged in homosexual acts. He argued that biblical authors could have had no knowledge of the homosexual invert, so biblical references to same-sex sexual behavior were describing perverts and not inverts. The Bible, he argued, quite simply does not speak to the question of whether inverts could enter into a monogamous sexual relationship.[13] According to this line of reasoning, the cultural distance is too great to apply biblical texts to mutual relations among inverts. While Bailey concluded that same-sex sexual practices among inverts were still likely sinful, those who followed his exegesis took his argument farther.

JAMES BROWNSON'S ARGUMENT FROM SIMILARITY

Among professing evangelicals today, the most rigorous presentation of an affirming paradigm has been James Brownson's 2013 *Bible, Gender, Sexuality: Reframing the Church's Debate on Same-Sex Relationships*.[14]

Brownson cautions against overusing an argument from cultural distance. The Bible, he argues, does speak into who we sleep with. He sees sexual expression properly set within a deliberate kinship bond between two people sharing similarity and a sense of mutual obligation. He writes, "I have offered a more complex moral vision, one that looks at sexuality through the central category of the exclusive one-flesh kinship bond and sees the core meaning of sexuality expressed in a delight in the other; a deep desire for gratification and union; the attendant call to honor and serve the other in committed bonds of loving mutuality; and a fruitful vision of committed love that overflows in many ways—in procreation, adoption, service to the community, and hospitality to others."[15]

Brownson argues that the narrative of Eve's creation focuses not on the complementarity of the man and woman but on their similarity over against the animals. He notes how each animal brought before Adam failed to be a suitable helper. Only when God created another human was that helper found. The emphasis of the passage, therefore, is on their similarity as fellow humans and not on their dissimilarity as male and female. This reframing opens the door for the possibility of Christian marriage being between two people of the same sex. Brownson concludes, "As far as the creation accounts are concerned, then, gender complementarity, viewed through the lens of the physical or biological difference between the genders, cannot be construed as the basis for the Bible's rejection of same-sex erotic relations."[16]

Brownson fails to address the Hebrew terminology used to describe the precise nature of the relationship between the man and the woman. The search was for an עֵזֶר כְּנֶגְדּוֹ. An *ezer kenegdo*. The Hebrew term *ezer* denotes a helper without necessarily implying any inferiority. In fact, quite the opposite can be implied. Commentators rightly note that God is called the *ezer* of Israel in Exodus 18, Deuteronomy 33, and countless psalms. Sixteen of nineteen biblical uses refer to God. But this was a search for a particular kind of helper, a particular type of relationship.

This sought-after *ezer* is also *kenegdo*. While *kenegdo* appears only once in the Old Testament, it likely denotes "corresponding," with a connotation of "complementary." Think equal and opposite. A mirror image. A counterpart. Alike and yet different in a way that complements the other. The best English translation is probably "a helper according to his complement." (Brownson does acknowledge this fact in an endnote, only to dismiss it, writing that "this aspect of difference remains undeveloped in the remainder of the passage.")[17]

The entire passage is about finding an *ezer kenegdo*, a helper according to his complement. When the woman is formed from the man's own flesh, that complement is at last found, and the two become family. Were the two identical, she would have been an *ish*, a man, but Adam calls her an *isha*, a woman. Within Genesis 2, the gender difference between the man and the woman—their sexual diversity—is at the heart of their complementarity. They are similar in their humanity yet complementary in their gender. A helper according to his complement. An *ezer kenegdo*.

One need not be a strict gender complementarian to recognize the sexual diversity at play between the man and his sought-after *ezer kenegdo*. In God's image, "male and female he created them" (Gen. 1:27) and instructed them to "be fruitful and increase in number" (v. 28). They are "a man" and "his wife" (Gen. 2:24).

This complementarity includes sexuality, which draws attention to the purpose of the chapter—to explain marriage and why there are two sexes. The chapter concludes with its summary. "That is why a man leaves his father and mother and is united to his wife, and they become one flesh. Adam and his wife were both naked, and they felt no shame" (Gen. 2:24–25). Genesis 3 then explains the fall—and the shame—with chapter 4 picking up the narrative. "Adam made love to his wife Eve, and she became pregnant and gave birth to Cain" (4:1). Brownson argues, "Such a reading of the physical complementarity of the genders is nowhere else directly affirmed (or even addressed) in Scripture."[18] Yet this entire passage is affirming just that sexual diversity, or complementarity, within marriage.

The entire Genesis 2 narrative is about a search for a complement to the man, culminating in the creation of the woman, their marriage, their being naked, their having sex, and their having a baby together. The text thus draws attention to their shared, coordinating reproductive system designed to function successfully only through the sexual union of one male and one female. They have coordinating parts through which they image God the creator by becoming cocreators with him in the creation of new humans. And they go from being naked together in chapter 2 to making love and having a baby in chapter 4. We cannot remove from this discussion the human reproductive system and the way God designed it to work.

The creation account in Genesis is the single most important canonical passage for understanding our heavenly Father's design for sexuality. Once we see what sexual union was intended to be before the fall shattered God's visage, we can see how all of God's nos to sex are given to protect his one overarching yes to sex. We moderns often naively think of sex as simply an exchange of bodily fluids or a benign act of personal self-expression. But anyone who has experienced sexual assault, abuse, or rape knows that sex is something far more than that. Sex was designed as something holy. Its abuse therefore becomes something profane.

Personally, what I find so convicting is this: As we look at the unfolding narrative of Scripture, we see that whenever sexual desire is cultivated outside of that original design—whether lust, sex with animals, sex outside of marriage, prostitution, incest, adultery, deserting a spouse, or, yes, sex with a person of the same sex—it is presented as something distorted. Something God doesn't want us to do.

Brownson relegates to an endnote the complementarity of the man and woman that is so emphasized in the creation account—a sexual diversity which sets the moral logic of all subsequent biblical teaching on sexuality. Without this biological complementarity, he is free to question from scratch the moral logic of each biblical passage that on the surface appears to instruct us against same-sex sexual expression.

REDEMPTIVE MOVEMENT AND CANONICAL TRAJECTORY

If Brownson's minimizing of the *kenegdo*, or sexual diversity, or complementarity, of the marital union at creation is a first step in reframing the debate about same-sex sexual unions, a second step involves a significant hermeneutical shift.

Constructing a social context in which homosexual acts were perceived as arising from uncontrollable passions, Brownson sees the moral logic of Romans 1:24–27 as a warning against out-of-control desire and licentiousness—a problem a modern gay couple might not have. Further, he relativizes the passage by placing it within a human honor-shame context and within first-century cultural assumptions about what was against nature. This may be, but for Brownson, the sexual acts were shameful and unnatural not because they violated the creation pattern in Genesis but because they violated the gender norms and expectations of antiquity. The homoerotic acts in Romans were not shameful because of their object but because of their excess. Brownson concludes, "The same-sex eroticism Paul envisions is either an expression of the monstrous ego of the Roman imperial house, or an expression of prostitution, child abuse, or promiscuity, an absence of mutuality, a neglect of the obligation to procreate, or a failure of persons to express with their bodies what they say with the rest of their lives."[19]

What about the Mosaic legislation?

Brownson acknowledges "From the perspective of Leviticus, to 'lie with a male as with a woman' is to reduce a male to the status of a female, which inherently degrades him and fails to honor his divinely given status as a male. For a male to willingly accept such degradation makes him equally culpable in the Leviticus author's mind." That much seems clear. He summarizes, "Leviticus concludes that 'lying with a male as with a woman' is an 'abomination' to both God and Israelite sensibilities, and its presence could not be tolerated within Israel." Agreed. But Brownson explains that the author of Leviticus was working within a relative social construct of honor and shame that shamed such sexual practices. Our modern Western social constructs are different, so the command does not apply to us. "We can appreciate the way the ancient writer is seeking to preserve the integrity of Israelite life in Leviticus without assuming that the same concerns are relevant to life today."[20]

There's obviously quite a hermeneutic at play here. What's going on?

Throughout, Brownson appeals to a looser version of what William Webb calls a "redemptive movement" hermeneutic. In doing so, he moves us beyond the ethics of the New Testament to an ethic that tolerates—if not fully embraces—committed monogamous same-sex sexual partnerships in the church. He does this by constructing a canonical trajectory that moves from an Old Testament emphasis on outward purity to a New Testament emphasis on inner purity. Brownson extrapolates that following this trajectory would imply that over time, the outward gender of a life partner becomes less important than the love and commitment that partner shares. Brownson's conclusion is in contrast to that of Webb, who sees in the New Testament no softening of the Old Testament's prohibition on homosexual practice.

Yet Scripture does not present itself as a set of trajectories for us to extrapolate in order to come to an ethical system better than what has been revealed in the New Testament. "Prophecy never had its origin in the human will, but prophets, though human, spoke from God as they were carried along by the Holy Spirit" (2 Peter 1:21). I fear that this is less an issue of hermeneutics than it is of posture. Do we see ourselves and the church above the Scriptures or beneath them? Theologically and morally, such a posture toward Scripture could get us anywhere we wanted, which is precisely the problem. Functionally, such a posture nullifies the moral authority of the entire New Testament.[21]

But even if we were to allow such a hermeneutic for the sake of argument, the Bible's canonical trajectory doesn't get us to Christian gay marriage. The redemptive movement of sexuality carries us in the opposite direction. In the Old Testament we see a nearly universal emphasis on heterosexual marriage, with a tolerance of polygamy among leaders. In the New Testament we see a new emphasis on celibacy as a gift equal to marriage, one that Jesus commends in Matthew 19. In 1 Corinthians 7, Paul expresses his wish that everyone could be celibate like himself. In 1 Timothy 3, we see heterosexual polygamy now expressly forbidden among leaders. In the coming age, as Jesus tells us in Matthew 22 and Mark 12, there will be neither marriage nor giving in marriage. Instead, Jesus says we will be like the angels in heaven. There is a very clearly defined redemptive historical trajectory concerning sexuality in the Bible. This is not a move toward increasingly diverse expressions of sexual union. To the contrary, Jesus tells us we are all moving toward celibacy. All of us will be celibate one day, when we will at last be in consummate union with Christ, to which sexual union was but a sacramental pointer. The canonical trajectory is moving away from human sexuality altogether. Celibacy is an intrusion ethic, an inbreaking of the ethics of the coming age into our present era.

The moral instruction of the New Testament is final and perfect. I must always place myself under the New Testament, never above it.[22] Turning back to the creational pattern revealed in Scripture, if Genesis 2 is a quest for a complementary partner and an explanation of why we have two different sexes with an interconnected reproductive system, of why men and women marry and have children, then each of Brownson's attempts misses the point. The biblical prohibitions on same-sex sexual acts are merely being consistent in pointing us back to God's original design for our relational, familial, and sexual flourishing.

DEFINING *ARSENOKOITAI*:
GAY SEX OR CHILD MOLESTATION?

Moving from Genesis into the New Testament documents, we find that much of the discussion surrounding sexuality has swirled around one word and its meaning. If much of the Genesis discussion centers on the Hebrew term *kenegdo*, much of the New Testament discussion centers on a word Paul used on two occasions to warn against a certain kind of sexual expression. Various proposals for its meaning have arisen.

Much ink has been spilled, and endless blogs and websites have been filled, with speculation about one word and its meaning. The apostle Paul used the term *arsenokoitai* in warning us against a certain sexual practice in 1 Corinthians 6:9–11.

> Do you not know that wrongdoers will not inherit the kingdom of God? Do not be deceived: Neither the sexually immoral nor idolaters nor adulterers nor [*arsenokoitai* nor *malakoi*] nor thieves nor the greedy nor drunkards nor slanderers nor swindlers will inherit the kingdom of God. And that is what some of you were. But you were washed, you were sanctified, you were justified in the name of the Lord Jesus Christ and by the Spirit of our God.

One of the two Greek words here translated "men who have sex with men" is *arsenokoitai*. The word is a coupling of the words for male and bed—as in the place to lie down, used of the marriage bed. The term *arsenokoitai* may have had earlier Hellenistic Jewish usage, though this is its earliest surviving use. But its components appear to have been lifted from the Greek Septuagint text of Leviticus 18:22—καὶ μετὰ ἄρσενος οὐ κοιμηθήσῃ κοίτην γυναικός βδέλυγμα γάρἐστιν—literally, "And with a male you shall not lie down in bed as with a woman; it is detestable" (translation mine). Both *arseno* (ἄρσενος, or male) and *koitai* (κοίτη, or bed) are there to be seen in the Levitical prohibition. The Septuagint was a collection of Greek translations of the Hebrew Scriptures, our Christian Old Testament, and was probably used by Paul and many of his Jewish contemporaries. The connection is even stronger in Leviticus 22:13, where they occur next to each other—ὃς ἂν κοιμηθῇ μετὰ ἄρσενος κοίτην γυναικός. "If one lies down with a male in bed as with a woman" (translation mine). Here ἄρσενος κοίτην or *arsenos koitain* means "with a male in bed." It certainly appears that whoever coined the term simply took the text of Leviticus and created a new word to describe what the Leviticus passage prohibited—*arsenokoitai*.[23]

Paul used this same term in 1 Timothy 1, where the New International Version translates it as "those practicing homosexuality" (v. 10). "We know that the law is good if one uses it properly. We also know that the law is made not for the righteous but for lawbreakers and rebels, the ungodly and sinful, the unholy and irreligious, for those who kill their fathers or mothers, for murderers, for the sexually immoral, for those practicing homosexuality [*arsenokoitai*], for slave traders and liars and perjurers—and for whatever else is contrary to the sound doctrine" (1 Tim. 1:8–10). The Timothy text echoes the Mosaic law and particularly the Decalogue, or Ten Commandments, listing them in order. Paul lists not being holy or religious—violating the fourth commandment to keep the sabbath holy. Then he lists dishonoring father and mother, a violation of the fifth commandment. Then Paul lists committing murder, the sixth commandment. Next Paul lists adultery, sexual sin, and *arsenokoitai*. Adultery is the seventh commandment. Next comes slave trading. The Greek word means a slave dealer, kidnapper, or man-stealer. The eighth commandment is, "You shall not steal." Then Paul lists lying and perjury. That's the ninth commandment, about bearing false witness in a court of law.

Brownson neglects this underlying structure of the Ten Commandments and chooses instead to argue that slave dealers are "acting as 'pimps' for their captured and castrated boys." He suggests that the Greek *pornos* refers to child sex slaves. They in turn service the *arsenokoitai*, "the men who make use of these boy prostitutes."[24] Such a reading neglects the fact that Paul is listing commandments four through nine in order. And the other nine uses of *pornos* in the New Testament refer to sexual immorality, sometimes to premarital sex as distinct from adultery. A *pornos* is one who engages in *porneia*, sexual immorality. The man-stealing is listed where it is because it was a most egregious form of stealing, not because it was stealing boys to castrate for pedophiles. The literary structure and context of the passage clue us into that.

Clearly, Paul considers *arsenokoitai* to be a violation of the universal moral law summarized in the Ten Commandments, with adultery, premarital sex, and sex with men all violations of the seventh commandment about sexual holiness. Paul considers Leviticus 18:22 and 20:13 still very much applicable.

Malakoi: Trafficked Boys, Dapper Dressers, or "Bottoms" in a Gay Hookup?

The Corinthians list pairs *arsenokoitai* with *malakoi*—Greek for "soft." The term had a range of meaning that could include being fancy in relation to clothing, lacking self-control, being effeminate, or being the passive partner in a sexual relationship between two men, whether that happened in a mutual relationship or in male prostitution. First-century Jewish philosopher Philo uses *malakoi* for the passive partner.

Some have suggested that *malakoi* here refers to children or youth slaves who were forced into prostitution against their will, with *arsenokoitai* being their clients. But that reading cannot stand in this literary context. If *malakoi* refers to those exploited and forced into sexual servitude against their will, then why does Paul stress their moral culpability? The people of whom Paul writes will not inherit the kingdom of God on account of their unrepentant violation of the seventh commandment. Clearly, Paul is speaking of someone willfully engaging in sexual sin, not a victim of human trafficking or rape.

Could *malakoi* here refer to someone in fancy dress or someone with a lack of self-control? Fancy dress might seem out of place in such a sin list. Someone lacking self-control fits in a sin list. But does it fit this particular location in this particular sin list in this particular literary context?

In the vice list in 1 Corinthians 6, *malakoi* is listed between sexual immorality, idolatry, and adultery on one side and by *arsenokoitai* on the other. Paul goes on to explain how sexual sin is idolatry because it violates the holiness of the temple of the Holy Spirit (vv. 18–19). This is a list of five consecutive terms describing sexual sin, grouped together as the seventh commandment, before the eighth.

These chapters are very much about sexual sin. In the preceding chapter, Paul had instructed the Corinthians about a case of incest (1 Cor. 5:1–8). Paul had charged the believers not to associate with sexually immoral people who claim to be Christians (vv. 9–13). In chapter 6, he made the point that believers should handle these cases themselves and not turn to outside courts (vv. 1–8). Paul then presents his vice list before continuing with his discussion of fleeing sexual immorality (vv. 12–20). William Loader explains, "It is likely that . . . the two words . . . refer to the passive and active participants in all same-sex relations."[25] In modern gay parlance, that would be the distinction between the "bottom" and the "top."

But we're getting ahead of ourselves. Before we simply apply this language to modern gay partnerships, we have to ask: in what context was this language used in antiquity?

How Was *Arsenokoitai* Used in Antiquity?

When speaking about same-sex sexual practices in the Bible and today, James Brownson argues from cultural distance that we're comparing apples and tangerines. He proposes that Paul had in mind only the Greek practice of pederasty—sex with a teenager. Brownson explains the difference between these pederastic relationships and modern gay sexual partnerships. He writes, "These pederastic relationships were transitory rather than permanent and committed; they were driven by the desires of the older partner rather than being mutual and shared; and they were often characterized by abuse, slavery, and prostitution." Such relationships, he argues, are very different from the same-sex unions of today.[26] And he makes a fair point.

Up to a point.

Abuse, slavery, and prostitution are very different foundations compared with the mutual love and commitment driving many modern gay partnerships. Much Greco-Roman sexuality involved abuse. Women were expected to be virgins at marriage and stay monogamous.[27] But among men, sex was often about power and personal self-fulfillment.

But is Brownson correct that all *arsenokoitai* was necessarily pederasty? And is he correct that all ancient Greek and Roman pederasty necessarily involved these negative qualities—transitory, abusive, prostituted, enslaved? Is he right that these relationships were never mutual? These are crucial historical questions.

The word *arsenokoitai* is a generic term and was certainly used to describe sex with teenagers. Sex with a younger man was the primary homosexual expression in the Hellenistic world. In that sense, *arsenokoitai* could be used as a substitute for *paidofuora*—sex with teenagers and young men. Paul could have used this term or other terms specific to pederasty, like *erastes* for the older lover and *eromenos* for the younger beloved.[28] These were all expressions of the larger category of *arsenokoitai*. But they were not the only forms of *arsenokoitai*. William Loader notes that Paul "might have used more specific terms if he had a narrower sense in mind."[29]

Since there are no earlier surviving Greek examples, we have to look at the patristic record to understand what range of behaviors *arsenokoitai* covered. What did the early Christian readers of Paul understand by the term?

How Was *Arsenokoitai* Used in the Early Church?

How did the early church use this term? The vast majority of patristic uses of the term *arsenokoitai* are either quotes of Saint Paul or just a prohibition listed without any context to help us ascertain its precise meaning. Those references can't help us know what range of behaviors the term covered. But there are a few instances in which patristic authors gave us more context or even an example of *arsenokoitai*. And they do not all involve adolescents or prostitution.

In his *Preparation for the Gospel*, begun around AD 313, Eusebius quoted the Parthian gnostic Bardaisan, from the previous century, about the difference in cultural practices between the Hellenistic world and Parthia. "From the Euphrates River . . . a man who is derided as a murderer or thief will not be the least bit angry; but if he is derided as an arsenokoitēs, he will defend himself to the point of murder. Among the Greeks, wise men who have male lovers are not condemned."[30] That last line was likely Eusebius's own explanatory note. Either way, Eusebius is defining *arsenokoitai* as "men who have male lovers." That sort of thing was okay in the Hellenistic world, but not beyond the Euphrates in Parthia—modern Iran and Iraq.

In numerous patristic vice lists, *arsenokoitai* or *arsenakoitia* is grouped with other sexual sins like sexual immorality *(porneia)* and adultery *(moicheia)*.[31] A collection of homilies traditionally attributed to Macarius of Egypt said that Sodom was destroyed because their men refused to repent of *arsenokoitia*.[32] There's room to debate the exact nature of the sin of Sodom. Rape. Poor hospitality. Being overfed. (It's listed in Ezekiel.) Trying to sexually penetrate males. Probably all of that and more. But I'm pretty sure those angels weren't kids. Here *arsenokoitai* refers to those seeking to penetrate grown men.

Hippolytus of Rome—martyred in the year 235 under the persecution of Maximinus Thrax—also used *arsenokoitai* to refer to an incidence of sexual penetration of an adult male, not a youth. In book 5 of his *Refutation of All Heresies*, Hippolytus describes the beliefs of the Gnostic Naasseni sect. He says this religious group believed that the evil angel Naas—whose name is a Greek transliteration of the Hebrew word for serpent—deceived and committed adultery with Eve. After he was done with Eve, Naas approached Adam and had sex with him as well. The text concludes, "From these origins came adultery and male sex with a passive male partner [*arsenakoitia*]."[33] Eve was the example of adultery. Adam and Naas provided the example of *arsenokoitai*, with Adam the passive partner. Clearly, Adam was not a child when Naas bedded him down. Adam was a married man at the time. We know this because the angel's sex with Eve is described as adultery on her part. The text does not specify whether Adam's involvement was consensual, though it seems less likely. Either way, this was not pedophilia.

The example documents two things.

First, the Naasseni were bonkers.

Second, *arsenokoitia* refers simply to a man penetrating another man, even if that most often involved pederasty, particularly in Greece. In this case, Adam was an adult.

A century earlier the *Apology of Aristides* had used *arsenokoitai* to describe Zeus penetrating the handsome young shepherd Ganymede. It was a retelling of a story familiar within Greek mythology. Zeus summoned an eagle to bring Ganymede to Mount Olympus, where he gave him eternal youth and made him cupbearer to the gods. In Virgil's *Aeneid*, the wife of Zeus sees Ganymede as competition for her husband's attention.[34] The relationship between Zeus and Ganymede was sexual.

So was Ganymede a child? No. In Greek art, Ganymede was depicted as a muscular young man—not quite as built as a Greek depiction of an athlete, but close.[35]

Arsenokoitai covered a broad range of male-on-male sex in the patristic era.

And when the early Christians translated *arsenokoitai* into other languages, they translated it as "sex between men." In his Latin Vulgate, Jerome translated it in both 1 Corinthians and 1 Timothy as *masculorum concubitores*—"those who lie with men." Earlier Latin translations of 1 Timothy similarly used *masculorum concubitores*. The Old Syriac text translates *arsenokoitai* in both passages with three words that mean "to lie with men." Both the Bohairic Coptic and Sahidic Coptic translations used two words that mean lying or sleeping with males.[36]

In Romans 1:27, where Paul writes of men engaging in unnatural sex acts with other men, it's *arsenes en arsenes*. He is speaking of *arsenokoitai*. The term had a range of meaning but almost always described the man playing the active role in sex with another male, whether with a teenager or with an adult.

The vision for sexuality revealed at creation unites two diverse sexes with shared, coordinating reproductive systems in procreative union. All the biblical nos to sex serve to protect God's one overwhelming yes to sex which was imprinted at creation. Paul uses language derived from Leviticus to instruct against men having sex with men—language the early Christians used to mean exactly that. It would seem that only a low view of biblical inspiration could justify a rejection of the historical understanding of biblical sexuality. Though there is one remaining possibility, the one outlined first by Ralph Blair and further developed by Brownson and Karen Keen.

I speak of course of the argument from cultural distance.

fifteen

Tackling the Argument from Cultural Distance

When they reach manhood they ... are not naturally inclined to marry or beget children. ... These are the people who pass their whole lives together.

—Aristophanes, Plato's *Symposium*

At its heart, the question of whether we got the biblical sexual ethic wrong—at least as argued today—is not simply a biblical or exegetical question. As we saw in the previous chapter, it is also a theological question in that modern affirming arguments rely on a low view of biblical inspiration. This view in turn allows for a redemptive movement hermeneutic that seeks a sexual ethic presumably better than the New Testament's. But equally, this is a historical question. Affirming arguments build on certain assumptions about gay relationships in antiquity, so we have to look historical-theologically at the Hellenistic sexual world in which Paul was immersed as Apostle to the Gentiles.

DID THE ANCIENTS HAVE A CONCEPT OF HOMOSEXUAL ORIENTATION?

The argument from cultural distance posits that since mutual, loving, faithful same-sex relationships were unheard of in the ancient world, none of the New Testament passages prohibiting same-sex sexual intimacy could have had modern same-sex relationships in mind. Brownson summarizes the line of reasoning:

Whatever specific behaviors and relationships the Bible is condemning in the "seven passages" cannot be used to condemn committed same-sex unions today. These ancient texts are speaking against pagan practices, against pederasty and abuse, and against violations of commonly embraced standards of decency and "normality" that were part of the ancient world. As such, they cannot speak directly to committed, mutual, and loving same-sex unions in the contemporary church.[1]

Karen Keen also follows this reasoning in her graciously written 2018 book *Scripture, Ethics, and the Possibility of Same-Sex Relationships.* "The biblical authors don't write about the morality of consensual same-sex relationships as we know them today," she writes. "To put it simply, to say that the biblical authors object to prostitution or pederasty is not to say that the authors object to monogamous, covenanted relationships. That would be comparing apples and oranges."[2]

But does the historical record support this?

Did anyone in antiquity have a concept of homosexuality as something constitutional? As a condition? As an emotional or aesthetic or relational or sexual orientation?

In Plato's *Symposium,* Aristophanes spoke of the *hetairistriai,* women who were attracted to other women. He also discussed men oriented toward other men. He described their origin in prehistory, when humans were round and had four legs and four feet and two faces looking in opposite directions. There were three sexes in that primeval age. The man was a child of the sun. The woman was a child of the earth. The third sex was the man-woman named Androgynous, who was a child of the moon. Each human had eight appendages. So strong were these four-armed quadrupeds that they rose up in force and made an attack upon the gods themselves. Seeing the intensity of their threat, Zeus devised a plan to cut these early humans in half in order to diminish their power.

So the humans were severed in two, each one becoming two people. Yet the smaller, weaker humans now spent their days looking for their other half. Those who had been Androgynous would pursue each other in marriages, with one man and one woman. Those who previously had been men would seek out other men. And those who previously had been women, once split asunder, would seek solace in the arms of other women.

Aristophanes describes it:

All the women who are sections of the woman have no great fancy for men: they are inclined rather to women, and of this stock are the she-minions [*hetairistriai,* courtesans of women].

Men who are sections of the male pursue the masculine, and so long as their boyhood lasts they show themselves to be slices of the male by making friends with men and delighting to lie with them and to be clasped in men's embraces. . . .

So when they come to man's estate [reach manhood] they are boy-lovers, and have no natural interest in wiving and getting children, but only do these things under stress of custom; they are quite contented to live together unwedded all their days. A man of this sort is at any rate born to be a lover of boys or the willing mate of a man, eagerly greeting his own kind. Well, when one of them—whether he be a boy-lover or a lover of any other sort—happens on his own particular half, the two of them are wondrously thrilled with affection and intimacy and love, and are hardly to be induced to leave each other's side for a single moment. These are they who continue together throughout life.[3]

Aristophanes explains that this kind of relationship was not primarily about the sexual intercourse. At the heart of their relationship was a "desire to be joined in the closest possible union," to "be made one," to "share a single life," to "be one instead of two," and to "be so joined and fused with his beloved that the two might be made one."[4] There was mutuality and companionship and love and fidelity. These relationships were permanent. "They . . . continue to live together throughout life."[5] This may be one of antiquity's closest descriptions to the modern concept of sexual orientation—or more accurately for Aristophanes, an emotional or relational orientation with a sexualized component.

Ancient writers frequently distinguished people according to sexual preference and seemed to have a concept akin to sexual orientation.

Was Paul Familiar with Classical Learning?

"But," you ask, "would Paul have had any knowledge of classical authors?"

Paul the apostle was born in Tarsus, the city where Mark Antony first met Cleopatra. Tarsus was a leading intellectual center famed for its academy. One of its foremost philosophers, Athenadorus Cananites, was tutor to the emperor Augustus. Paul described himself as a Roman citizen "from Tarsus in Cilicia, a citizen of no ordinary city" (Acts 21:39). He obviously knew what the city of his birth was known for. Even first-century Jerusalem was highly Hellenized. Paul was a student of Gamaliel I. We know that Gamaliel's family were well versed in Greek philosophy—even though they rejected it—on account of their need to interact intelligibly with the Roman government. According to the Talmud, Gamaliel's son (or possibly grandson[6]) later had a thousand students, half of whom studied

Greek philosophy while the other half studied Jewish Scripture and tradition (Sotah 49b:8–15). From the time of Paul's return to Tarsus, he was immersed in Hellenistic culture, no longer living separately as a Pharisee. Certainly, Paul had no formal philosophical training as in the academy. But his knowledge of Greek literature was typical of educated Hellenistic people of his day.[7]

In Athens, Paul spoke with Epicurean and Stoic philosophers. Paul addressed the Areopagus. Throughout his ministry, he freely quoted from fourth-century BC Greek dramatist Menander (in Acts and 1 Corinthians) as well as fourth-century BC Greek poet Aratus and the mythical Greek philosopher Epimenides. Paul seems strongly at times to allude to Seneca. Given that Platonism had been the single largest intellectual force behind the process of Hellenization in Judea for the previous three hundred years, it's highly plausible that Paul knew about Plato, though we can't know whether he was familiar with the *Symposium*.

It's sort of like when you see someone wearing a black turtleneck and reading Sylvia Plath. It's safe to assume they've probably heard of William Shakespeare, though you can't know which of his works they're familiar with.

The description in the *Symposium* was not the only such description of what we might call sexual orientation. Aristotle similarly saw a biological basis for the condition.[8]

They Knew about Gay People

Centuries after Plato, early in the first century AD, the Roman fabulist Phaedrus offered a different explanation. He proposed that the mythological figure Prometheus had worked all day long fashioning male and female genitalia. Prometheus then headed out to a dinner party and got smashed. Stumbling home too drunk to know what he was doing, he accidently slapped some male genitalia onto some females and some female genitalia onto some males. It was an honest mistake, if costly to some of us. The children of Prometheus's blunder therefore would have their sexual preference mismatched to their sex.[9]

The early second-century AD Greek physician Soranus, who was active in Rome, commented on the many in antiquity who believed same-sex orientation to be inborn.[10]

The second-century AD sophist Polemon explained that you could spot the man inclined toward passive homoeroticism by his physiology. In his *On Physiognomy*, which survives only through its Arabic translation, Polemon included a chapter titled "On the Signs of an Effeminate Angrogene"—terms most often used of the passive male partner. Among the chief characteristics of such a man were his "moist gaze . . . heavily moving his eyebrows and cheeks, neck inclined, frequently moving his back and limbs, as if they were all slack, . . . his voice thin, sharp, and drawn out, with emphatic movement of the head." Other than being overly expressive and a bit lispy, Polemon added, such a man was "frequently gazing upon himself and the limbs of his body."[11]

Around AD 330, astrologer Firmicus Maternus found that passive male partners were determined by the stars. Such men, he explained, also "dance on the stage and act in ancient fables, especially if Mars is in square aspect."[12]

I do wish Firmicus would quit peddling these twenty-first-century Western stereotypes.

This was the world of Saint Paul and the early Christians. Firmicus, for the record, revised his views about what determines the outcome of history, after his conversion to Christianity. He went on to become a prominent Christian apologist.[13]

Despite the dizzying array of explanations for it, there were understandings of sexual orientation in the Gentile world to which Saint Paul was called as a missionary.

Think of these pages as a guided tour. A visit to antiquity. A journey through the apostle Paul's neighborhood. Sightseeing along the streets through which Paul walked as Apostle to the Gentiles. There we find a sexually polymorphous culture that looks surprisingly like our own.

TEENAGE GREEK BOYS AND THE MEN THEY MELTED

The most common form of same-sex sexual practice in antiquity was pederasty. But what exactly was pederasty? Was this the abuse of helpless children? What we find in the historical record is admittedly a bit grisly for any Christian to read about. Consider yourself forewarned.

While pederasty was never a primary form of same-sex expression among female lovers, it was common and socially accepted for a Greek man to have a teenage male lover.[14] In the Hellenistic world of the eastern Roman Empire—Paul's world—both partners would typically be freeborn.

Fifth-century BC lyric poet Pindar's *Tenth Pythian Ode* noted how one young athlete might occasion sexual desire by "both his age-mates and old men," while also being "a heartthrob for young maids."[15] Greeks embraced all of these. And such relationships were not always mutually exclusive. In his treatise *The Art of Love* from around the year 1 BC, Ovid put words to the helplessness some young wives felt. "What can a woman do when her husband has skin silkier than hers and can snare more men?"[16]

By contrast, Roman general and later emperor Galba preferred his men older. Suetonius explained, "As for his sexual desires, he was more inclined to males, and among males only to the very strong and experienced."[17]

A lot of confusion arises when people speak of Greek and Roman pederasty. Because we moderns marry late, we associate ancient pederasty with pedophilia. They were in fact very different. Much homoerotic imagery on Greek pottery shows male lovers who appear relatively close in age.[18]

I write not to justify pederasty but to help us understand the apostle Paul's context in his Hellenistic world. Marriages in antiquity typically involved a significant age difference, as the man needed to be able to support his wife and family. Women in Greece married between age fourteen and sixteen. Men typically married at thirty. They married women half their age. This was normal. When men sought out male lovers, they typically pursued young men the same age as a potential wife or a bit older, typically fourteen to eighteen. In Rome the legal age to marry was twelve for women and fourteen for boys.[19] Average age at first marriage in Rome has been a hotly debated subject. Literary evidence suggests that Roman women first married between age twelve and fifteen, with men marrying when they were about six years older, though literary sources give a picture only into the lives of Roman elites. The epigraphic record suggests that most Roman men followed the Greek pattern and did not first marry until their late twenties.[20] Census records in Roman Egypt suggest men waited five to ten years longer than women to marry.[21]

All of this is to say that in antiquity there were a lot of unmarried men under thirty, and when they did first marry, they typically married someone age twelve to eighteen. This age differential has four profound implications for discussion of pederasty in antiquity. First, Greek young men had on average an extra sixteen years to experiment sexually before marrying. Roman men had perhaps an extra decade to do so. That's a lot of time to experiment in a pagan civilization that had a very different sexual ethic than that of the early Christians. Second, this age differential meant that when Greek or Roman men looked for a male sex partner, they would have idealized teenage young men because that's the age of a wife they would eventually seek, though the most desired young men in Athenian oratory were all *meirakia*, age eighteen to twenty-one.[22] Third, it means we should not filter this through a modern Western paradigm that considers a normal wedding to be between two twentysomethings, with anything under age eighteen a species of pedophilia. As disturbing as this thought is to us, remember that Jewish women married at age twelve and a half. The Virgin Mary was likely twelve or thirteen while she carried our Lord in her womb. Our concept of a delayed adolescence is very modern. This was not pedophilia by the standards of antiquity. And fourth, this means we should not apply a filter of sexual abuse to all pederastic Greek and Roman relationships. Sixth-century BC poet Theognis of Megara wrote, "With a boy there must always be mutual favor."[23]

Greek literature emphasized the power the youth had over his older courters. "To the extent that literary texts display a power differential," writes classicist Thomas Hubbard, "it is rather to emphasize the powerlessness and even emotional helplessness of the lover and a privileged position of control occupied by the beloved youth."[24] Pindar captures the experience of many Greek men whose hearts were melted by the beauty of teenage boys. One *skolion*—a drinking song sung at symposia—praises the beauty of young Theoxenus.

> Ah! But any man who catches with his glance
> The bright rays flashing from Theoxenus' eyes
> And is not tossed on the waves of desire,
> Has a blackened heart of adamant or iron. . . .
>
> But I, by the will of the Love Goddess, melt
>   Like the wax of holy bees stung by the sun's heat,
> Whenever I look upon the fresh limbed youth of boys.[25]

My, how those Greek men melted.

One might argue that such poems—and tons of them survive—reveal only the voice of the men pursuing the teens. And that is a fair concern. Yet in ancient graffiti, young men bragged about their beauty and their pride in being courted by men.[26]

Pederastic relationships typically were not permanent. The youth would get older, grow a thicker beard and increasing amounts of body hair. So men often would lose interest. In his twenties, a Greek man might switch roles and become the man pursuing a teenage lover. Around thirty, he would settle down with a teenage bride.

WERE THERE MUTUAL, LONG-TERM HOMOSEXUAL RELATIONSHIPS IN ANTIQUITY?

We have already seen from Aristophanes a description of loving, mutual, life-long same-sex relationships, relationships in which two men lived together for their entire lives without marrying, relationships that were deeply emotional and sexual.

But even pederastic relationships could become permanent. In Plato's *Symposium*, Apollodorus speaks of a dinner party or symposium around 416 BC held in honor of Greek tragedian Agathon. Agathon, one of the most prominent of the tragic writers, was celebrating his victory in a drama festival. Young and beautiful, he was there alongside his older male lover Pausanias. Pausanias and Agathon were one such couple who, beginning with a structured Greek pederastic relationship, chose to violate that convention by becoming a lifelong committed monogamous couple. The couple had first been mentioned as such seventeen years earlier when Agathon was in his late teens.[27] Later, when Archelaus of Macedon—a noted patron of the arts—summoned Agathon, both he and Pausanias moved to Macedon together as a couple.

As a public figure, Agathon faced ridicule for violating the social convention, continuing in the passive sexual role later than the structures of Greek pederasty typically approved. At one point, a rival playwright staged a play in which a character named Agathon came out on stage and asked if any men were willing to penetrate him. But theirs was a mutual, monogamous, lifelong same-sex partnership. And it was a very public relationship. It was immortalized by Plato.

Aristotle also commented on erotic relationships between males sometimes continuing indefinitely. "Many couples continue the relationship, if, as a result of spending time together, they come to love each other's character, because they are of similar character."[28]

Let me note again why I am developing this argument. I am not developing this argument to conclude that these were biblical relationships. The whole direction of this chapter runs counter to that. Rather I am outlining this historical record to counter the argument from cultural distance. If there were in fact nonabusive, nonprostituted, mutual homosexual relationships in the first century, then one cannot use their absence to argue that the apostle Paul knew nothing of them and therefore could not have been speaking into them. I am providing the historical context that I believe demonstrates that the church has historically gotten the basic biblical sexual ethic right.

Strangely, affirming writers advocating for an argument from cultural distance try to erase the experience of mutual same-sex couples from antiquity. They have borne their eraser every bit as firmly as the ex-gay movement ever did. It's a historiographical *Boy Erased*. In an irony born of theological agendas, supposedly "open and affirming" authors have to erase queer couples from ancient history to fit their biblical interpretation.

Pardon me if I don't find that very progressive.

We have an actual historical record.

Same-Sex Couples during Paul's Lifetime

During Paul's life as a Pharisee, the Jewish philosopher Philo of Alexandria lamented the prevalence of long-term homosexual relationships among Greeks and worried the human race would have been extinguished had such unions become too common. "Men mounted males without respect for the sex nature which the active partner shares with the passive; and so when they tried to beget children they were discovered to be incapable of any but a sterile seed." With same-sex couples spreading, population would inevitably decline. He continued, "Certainly, had Greeks and barbarians joined together in affecting such unions, city after city would have become a desert, as though depopulated by a pestilential sickness."[29] It seems gay couples were common enough to worry Philo.

One of the more infamous of Rome's emperors was Nero. Nero became emperor of Rome in the year 54, while Paul was ministering in Ephesus. Nero ruled over the empire for the rest of Paul's life on earth. By the year 60, Paul may have been under house arrest in Rome, awaiting his judicial appeal to Nero. It was likely the previous year that Paul had exercised his right as a Roman citizen to appeal to the emperor to adjudicate his case.

In the year 64, Nero married his first husband, Pythagoras, in a ceremony described by Tacitus as having "all the forms of regular wedlock. The bridal veil was put over the emperor; people saw the witnesses of the ceremony, the wedding dower, the couch and the nuptial torches; everything in a word was plainly visible."[30] Nero was the passive partner in the relationship. A murderer, but not likely insane, Nero was in fact deeply romantic. He fell in love five times in his life and married all five—three women and two men. Suetonius also records the marriage to Pythagoras, though he misidentifies his name. It was the talk of the empire. Paul was in Rome at the time.

Both Tacitus and Suetonius describe how Nero later that year tortured Christians after the great fire of AD 64 on account of their superstitions. Some historians believe that Paul died during this persecution. Paul may have been buried along the Via Ostiensis outside the walls of Rome. Some historians believe Paul may have survived but been martyred in AD 67.

That was the year Nero married his second husband, Sporus—a Roman freedman, according to Cassius Dio. In this marriage—concurrent with the marriage to Pythagoras—Nero was the dominant partner. Likely in his late teens, poor Sporus ended up being castrated in an attempt to preserve his youthful looks. (This was back before Botox and fillers.) The power differential between freedman and emperor raises questions about just how mutual such a marriage could be; this may have been very different from the relationship between Pausanias and Agathon. Nevertheless, Sporus remained at Nero's side until Nero's suicide.[31]

Many emperors had their young men. The young Bithynian Greek man Antinous was between sixteen and eighteen years old when Emperor Hadrian took him as his lover. From that point on, Antinous traveled with Hadrian as his personal companion. They attended the annual Eleusinian Mysteries together, and Antinous was with Hadrian when the emperor killed a lion in Libya. Their relationship came to a tragic end on a trip to Egypt, when Antinous drowned in the Nile. Hadrian subsequently had Antinous declared a god. He named a city after him and set up a religious order to worship him.[32]

Roman Same-Sex Couples

While the Latin-speaking Romans borrowed heavily from Greek culture, their sexuality played out somewhat differently. With marriage often delayed for Roman men, it was not uncommon for a Roman man to have a male *concubinus* right up until his wedding day. Typically a slave—unlike in Greece—the *concubinus* had "a stable sexual relationship, not exclusive but privileged."[33] Roman fiction certainly had a place for mutual same-sex sexual relationships. In his second-century *Ephesian Tale*, Xenophon's character Hippothoos reminisces about his relationship with his lover Hyperanthes. They were both young men at the time.

The late-first-century Roman poet Martial wrote a fictional account about a Roman wedding between two men, a rugged Roman named Afer and a bearded Greek Stoic named Callistratus. Martial had moved to Rome the year Nero married Pythagoras, and one can speculate about their connection. Martial's friend the Roman poet Juvenal took the account farther by making both spouses Romans and making the wedding one of the social events of the season. The Roman Gracchus replaced Callistratus. Juvenal added a second similar marriage involving a Roman man of distinction as the bride. The two poets differed in the intentions of their satire. While Martial presented his account as something humorous, Juvenal saw nothing funny about homosexual marriage. He proceeded to launch into a diatribe against the perversion which was threatening Rome itself.[34]

Were this all strictly fictional, he would not have launched into a diatribe.

We have fewer accounts of lesbian relationships from antiquity, though to be fair we have fewer accounts of women altogether. We have surviving records of magical spells to allure same-sex liaisons between men and between women.[35] The second-century satirist Lucian of Samosata wrote of women in mutual sexual relationships. In his *Dialogues of the Courtesans,* he spoke of the women of the Greek island of Lesbos who would not suffer to share their beds with men but preferred the company of women. The second-century Syrian writer Iamblichos wrote a widely popular story about an Egyptian king's daughter and her female lover. In *Babyloniaka,* he described how Berenike slept with and then married the woman named Mesopotamia.[36]

Paul was Apostle to the Gentiles. This was his neighborhood. This was the cultural context for his missionary endeavors, the Hellenistic tableau upon which he penned his letters to the Corinthians, the Romans, and Timothy.

RETHINKING THE ARGUMENT FROM CULTURAL DISTANCE

So what of the argument from cultural distance? The argument that there were no mutual, committed same-sex relationships in antiquity? The argument that Paul could not have conceived of such a thing and therefore could not have spoken into it?

There are certainly differences between then and now. Brownson frequently mentions that ancient homoerotic sexual relationships were marked by differences in social rank and status. The older partner of higher social rank played the active role. The younger partner of lower social rank played the passive role. And that does appear to be a common pattern. There were plenty of exceptions, though, including the emperors Nero and Elagabalus. They had the highest possible social rank yet were content to be the passive partner. But while there was usually a differential in social rank and status between active and passive male partners, the same could be said of nearly all heterosexual partnerships in the ancient world. We late moderns tend to think about power very differently. Nearly all sexual relationships in the ancient world had a power differential. That was true with everything from heterosexual marriages to a same-sex temple prostitute. It was only in later antiquity that the Christians introduced a theology of sex that was all about self-giving love. But it is a stretch to say that because of that difference in social status, men and women never entered into sexual relationships—including same-sex relationships—out of mutual love.

The historical record simply doesn't bear out the narrative of the argument from cultural distance.

There were both mutual lifelong partnerships and short-term ones. It was not uncommon for well-to-do Greek and Roman men to have a series of consecutive two-year sexual relationships with younger men. Mostly, the ancients preferred their male same-sex partners young, muscular, and smooth. A well-off Greek or Roman man could easily draw a male partner half his age.

These things happened.

It's history.

And from where I stand, I think I can say that's a pattern any gay man today would instantly recognize. It's almost a cliché. The partner half your age is a fantasy most gay men have entertained on more than one occasion. And in two thousand years, the shelf life on such relationships hasn't gotten much longer. When they're half your age, two years is about right. And gosh. After all this time, still nobody is chasing after the geezers.

I hear some well-to-do straight men have a similar thing about women half their age.

The cultural distance may be less than it at first appears.

DID WE GET THE BIBLICAL SEXUAL ETHIC WRONG?

Did we get the biblical sexual ethic wrong? Those who argue that we did get it wrong seek to open the door to allow for monogamous same-sex sexual unions in the church. Their arguments tend to follow along a series of propositions. They argue that we can surmise a canonical trajectory to project an ethic beyond that of the New Testament. They see the Genesis 2 creation account as a search for a helper who is fundamentally like—not complementary to—Adam. They understand the Levitical legislation prohibiting sex among members of the same sex to no longer apply in our era. And they argue that Paul the apostle could never have imagined mutual, faithful, loving relationships between two members of the same sex. His prohibitions must therefore be against sexual abuse, prostitution, and the like.

Many have found this line of reasoning or something close to it convincing, including evangelical left leader Tony Campolo, former *Christianity Today* editor David Neff, evangelical Anglican bishop David Atkinson, ethicist David Gushee of the Center for Faith and Public Life, popular author Jen Hatmaker, *Sojourners* magazine founder Jim Wallis, the late Rachel Held Evans, and recent authors publishing on the topic with Eerdmans. These are all people (and a publisher) I respect.

In asking whether we got the biblical sexual ethic wrong, I have cautioned us against trying to use speculation based on canonical trajectories to reach a new ethic that is better than that of the New Testament. This is not about employing a slightly different hermeneutic. This is about our fundamental posture toward Scripture. I have argued that the Hebrew of Genesis 2 emphasizes the complementary nature of the relationship between the woman and the man as a diverse union of similar yet different equals. I have argued that Paul's use of *arsenokoitai* in his letters is his application of the wording of the Septuagint Greek text of Leviticus condemning the act of a male lying with a male, and was understood thus by the early church. And I have documented the presence of mutual same-sex relationships in Paul's world, in its culture, in its history, and in its literary imagination. Because this was Saint Paul's mission field—he was Apostle to the Gentiles—the presence of these relationships calls into question the plausibility of the argument from cultural distance.

This leaves me to conclude that we did not get the biblical sexual ethic wrong, at least not on the question of whether Jesus wants me to have a husband. (He does not.)

Given the emphasis on complementary sexes in Genesis 2 in connection to their nudity and procreation, given that every sex act that deviates from that creational pattern is presented as something negative, given that mutual same-sex relationships were widely known in the ancient world, given Paul's use of the Septuagintal language of the Levitical prohibition [*arsenokoitai*], given his basis for the prohibition being that such acts are against nature, and given the canonical and redemptive historical trajectory from marriage to celibacy, I can't in good conscience sanction any Christian same-sex sexual union in the church.

REALIZE WHAT'S AT STAKE

Realize the stakes are high. Paul says that unrepentant *arsenokoitai* and *malakoi* —like adulterers and those sexually active outside of marriage—will not inherit the kingdom of God (1 Cor. 6:9–10).

And in a culture that elevates romance and sex—being coupled—as things that make life worth living, this can be a very hard conclusion for some of us to hear. I have only ever had romantic or sexual feelings toward other men. Family members tell me they wish I had a special man in my life, someone to walk through life with.

And I tell them I do.

He's my Lord, Jesus. And he's not all. I have lots of other special someones whom I've been walking through life with all these years.

The reality is this. I am convinced that for me to engage in a loving, nonabusive, mutual, long-term sexual relationship with another man—for me to grab hold of his hand—I would have to let go of Jesus' hand.

There is not a man on the planet who's worth that.

If I am going to have any real relationship with God, he has to be able to tell me I'm wrong. That's the cost of any real love relationship.

Still, being a big, shameful sinner puts me in the best possible position.

Sinners are the only class of people Jesus came to save. Jesus was a friend of sinners. One of my biggest spiritual concerns for friends who have bought the affirming argument is its inherent self-righteousness. ("There is nothing wrong with my sexuality!") I find it so much more liberating just to own the big, shameful label and let Jesus love me.

sixteen

Is the Biblical Ethic Inherently Violent to Gay People?

Lesbians and gays who reported that religion was important to them were 38 percent more likely to have had recent suicidal thoughts. For lesbians only, religion was associated with a 52 percent increased likelihood of suicidal thinking.

—Anne Harding, Reuters

After the 2016 Orlando Pulse nightclub shooter gunned down forty-nine people, Eliel Cruz of Faith in America penned an editorial which expressed the feelings of many when they heard conservative religious leaders express sorrow over the massacre. "When those who heavily influence our policies and culture espouse the very rhetoric that causes LGBT people violence, they must be held accountable. They cannot encourage this traditional theology and wash their hands of the harmful, and even deadly, effects."[1] It is a powerful argument born of much pain.

And it raises a question worth considering: Is the biblical sexual ethic inherently violent to gay people?

We know that a tidal wave of men and women left the ex-gay movement and eventually—in their words—came to terms with their sexuality, accepting it as a healthy and even good part of how God made them. Many of these describe themselves as affirming Christians. Others want nothing to do with Christianity. Many of them will tell stories about how repressed they felt in the ex-gay movement. They will speak of the self-loathing they endured because of the expectation of heterosexuality. You will hear stories of youth being cast out by their families and rejected by their churches. Many protest the unfairness of what they see as mandatory celibacy. They perceive any biblical vision that limits sexual expression to a marriage between a man and a woman as inherently violent to gay people.

No one can deny that there has been a history of abuse inflicted on gay people within churches. Only the active abusers deny that. Nothing I can say can negate the tears that have been shed, the wounds that have been inflicted, or the rejection that has been endured. I believe that our churches and ministries have much to repent of. It's not always possible to separate the biblical sexual ethic from the abuse suffered at the hands of communities that profess that same biblical ethic. And even when we can attempt to untangle the two, there is conflicting data.

PERSPECTIVE 1: IT'S STILL DANGEROUS TO BE CHURCHED IF YOU'RE NOT STRAIGHT

On the surface, there is evidence that the biblical sexual ethic, as it has often been applied (or misapplied), can do psychological damage to gay people. Personal accounts speak of depression and suicidal ideation. In a 2016 BBC report, a Belgian man named Sébastien explained why he had requested euthanasia on account of extreme psychological suffering because he could not reconcile his homosexual orientation with his Catholic faith. After seventeen years of therapy and medication, he spoke of "a constant sense of shame, feeling tired, being attracted to people you shouldn't be attracted to—as though everything were the opposite of what I would have wanted." Asked whether he would reconsider, he replied, "If someone could give me some kind of miracle cure, why not? But for now, I really don't believe it anymore." You could hear the despair in the thirty-nine-year-old's words. "The moment when they put the drip in my arm—I'm not worried about that. For me, it's just a kind of anesthesia."[2]

One could argue—as many of Christianity's critics do—that the Bible constructs sexuality and gender in such a way as to be inherently violent to gay people. Along this line of reasoning, it's an ethical system that systematically favors straight people and marginalizes and oppresses nonstraight people. Further, one could argue that an ethical system that identifies the unchosen longings of a minority group as particularly aberrant and unnatural inevitably creates an atmosphere conducive to violence against them.

Is the biblical sexual ethic, as it has often been applied, inherently violent toward people who aren't straight?

A study of 21,247 college students examined the correlation between sexual orientation, religious faith, and suicidal ideation. Using data from 2011, researchers found that 21–28 percent of LGBT students rated religion very important. While 3.7 percent of straight students had recent thoughts of suicide, 6.5 percent of gay and lesbian students had recent thoughts of suicide—a significant increase in comparison. Lifetime suicide attempts were three times as high for gay students as for straight. But religious faith added another layer to the data. Religious faith lowered suicidality among straight students. But only for the straight ones. "Lesbians and gays who reported that religion was important to them were 38 percent more likely to have had recent suicidal thoughts. For lesbians only, religion was associated with a 52 percent increased likelihood of suicidal thinking." The same correlation was found with suicide attempts.[3]

Such statistics do not distinguish between conservative and liberal church involvement or between Christianity, Judaism, Islam, and other religions. Given the prevalence of Christianity in the United States, however, one cannot deny a link between suicide and growing up gay in some sort of church. What we are not able to document is whether the biblical sexual ethic itself accounts for this difference. Could it not be some other constellation of factors within American church culture?

I recall one Sunday morning in 2019 when, as I was getting ready to preach, I noticed a tweet addressed to me. It simply stated, "Die fag, die." It had been decades since anyone had called me a fag. The account was from a conservative, religious Presbyterian man who frequently posted comments on evangelical so-called discernment blogs. His religious culture had only fueled the fire of his violence. Perhaps it was a drunk tweet, I don't know. He never apologized. The previous year, a man commenting on a Facebook page affiliated with a ministry based in Moscow, Idaho, wrote of thrusting me through with a spear. I don't take internet death threats too seriously unless they attach a photo of my license plate. But no one can deny that these are instances of religiously fueled violence at the level of the heart and tongue. If this is what virgins get for being attracted to members of the wrong sex, I hate to think what others face.

Statistically, by 2014 LGBT people were more likely to experience hate crimes than any other group—more than twice as likely as people of color.[4] How many of those crimes are religiously motivated? It's hard to say, though it would be difficult to deny that some are motivated by their reading—or misreading—of the Bible. This seems to present a sobering narrative. In a nation heavily influenced by Christianity, it's still dangerous not to be straight.

PERSPECTIVE 2: DATA SUGGESTS MANY GAY BELIEVERS DO WELL IN NONAFFIRMING CHURCHES

At the same time, there has been research on the emotional and psychological health of celibate Christians who are oriented to members of their own sex. A 2012 study in the *American Journal of Orthopsychiatry* examined the psychological well-being of 355 gay, lesbian, and bisexual people in traditional (nonaffirming) religious settings. They found that "participation in nonaffirming religious settings was not related to adverse mental health outcomes." They suggested that the negative effect of the higher level of documented shame among participants was offset by the "salutary effect through improved social support." The authors also noted that sexual minorities with a strong religious faith were 2.5 times more likely to attend a traditional nonaffirming church than an affirming one.[5]

In 2019, Mark Yarhouse and Olya Zaporozhets published their quantitative study of three hundred Christians "who experience same-sex attraction [and] have not experienced a change in their sexual orientation, yet . . . report an ongoing conviction to refrain from same-sex sexual behavior."[6] The study analyzed milestone events in sexual identity development, emotional well-being, psychological distress, attachment, and religiosity among these Christians who were gay but celibate or in a traditional marriage.

Were they repressed and self-loathing? Did they have higher levels of depression and suicidal ideation?

On the Depression, Anxiety, and Stress Scale (DASS-21), just less than 80 percent scored in the normal range for depression. About 9 percent scored in the moderate (8 percent) or major (1 percent) range, compared with roughly 7 percent of the general population. For anxiety, 93 percent fell in the normal range. For stress, 94 percent fell in the normal range. Participants who were unmarried were more at risk for depression, with nearly a third with mild or moderate signs of depression, and 67.7 percent in the normal range.

Examining overall well-being, the researchers found that gay celibate Christians ranked high in some areas but not in others. In areas of safety, standard of living, and personal spirituality or religion, they ranked high. But in areas of personal relationships, feeling part of your community, and future security, they scored medium, likely reflecting the double challenge of being neither married nor straight in churches often centered on marriage and family. Still, the median score for satisfaction with life as a whole was more than 70 percent, which is considered high.

A Ryff-54 assessment looked at participants' personal growth, purpose in life, and self-acceptance. Participants tended to be quite normal in the first two categories. But they were more likely to struggle with self-acceptance. Among those strictly celibate from all romantic relationships, only 52.3 percent were in the normal range.

All of this tells us something. When examining nonstraight people in conservative Christian spaces, by and large they're doing better than expected. Those committed to celibacy are the most likely to struggle to feel accepted by God. They will also more likely struggle to feel connected to their community and will face challenges in building meaningful relationships. But they don't seem very repressed or self-hating. The challenges Yarhouse and Zaporozhets document tie in closely with an alternate approach to this question of whether the biblical sexual ethic is inherently violent to gay people.

PERSPECTIVE 3: A BIBLICAL PARADIGM

There's another perspective in the New Testament, and I think it can help weave together these disparate data. It is this.

Biblically, God's moral law—apart from his grace—kills. This is the language the apostle Paul used in 2 Corinthians 3, where he contrasts God's law with the Holy Spirit's gospel ministry. Paul describes God's law in strong terms: "The letter kills," he explains (v. 6). The commandments that were "engraved in letters on stone" (v. 7) performed "the ministry that brought condemnation" (v. 9). God's moral vision is a mirror showing us how humanity's fall into sin has damaged us all.

This is what theologians have called the pedagogical use of God's law. God's commands are a tutor. The biblical sexual ethic, like the rest of divine law, was not given so that it "could impart life" (Gal. 3:21). No. By contrast, "Scripture has locked up" everyone—straight people, gay people, everyone—under sin (v. 22), leaving us all prisoners in need of grace. The moral vision of the Bible shows us how poorly we measure up. It exposes our shame. And in so doing, it shows us how desperately we need a savior. God's law was put in charge to lead us to Christ "that we might be justified by faith" (v. 24).

Without the radical grace of Jesus, this biblical sexual ethic is inherently violent to all people—not just gay people—because it exposes our shame. When Paul in Romans 1 exposed sex acts among people of the same sex, both Jew and Roman moralists would have turned around in disgust, particularly at the women and the passive male partners. Paul used that as his gotcha moment.

Once Jew and Gentile alike were fueled up in their righteous indignation, Paul then turned those big guns on them. He explained that God handed all of humanity over to a depraved mind. He then illustrated that depravity with a list of twenty examples. Envy. Strife. Deceit. Slander. Gossip. Arrogance. Boastfulness. (See Rom. 1:28–31.) These were the classic sins of religious people. They still are. God's moral vision is the great leveler because it shows us that there is no difference. Paul's three-chapter argument hits its crescendo with these words: "There is no difference . . . , for all have sinned and fall short of the glory of God" (Rom. 3:22–23).

The biblical sexual ethic is inherently violent to my pride. Violent to my delusional insistence that I'm one of the good people. Violent to my self-righteousness. Violent to my vain attempt to build an identity for myself that will last. Violent to my confidence that I know what's best for me. Violent to my desire not to need a savior. There was a Greg Johnson who had to die in order to become alive to God.

This pedagogical use of the law points us to Jesus. "There is no difference . . . , for all have sinned and fall short of the glory of God, and all are justified freely by his grace through the redemption that came by Christ Jesus" (Rom. 3:22–24). To be justified is to be declared righteous. It means that just as your sin and shame were transferred to Jesus on the cross, so his righteousness was transferred to you when you trusted him. That means you have Jesus' resume.

It means that you fed the five thousand. You raised Lazarus from the dead. You always did what pleased the Father.

To remove the biblical sexual ethic from its pedagogical context leading us to Jesus is to weaponize the law of God in ways that the New Testament does not. Divorced from this message of radical grace and acceptance in Jesus, the biblical sexual ethic can easily crush gay and lesbian people. Divorced from the biblical context of the gospel, the biblical sexual ethic can lead to despair, self-hatred, morbid introspection, and overwhelming feelings of guilt and shame.

When the biblical sexual ethic is not wrapped in the compassionate and gentle embrace of Jesus, it can drive people to suicide. And it has done just that. That's what law without gospel can do.

In that sense, the biblical sexual ethic—when robbed of its gospel-oriented pedagogical use—can be violent to all people, leaving us exposed and ashamed, without excuse, despairing of our unworthiness and without hope. It is the gospel that is the power of God to save. Not the law.

The biblical sexual ethic must be bathed in radical grace for it to be truly life-giving. Unless a gospel culture permeates a church or ministry, any discussion of the biblical sexual ethic will abuse and beat down and not inspire anyone to pursue holiness. Until we know that our Father actually likes us, we will lack the ability to get outside of ourselves enough to see the beauty of God's law, particularly at the point at which it tells us we are defective.

THE MISSING PIECE: GOSPEL CULTURE

I have heard many horror stories about growing up Christian and realizing you're not straight. A common thread in people's stories is that their church was not a safe place to be a sinner loved by Jesus. They lacked the gospel culture that could have made God's law profitable in their life.

That was part of what made the ex-gay movement's focus on orientation change so problematic. At times, the emphasis on change obscured the gospel from gay people. It did this in two ways.

First, the emphasis on sexual orientation change kept the gospel from reaching the people who really needed it, like me. It was the same-sex-oriented Greg who needed to know he was loved by God. It was the homosexually inclined Greg who needed to know his shame was covered. It was the nonstraight Greg who needed to know that he was seen and supported. It was the homophile, Uranian, friend of Dorothy, gay, inverted—whatever term you prefer—Greg who needed to hear that his name was carved into the palm of God's hand, that his Father in heaven delighted over him in song, and that nothing would separate him from the love of God. The actual Greg was denied all of that. Only the Changed Greg™ qualified for all of that. So, like so many others, I tried to convince myself that I was a straight man with a little bit of a struggle. And the make-believe Greg Johnson Mask™ felt accepted by God. But the actual Greg Johnson too often was alone with his shame.

Constantly telling ourselves and others that we weren't gay anymore left many of us feeling completely isolated in our experience. It is so much healthier to be the big, shameful sinner and let the gospel wash over you than to pretend you've been cured and be alone in that lie. The change-centered message obscured the gospel.

Second, the emphasis on sexual orientation change redefined spiritual growth as the absence of temptation. To be mature was to no longer experience sexual temptation. That was a standard no straight person was ever put under. I've known plenty of octogenarian brothers in Jesus who tell me they are still distracted when a beautiful woman walks in the room. It was perfectly normal (so it seemed) for straight men to experience sexual temptation.

But not for us. As we grew in Christ, we were told that sexual temptation would diminish and eventually disappear. When temptation didn't disappear, that left us questioning whether we were really Christians. That pressure to see temptation disappear put many of us on a performance treadmill, trying to become untemptable, trying to become changed. We felt so much pressure to become *changed*. And by changed, we didn't mean lusting less. We meant becoming straight or at least bisexual in orientation, or perhaps asexual. That kind of change is what would confirm that God was working in our lives. We were denied the freedom to just be a repentant sinner loved by Jesus. That's what the gospel does for everyone else. But for us, we had to be changed in one very particular way. So again the gospel was obscured.

I have heard the siren call of a secular culture that tells me to embrace my homosexuality with a gusto and find myself a boyfriend or three. I have also heard the siren call of religious pharisaism that tells me to fake it 'til I make it. I have followed that latter call and found it wanting. It's like the two brothers Jesus described who both wanted their Father dead. I feel the call of the prodigal to a far off country, but I grew up in that country and found it wanting. However, I have also heard the siren call of the elder brother. I followed that call and found it, too, wanting. I have found life in the call of Jesus, a third way distinct from the other two. In Jesus I have found the embrace of divine love just as I am, without one plea.

Is the biblical sexual ethic inherently violent to gay people?

To the degree in which it is immersed in a biblical culture of radical grace, it is not.

To the degree that it is removed from that biblical gospel culture, however, it becomes weaponized and cannot help but do violence to gay people. A church or ministry cannot responsibly have a discussion of sexual ethics apart from a discussion of the gospel. Any attempt to present a biblical view of homosexuality will do harm unless it is couched in a larger discussion about Jesus' love for gay people as image bearers and as objects of redemption in Christ. Any writing about homosexuality is in essence writing about gay people. And the bare minimum to make such writing nonviolent involves stating very clearly from the outset, "We're so sorry for what you've been through. We're sorry for where we've made it even harder. We love you. You have dignity as an image bearer of God. Jesus really loves gay people. Jesus loves you. His gospel is for gay people. His salvation covers all our shame." If it doesn't start there—or someplace very close—there is a high likelihood that anything written or said on the subject of homosexuality will inherently be experienced as violent by many. But if you keep it Christ-centered, even the bad news can be experienced as good news in Jesus.

part four

A Path Forward

seventeen

Confronting the Walking Dead

When a single mother of three small children identifies as such,
she is probably looking for help or support or understanding.
—Jill Rennick, Volunteer Coordinator,
Exodus International

Perhaps it just wasn't a good fit. He was getting frustrated. So was she. A friend of mine once decided to go to a counselor because he was depressed. The counseling sessions didn't seem to be going very well. He was wondering whether the counselor was a good fit, because she kept zeroing in on his relationship with his father and his sexuality. Finally, after three or four sessions, the Christian counselor stared at him intently. After a long, pregnant pause, she spoke the telling words. "Oh. I think I'm beginning to understand. You're not here because you want me to help you understand why you're gay and figure out how to become straight."

"No. I'm here because I'm depressed."

The fact that a licensed Christian professional would have such a strong assumption that sexuality was the issue says everything about the continuing effects of the ex-gay movement. It walks dead among us today. The ex-gay movement as we knew it died in 2013 with the closure of Exodus International. Some ex-gay ministries tried their hardest to stick around. Love in Action rebranded as Restoration Path in 2012 and changed its ministry focus to sexual addiction, but by 2019, the ministry no longer had a website or Facebook presence. Homosexuals Anonymous still has a website, but it hasn't been updated since 2017. It lists three chapters remaining in the United States, with a director in Germany. The Hope for Wholeness Network—with fifteen remaining former Exodus ministries—dissolved in 2020. I can't remember the last time I met someone who identified as ex-gay. What had been a massive movement of ministries, organizations, and therapists is now pretty much a memory.

Reparative therapy seems to have come to a similar demise. In 2019, Warren Throckmorton observed the near total collapse of reparative therapy among professional psychotherapists. "In my opinion, within psychotherapy, the war is actually over and change therapy has lost," he wrote. "No training programs teach it. I know of no Christian training programs that teach it."[1]

The closure of Exodus had a huge impact on its affiliate ministries, which relied on Exodus for referrals. Many of the remaining former Exodus affiliates chose a path of care, not cure. But the changes were not easy. "Most of our referrals came through the Exodus network," explains Richard Holloman of Sight Ministry. After Exodus closed, it was up to them to get the word out about who they were. "We started doing fewer groups. The focus shifted to provide more training for churches in how to be more redemptive and have a better understanding of homosexuality and how to love gay people."[2]

While Exodus in the United States is largely buried and dead, change-focused ministries continue to exist. And in much of the world, the ex-gay movement is still very much alive.

As we ask what a path to care looks like for gay people who become Christians, we have to confront the ways the ex-gay movement is still moving about undead among us. The relics of the ex-gay movement continue to foster emotionally unsafe and even abusive spaces within conservative Christianity. Any path to care must root out the emotional abuse within our churches and ministries.

THE WALKING DEAD

In much of the world, the ex-gay movement is still very much alive. The walking dead can be seen organizationally in the Exodus Global Alliance. When Exodus International closed in 2013, its international wing continued as Exodus Asia Pacific, Exodus Brasil, and Exodus Latinoamerica. Exodus Global Alliance had been formed in 1995 to help resource ex-gay affiliates, mostly in the developing world.

In North America, the Restored Hope Network (RHN) includes a few more than thirty affiliate ministries, including the former Exodus affiliates that had been most focused on change. Key figures include Anne Paulk and Andy Comiskey. Their approach in many ways is that of the Exodus of the 1990s, before Alan Chambers took over. Affiliates might use the Living Waters or similar curriculum. They do not like to be characterized as conversion therapists—a term they see as pejorative. But they do seek to change underlying predispositions "regardless of whether residual struggle remains or returns on occasion."[3] The leader of one affiliate, Stephen Black—also formerly head of Restored Hope Network—explains, "There is sure hope that one can enjoy freedom from driving homosexual temptation and the pounding desires of same-sex lust, which many call same-sex attraction."[4] Whatever name they give it, this program is still very much focused on the promise of sexual orientation change.

On a Christian FM radio network, Black has claimed a 72 percent success rate in freeing people from homosexuality.[5] The effectiveness survey at the end of his book documents his results. Here's a hint to his success rate. In answer to question 19, 84 percent of surveyed clients with more than a year of treatment stated, "I have same-sex attractions and do not consider myself gay or homosexual."[6] The ministry counted those former clients as successfully changed. Even though they're still attracted to members of the same sex.

I don't see how that's a successful change in sexual orientation. It seems to me, that is a successful change in sexual orientation terminology.

Such equivocation leaves unknowing listeners assuming he's talking about people becoming straight. From his own survey results, it's not clear that any of his clients have found freedom from same-sex longings. Yet major Christian radio shows continue to platform him and his misleading claim of a 72 percent success rate.

Another new ex-gay push comes to us from the West Coast.

Charismatic megachurch Bethel Church in Redding, California, and its pastor Apostle Bill Johnson (no relation) has launched an attempt to resurrect and rebrand the movement with its ex-gay ministry Equipped to Love. The ministry's CHANGED Movement uses hashtag #*oncegay*. They've even appropriated the old Exodus motto "Change is possible." The polish of the rebranding effort is impressive. But among the "ministries we love" listed on their website are the Restored Hope Network and many of its affiliates. Behind the trendy fonts and professional graphics, this is the old-school, unreconstructed 1990s ex-gay movement.

THE TERMINOLOGY WARS

While disguised ex-gay ministries are the obvious remains of a once large and vibrant movement, there are more subtle and sometimes more damaging ways the ex-gay movement walks undead among us today.

One way the ex-gay movement continues to shape evangelicalism is through what some have called the "terminology wars"—the attempt to promote or suppress various sexuality labels. As I mentioned in my note at the beginning of this book, all available labels have their issues. My sense is that most non-straight believers are very thoughtful and intentional about how they choose to describe their experience of their sexuality.

There are perfectly good and valid reasons why many followers of Jesus choose to describe themselves as same-sex attracted. They may not want to be associated with baggage that comes with the term *gay*. They may have built their identity on their gayness in the past and are trying to break free of that. I have a friend who says, "Homosexuality was my identity until I met Jesus." He wants nothing to do with the label *gay*. He wants to get as far away from it as he can. Others may prefer the phrase because it seems more descriptive and less tied up in issues of personal identity. Some others use the phrase because their spouse could never live with the alternative. Still others may choose to identify as same-sex attracted because they inhabit conservative religious spaces in which calling themselves gay will be misunderstood or misrepresented. They choose to use a term that is best understood within their context. They may consider that the more loving option, from where they stand. They may also want to avoid a naivete about the potential for LGBTQ narratives to exert an influence they don't want in their lives. There are lots of good reasons believers have for describing themselves as same-sex attracted.

There are also very good and valid reasons why many followers of Jesus choose to describe themselves as gay and celibate. They may be speaking phenomenologically, using the term *gay* in its descriptive sense, not in a prescriptive or ontological sense. They may not be saying, "This is who I am at core" but be merely saying, "This describes my experience." They may find the association between the language of same-sex attraction and the ex-gay movement disturbing. They may have gone through reparative therapy and feel retraumatized by a label they were told to adopt under false pretense. If someone had been closeted and hiding behind a mask her entire life, her saying she is gay might be a healing step toward personal integration. Someone else may be thinking missiologically and therefore prefer to use the language of the culture they are trying to reach. They may be wanting to emphasize their commonality with secular LGBTQ people in order to build bridges for the gospel. They may see it as a subversive way to tell an unbelieving world that there's a different way of being gay, a way that's all about finding life in Jesus. They may prefer *gay* because it maps onto sexual orientation and not just attraction. A homosexual orientation includes more than just same-sex sexual attraction. It also includes the lack of sexual attraction to members of the opposite sex, which for a Christian can be the far more painful half when we consider our human longing for a life partner. There are lots of good reasons believers describe themselves as gay and celibate.

They may just be trying to speak modern English. The phrase *same-sex attraction* is unfamiliar to secular people. I recall a counseling class at a seminary, in which a respected local counselor was brought in to teach a unit. One student raised her hand and asked, "How would this situation play out if the couple were same-sex attracted?" The counselor was confused. "They were what? Same-sex attracted? I've never heard of that phrase. Do you mean they were gay?" Johanna Goth Finegan has described a conversation in which she tells a secular friend she is same-sex attracted. "You mean you're gay?" "No. I'm not gay; I just am attracted to other women." "So you're gay." Finegan concluded, "There is no other way that conversation is going to go."[7]

There are good reasons why some believers don't like either label, and that too is a perfectly good and valid option. These are personal decisions about how one describes one's experience. Terminology is an area for Christian freedom. My approach has been to try to use the language that will be best understood by those to whom I am speaking. Terminology isn't about my building an identity for myself. God gave us communication to speak love and life into others. It has to be about how best to care for and be understood by the other person.

You say, "Greg, this isn't really about terminology. It's about identity. Why would anyone want to identify with their sin? Your identity is in Christ."

Ah yes. Here we go.

DO WE MEAN IDENTITY . . . OR IDENTITY?

When we're discussing questions of identity, a lot depends on what concept of identity is in operation. Building one's identity on something is not the same thing as identifying as something. It's too easy to talk past each other.

If by identity you mean the core identity that defines me, the identity that then becomes what I aspire more fully to be, my defining narrative, then no Christian should have a sexual orientation as their core identity. Our core identity as Christians is that we have been adopted as sons and daughters of the Father into his family. That's the objective identity that names and claims me and to which I owe my life, my love, and my treasure.

This is the way that Mark Yarhouse in 2005 distinguished between sexual attraction, sexual orientation, and sexual identity.[8] Attraction is merely descriptive of an experience that may be fleeting, like the possibly 20–30 percent of kids who experience a homoerotic attraction at some point during adolescence. Most still grow up straight. Orientation is more deeply rooted than attraction. When sexual attractions are consistently and persistently toward members of the same sex, then we're speaking of a homosexual orientation. Attraction and orientation are both descriptive terms within Yarhouse's 2005 paradigm.

Within this tripartite framework, sexual identity is more prescriptive. Identity in this case is who you see yourself to be at the core. It's the defining narrative you place yourself in. It is both descriptive and prescriptive, or aspirational. You adjust your beliefs and behaviors to align with your identity.[9] Within this framework, gay identity means an acceptance of what Yarhouse called the "gay script," which says that this is who I am, and I will be truly free if I embrace this part of myself as my core and live it out accordingly. The controlling narrative moves from the oppression of the closet to liberation.

And that puts it in the place of Jesus, who offers an alternative defining narrative that moves from lost to found.

Johanna Finegan, a PhD in philosophy from MIT who did her own stint in the ex-gay movement after her Christian conversion, offers points of spiritual caution about allowing the secular LGBTQ narrative to define us at our core: "How we think about ourselves, how we interpret our experience, the stories we situate ourselves in, the ways we perceive the world, and how we fit into it has enormous impact on us."[10] The secular LGBTQ community has cultural liturgies of its own. These liturgies can reflect the image of God and echo a very human longing for redemption. They can provide points of contact, bridges for the gospel. But we ought not naively or uncritically embrace them. As always, Christian discernment must distinguish the good from the bad.

Modern expressive individualism conceives of sex as a means of self-expression. I am told that I have to be true to myself, by which our culture means I have to be true to myself as a gay man, which is what I fundamentally am in this narrative. Notice how sexuality has now been moved to the very core of selfhood. To be true to myself as a gay man, the paradigm goes, I have to be in a romantic relationship with another man. It's in that context that I can engage in sexual self-expression. Sadly, according to this narrative, I have really stunk at being a gay man. I never made it to first base, because I didn't want to make it to first base. That means I must be repressed and self-hating, since I am not expressing myself sexually. Acting on one's sexual longings is what makes a person authentic.

After all, you have to be true to yourself. To who you are. Follow your heart.

It worked for Hitler.

Sorry. But I think you get the point. The logic works only if your heart is unfallen.

The narrative of expressive individualism is incredibly powerful. Most Westerners adopt this paradigm uncritically.

But within a Christian paradigm, is sex really about personal self-expression? Or is it rather about self-giving love? Is it transactional? Or is it a sacramental enactment of a lifetime commitment within a bond between two people of diverse sexes who will never, ever leave each other?

I don't want an impoverished twenty-first-century Western concept of sex to dictate my life. As I've written elsewhere, "My sexual orientation doesn't define me. It's not the most important or most interesting thing about me. It is the backdrop for that, the backdrop for the story of Jesus who rescued me."[11] The gospel gives us a better identity—a core, governing identity, an identity grounded not in our feelings, not in our accomplishments, not in what other people think about us, not in our individualism or expressiveness, but in our adoption into the family of God.

Modern identities are very fragile. Jesus provides an identity that cannot fade as you age, an identity that provides forgiveness when you fail, an identity that places the lonely in families and cannot be taken away by death.

So there is wise caution about adopting a gay identity, if you mean the narrow sense of core identity or defining narrative. That is Jesus' role. He is not willing to share you.

A MORE COMMON IDENTITY PARADIGM

But there is another way—a far more common way—that we speak about identity. Sometimes we use identity to include all the things we see as true about ourselves. One may identify as a Republican or a Democrat without building one's identity on politics. "When a single mother of three small children identifies as such," explains Jill Rennick, "she is probably looking for help or support or understanding."[12] One can identify as British and as a Christian, even while believing that one's ultimate citizenship is in heaven. Paul identified as a Roman citizen. Paul identified as a Christian. There was complexity to his identity.

"Ah," you chime in, "but those are morally neutral things. Not sin. Someone saying they're gay is identifying with sin."

But, I ask, how is my saying I'm same-sex attracted any different? Is that not also identifying with my sin?

We know Saint Paul identified with his sin. He identified with it more the longer he ministered. He identified as a sinner. He even identified as the chief of all sinners. Not former chief. Not chief emeritus. Chief. Paul identified as the CEO of depravity.

All of these things were true of him. Identity in this second sense is complex.

That's why centuries later the New Testament still calls Rahab a prostitute. The thief on the cross next to Jesus was not called the ex-thief.

Paul David Tripp speaks of the "two identities of every Christian." He explains, "These identities are 'sinner' and 'child of grace.'" He adds, "To recognize their existence and understand what it means to possess them both, together, is to see yourself as you truly are." He continues, "This will profoundly shape your fundamental sense of self and radically influence for the better how you live in the here and now, somewhere between the Fall and Destiny."[13]

This means a Christian who is an alcoholic can identify as such, not because he wants to glorify drunkenness but because he wants to be honest and be known in his weakness.

This approach to identity is the one Martin Luther took when he claimed that a Christian is *simul justus et preccator*, simultaneously saint and sinner. This was an understanding of the believer's dual identity that Johannes Oecolampadius had come to twelve years earlier in Basel. "The apostle is still a sinner while justified and has the desire to sin."[14] Here, with Paul and Oecolampadius and Luther, we see the believer identified with his temptations and sins as well as—supremely—with Christ.

The gospel doesn't erase this part of my story so much as it redeems it.

WEAPONIZING IDENTITY IN CHRIST

The believer's identity in Christ is frequently weaponized against nonstraight people in our churches, in ways we never would use it against straight people. In her study of people having undergone ex-gay treatment, Jan Gelech describes Brad. He said, "I started . . . saying, 'You know what? I'm gay. . . . I'm not going to be in a relationship, but I don't have to be in denial of who I am.' . . . [But] they [leaders] called it idolatry . . . taking on a false name. . . . You had to always call yourself straight and . . . work towards change."

How many times have I heard such conversations play out?

Christian: I'm gay.

Well Intentioned: No, you're not. Your identity is in Christ.

Christian: Well, of course Jesus is everything to me. That's my core identity. But I'm also attracted to members of the same sex.

Well Intentioned: You shouldn't identify with your sin.

Christian: My sexual orientation tempts me toward different sins than yours does, but it encompasses more than sexual desires. My orientation encompasses my complete lack of sexual attraction to members of the opposite sex. That's not indwelling sin, is it? My orientation also brings in certain shared experiences. I'm not talking about some intangible quality of gayness. I'm talking about the feeling of always having been different. The common experience of growing up closeted and afraid. The process of being honest and opening up about my story. Taking off the mask.

Well Intentioned: You still shouldn't identify with your sin. Your identity is in Christ.

Perhaps this is a bit of a caricature, but notice what is absent from this conversation.

Well Intentioned has not made any attempt to understand, let alone move toward and accept, the Christian in question. Without realizing it, Well Intentioned is functioning to police terminology, not to empathize or understand. Even if the intention is to help someone, the effect is that the sister or brother in Christ feels judged or controlled instead of feeling seen and known. I guarantee a Christian will experience such conversations as emotional abuse. From where they stand, they will feel that their existence within the church is threatened. That will make it even harder for them to know who they can trust.

This flattening of identity—identity as erasure of everything about you except Christ—sounds strikingly familiar to those of us who experienced the ex-gay movement. In a cassette tape titled *Introduction to Love in Action*, Frank Worthen explains, "Does Christ's life-changing power mean that I will suddenly become heterosexual? No, it certainly does not mean that. What will I be then? Neither homosexual nor heterosexual. You will be a new creature in Christ."[15] That's an unwillingness to accept the ongoing reality of sexual temptations. That's identity as erasure.

To clarify, saying you're gay or homosexual or same-sex attracted is not identifying yourself as a homosexual offender. None of the biblical terms for people who have gay sex—*arsenokoitai, malakoi,* and so on—describe sexual orientation or prevailing propensity. They describe certain types of sinful sex acts. They do not map onto orientation as a category, only onto what might tempt someone with that orientation. Now if someone were approaching me and saying, "Greg, I am a Christian and I want to build my life on receiving as much sex as I can from men, with me in the passive role," I would answer, "Ah, that's *malakoi*," and I would conclude that they were building their identity on their sin.

An alcoholic who celebrates drunkenness and lets it drive his life is identifying with his sin in an unhealthy way. An alcoholic who has been twenty years sober but says he is still an alcoholic is identifying with his sin in a healthy way. His terminology has not put him on a slippery slope toward getting drunk. Identifying himself as an alcoholic was his first step toward a new life. That new life began with honesty.

A HISTORY OF IDENTITY IN CHRIST

The language of identity in Christ is quite recent. You won't find it in Augustine or Luther or any of the creeds or confessions. Other than the occasional mention in works on Christian ethics—typically in discussing Paul's discourse in Galatians—the concept of identity in Christ received little attention until the 1990s. It's a recent theological construction.

Bestselling author and professor of practical theology at Talbot School of Theology Neil T. Anderson began introducing evangelicals to the concept in a series of books and a devotional between 1990 and 1996 and followed with more. Steve McVey followed in 1995 with a bestselling devotional, then a trickle of others jumped in, including the much-televised Southern Baptist powerhouse Charles Stanley, who wrote a 1999 Bible study titled *Discovering Your Identity in Christ*. Theology has its fads, and beginning in the 2000s, we see books on identity in Christ from everyone from Campus Crusade for Christ founder Bill Bright (2002) to disgraced Acts 29 pastor Mark Driscoll (2013) to Word of Faith evangelist David E. Longenecker (2012) to Tony Evans (2013) to Bill Hybels (2009) to John MacArthur (2010) to prosperity preacher Creflo Dollar (2010) to Jerry Bridges (2012). For the most part, these authors were not developing the concept of identity in Christ to erase other aspects of human experience. Their intent was to free Christians from the performance treadmill of legalism.

Goodness knows I have preached a ton of sermons about our identity in Christ. But identity in Christ can be a rather vague concept. Often we use it to lessen or negate the importance of other things. "I dropped the ball at work today." "Don't worry, your identity is in Christ." "My girlfriend dumped me." "Just remember, your identity is in Christ."

What does it mean? And why do we press it into action so often to negate powerful experiences?

I prefer the older biblical concepts like being justified before God, being forgiven and clothed in Christ's righteousness, being adopted as children of our heavenly Father, being mystically united to Christ our brother, bearing the seal of the Holy Spirit, being an heir, being part of Christ's body, the church. These truths all have teeth. These all shape me powerfully.

However well-intentioned the attempt to put losses in context, the negative use of the language of identity in Christ ends up minimizing the calling of God on our lives. I am an image bearer of God. I am united to Jesus Christ in saving union by his grace. I am unmarried. I am a pastor. I have no physical children. I have had many spiritual children. I am an American. I am a Washingtonian by birth and a Saint Louisan by adoption. I am a doctor of philosophy in historical theology. I am a diabetic. God has called me to steward my sexual orientation in obedience to him. All of these are who I am. We speak as if God's only calling on my life is to have my identity in Christ. All of life is a calling from God and becomes a part of our story, part of who we are, part of our (lowercase) identity as human beings called by God.[16]

But too often, well-meaning believers are unfamiliar with the nuance of these discussions about primary and secondary identity, phenomenological gayness, and the risk of erasing someone's story by weaponizing their identity in Christ. Too often, well-intentioned Christian siblings default to the paradigm they heard for four decades, without realizing it, in stories, sermons, and testimonies. They default to policing the ex-gay script.

eighteen

Ending (Unintentional) Emotional Abuse

Descriptive language has been wielded. It shouldn't be. It was intended as a resource. . . . It was never my intention that it be weaponized.

—Mark Yarhouse

"You shouldn't identify with your sin." "Your identity is in Christ." "You may start out there, but God won't leave you there." "You're minimizing the power of the gospel to change you." "You can't be gay and be a Christian." We hear these statements constantly from our spiritual siblings who are oblivious to the emotional wounds they inflict.

Here let's translate. "Get back in your closet." "Fake it 'til you make it." "The reason you haven't become straight is because you don't try/pray/believe hard enough." "You're unbelieving." "You are not saved."

When a family system is deeply dysfunctional, those within that system unwittingly maintain the dysfunctional status quo in a constant attempt to keep the system in equilibrium. And frequently their well-meaning efforts are experienced as emotional abuse by those whom the family system cannot accept as they are. I speak of course of the spiritual family that is the church.

The church in America maintained an abusive ex-gay status quo for decades. There is no path forward that doesn't name and forsake that pattern of abuse.

Take Brad, for example. He "considered renouncing all change efforts and pursuing a life of devout celibacy," explains researcher Jan Gelech. His efforts at orientation change had been unfruitful, and he was weary. When he expressed this desire, his ministry leaders refused. They "insisted he continue working toward sexual change."[1] Sadly, even though a lot of ex-gay ministries have closed, these kinds of conversations continue to make conservative religious spaces unsafe for a lot of our fellow Christians.

At the heart of the ex-gay movement was the ex-gay script, the testimony of change from gay to not gay. Even after the movement collapsed in abject failure, its history still shapes how we expect people to speak about their sexuality. It's an illusory truth effect.

THE ILLUSORY TRUTH EFFECT

First documented by Hasher, Goldstein, and Toppino in 1977, the illusory truth effect is the scientifically observed tendency to believe things to be true on account of repetition.[2] The illusory truth effect explains why people think that we use only 10 percent of our brain. Or that Native Alaskans have a hundred words for snow. Or that Einstein failed math. Or that you can see the Great Wall of China from space. Or that if you touch a baby bird, its mother will reject it. Or that iron maidens were an actual torture device. Or that Napoleon was short. Or that you can't eat and swim. Or that it takes seven years to digest chewing gum. Or that Benjamin Franklin wanted the turkey to represent America. Or that there were three magi.[3]

None of these "facts" are true. We just believe they are, because we've heard them so frequently. Because repeated statements are easier to process, we perceive them to be more truthful.

Through four decades of the ex-gay power of repetition, Christians have come to believe as truth teachings that were at the core of much ex-gay ministry. Your fellow believers may no longer be questioning whether you can change your sexual orientation. But they may still think you can't say you're gay and be a Christian; you shouldn't think of yourself as homosexual. Ex-gay therapy might be on the outs, but somewhere along the way, the ex-gay script took on a life of its own.

This is not to say that everyone who raises questions about gay identity and terminology is merely parroting what was repeated for several decades. Commentators have raised many thoughtful and often valid concerns about gay identity, about the relative helpfulness or unhelpfulness of various labels. These are often concerns with which I agree in part if not in full. As we've discussed, much depends on what one means by identity.

But most often, the ones policing the ex-gay script are well-intentioned believers who have no idea what it was. They seldom realize they're doing this. To them, there just seems to be a certain way Christians should speak about sexuality—a way that through repetition has come to feel comfortable and therefore right. We hear it. "You shouldn't identify with your sin." "You're minimizing the power of the gospel to change you." By repeating the ex-gay script over and over again for decades—like me in 1997 telling the painter, "I used to be gay"—we have trained Christians in America and much of the world to expect some version of an ex-gay narrative. We expect to hear someone say, "I used to be gay, but I'm not anymore. I might still struggle with temptations on occasion, but Jesus has set me free from homosexuality." That expectation looks to me like the illusory truth effect.

And when believers police it, no matter how sincerely, it is experienced as emotional abuse.

POLICING THE EX-GAY SCRIPT

All of this places extrabiblical expectations on gay people when they follow Jesus. And if they don't live up to those expectations, they may very well find themselves on the wrong end of a well-intentioned terminological enforcement measure.

At one point, the ex-gay script really made sense. In 1976, when ex-gay leaders believed that significant orientation change was to be expected for most people and possible for all, it made sense to signal that hope of change terminologically. But with orientation change now known to be very rare, the logic of the narrative no longer carries.

Renouncing a homosexual self-perception long had been a mainstay of the ex-gay movement and reparative therapy. Gabriel Blanchard writes, "By the mid-2000s, it was increasingly clear that those who had left [the ex-gay movement] ... had recognized that orientation change was not a realistic goal and that attempts to effect it were doing at least as much harm as good." But this led "largely not to a frank admission of failure and apology for hurts caused, but to a quiet decision to redefine what the goal was. Heterosexual attraction, which could not be achieved, was shelved, in favor of heterosexual self-concept, which could."[4] Again the script took on a life of its own.

The development of the language of same-sex attraction as it interacted with the ex-gay script meant that the distinction between being gay and being same-sex attracted had by the late-2000s become unclear. What does it mean to repent of a homosexual self-perception if you're freely admitting that you're exclusively attracted to people of the same sex and likely will be for the rest of your life?

And to complicate matters, the meaning of the term *gay* was shifting. Joseph Nicolosi had been able to speak about the "non-gay homosexual" as someone who experienced attraction to members of the same sex but was not looking for gay sex. The term *gay* to him and many older generations had been tied up in a cultural movement filled with bathhouses and bear bars, and carried with it the assumption of a non-Christian sexual ethic. But to most of those raised in the 1990s and later, the term *gay* was simply the opposite of *straight*. It was a box you would check on a doctor's medical questionnaire.

That shifting meaning for the term *gay* made it all the more difficult to discern any real meaning in the ex-gay narrative beyond semantics. For many, maintaining the ex-gay script meant changing which term you use, and not really much else. This meant that a gay person who repented and followed Jesus and gave up sex and porn and lust and walked with God and called themselves same-sex attracted was a godly Christian.

But a gay person who repented and followed Jesus and gave up sex and porn and lust and walked with God and called themselves gay was probably not walking with God, definitely was immature, and clearly needed pastoral attention.

The competing sexuality labels have become what D. A. Carson has called the "shibboleths of our day."[5]

Molly Worthen has described how later fundamentalists shifted from being apologists to being polemical. "Winning the war against modernism became more important than illuminating orthodoxy."[6] Matthew Lee Anderson notes how conservative evangelical discourse on sexuality has revived this very pattern. Whether on blogs or in books, he explains, "Increasingly, evangelical teachings on marriage and sexuality don't function as a framework meant to shed light on *all* of reality, including that of the people in the pews. Instead, they are a litmus test, and used to smoke out the putative compromisers." He adds, "To borrow a quip from Chesterton, the most important rule of doctrines is that they should be *doctrinal*, rather than effectively social demarcators or shibboleths."[7]

Our evangelical fixation on external identity labels as social demarcators ties in very well with the legalistic history of American fundamentalism. Legalism focuses on externals in order to gain a spiritual growth that is measurable. You know how this goes. Wear dresses, not pants. Drink Sanka, not Budweiser. Go natural, don't wear makeup. Go to G-rated movies, not R-rated movies. Listen to Christian music, not secular music. Play Uno, not poker. Go to a square dance, not a barn dance. Say same-sex attracted, not gay.

What all of these rules have in common is that they are surface changes that are easy to make, allow us to measure our spiritual growth, yet are of no value spiritually. "Such regulations indeed have an appearance of wisdom . . . but they lack any value in restraining sensual indulgence" (Col. 2:23).

Despite the death of the movement that wrote it, the ex-gay script seems to continue as a relic of reparative therapy and the ex-gay movement. I wonder whether it has long since lost its original function. But it keeps popping up.

A FAMILIAR-SOUNDING CATEGORY RESURFACES IN NASHVILLE

In August 2017, the Council on Biblical Manhood and Womanhood (CBMW) hosted a gathering of conservative evangelical leaders at the Opryland resort outside Nashville, Tennessee. Their purpose was to finalize a draft statement on biblical sexuality. Twenty-four thousand signatories eventually added their names to the statement, including many of the most accomplished, most artic- ulate, and most recognized figures in conservative evangelicalism. The intent was to stake out a list of biblical affirmations and denials in a post-Christian culture that was rapidly rewriting what it means to be human.

They wanted to help the church maintain her countercultural witness. Christians had faced strong and rapidly changing headwinds that had radically reordered cultural values surrounding sexuality in general and homosexuality and gender in particular. These changes came with a speed and thoroughness in which our surrounding culture abandoned biblical sexual norms and began celebrating all things queer. On top of this, mainline denominations started ordaining people in active same-sex sexual relationships and performing gay weddings. Many evangelical churches stopped teaching about or providing discipline for sexual sin, whether heterosexual or homosexual. These have been seismic shifts all around us. The increasing visibility of celibate gay Christians also raised questions about the nature of same-sex orientation.

The Nashville Statement sought to provide an anchor to prevent the church from drifting away.

Formed in 1987 to combat the influence of evangelical feminism in the church, CBMW had begun giving more and more attention to issues of sexu- ality as Western culture shifted its views. The degree to which homosexuality and gender had become the battle lines in American culture and increasingly in the church are evident on the ministry's website. A search of sexuality- related terms topped out with 469 combined mentions of *gay, homosexuality,* and *same-sex attraction* and 183 hits for the word *transgender*. This was clearly where they saw the battle lines. *Adultery* was mentioned 62 times, *porn* 86 times, *cohabitation* 12 times, and the word *premarital* 11 times.[8] I have to think that this reflects the fact that Christians were talking primarily about gay and transgender questions.

The first time I read the Nashville Statement, I mostly agreed with it, but I also thought it felt weird. I couldn't figure out what felt off about it. It wasn't trying to be a pastoral statement, so of course it didn't feel pastoral. So that wasn't it. The intent of the statement was to have something—a creed, a statement of belief—that a church could add to their bylaws (1) if they had nothing and needed a place to start with questions of sexuality and gender, and (2) as legal protection in case they ever got sued for refusing to do a wedding or firing an employee for sexual sin. This document wasn't trying to be public theology or to offer an apologetic, so I don't think I was expecting that. Still, something about it was staring me in the face.

Finally, I figured out what it was. In the middle of its brief summary of biblical views on sexuality and gender, the Nashville Statement, in article 7, stated, "We deny that adopting a homosexual . . . self-conception is consistent with God's holy purposes in creation and redemption."[9]

Homosexual self-conception.

Suddenly it stuck out like a sore thumb.

It sounded like Alan Medinger of Exodus speaking of "a change in self-perception in which the individual no longer identifies him or herself as homosexual."[10] It sounded like the Homosexuals Anonymous conviction that we "had accepted a lie about ourselves, an illusion that had trapped us in a false identity. . . . We are part of God's heterosexual creation, and he calls us to rediscover that identity in him."[11]

As an ex-gay, I had spent years telling myself I was a heterosexual, in an attempt to change my orientation. How could I see this as anything but a holdover from the ex-gay movement? "Wow," I thought, "they're still enforcing that?"

THE ILLUSORY TRUTH EFFECT STRIKES AGAIN

Was this repetition of language and categories so central to conversion therapy intentional on their part?

I don't think it was. I haven't heard anyone involved with drafting the Nashville Statement suggest intent. When I have asked them about the connection their language has to reparative therapy and to ex-gay approaches, some have told me they wouldn't have signed it had they thought it was meant to reinforce ex-gay therapeutic approaches. The statement said nothing about reparative therapy or orientation change. Heath Lambert and Denny Burk, the statement's primary authors, had opposed reparative therapy during a debate against Robert Gagnon at a meeting of the Evangelical Theological Society in 2015. The Nashville Statement was clearly not intending to be an endorsement of that.

Rather the authors' intent with article 7 was to locate the origin of homo-erotic desire in the fall and not in God's original design of creation. Their opposition was not to acknowledging same-sex desire but to embracing it.

I doubt many of those drafting and signing the Nashville Statement had any idea what kind of backstory lay behind this idea of renouncing homosexual self-perception, or its prominent role in the church's failed attempt to cure homosexuality.

An early draft of the document had focused instead on gay identity. Had that version moved forward, it might even have been suggestive of Mark Yarhouse's tripartite distinction between attraction, orientation, and identity. Within that framework, such a statement might have simply cautioned against believers making their sexuality their core identity. But in the revising process, there were concerns that identity could mean too many different things. The final draft switched out gay identity for homosexual self-conception, self-concept having previously been used by Alastair Roberts in a discussion of the experience of transgender people.[12]

In making the switch, though, they had perhaps inadvertently swapped out a potentially prescriptive concept of core identity with what on the surface appeared to be a descriptive concept of self-conception. By adding the notion of "adopting" the self-conception, they perhaps hoped to bring back in some of that sense of it being prescriptive and not merely descriptive of personal experience. I could imagine such terminology might even have sounded familiar, given its coming after four decades of ex-gay testimonies and teaching in the conservative evangelical spaces from which many of the various contributors hailed.

Without knowing it, they were demonstrating the degree to which we all have been cut from a conservative evangelical cloth that for four decades was steeped in a vat of ex-gay tea.

While the intent of the document was never to deny the ongoing presence of homoerotic temptations, the statement's Christian detractors can't help but see article 7 in light of four decades of evangelical ministry to sexual minorities in which renouncing a homosexual self-perception was central to changing sexual orientation. If you never were told to stare into a mirror, repeating to yourself over and over, "I am God's heterosexual child," then you may not grasp what some of us hear in article 7.[13] It seems to me that the church's failed attempt to cure homosexuality remains a backdrop for this whole discussion about terminology, self-perception, and sexual identity.

While the Nashville Statement may not have intended to say a person can't (on any level) acknowledge a homosexual orientation, I can say the statement has been used to do just that. I have been denounced publicly for acknowledging my ongoing homosexual orientation. An open letter from a group of church leaders in August 2020 spoke of "what our self-conception should not be. . . . Christians need to be consistent on this point. A believer must not have a self-conception as a homosexual."[14] For these church leaders, article 7 of the Nashville Statement represented a welcome codification and reinforcement of the ex-gay script, one they would use to try to remove noncompliant ministers from ministry.

Again, we cannot overemphasize the relative novelty of renouncing homosexual self-perception. In 1954, C. S. Lewis could write of a "pious male homosexual."[15] In the 1960s, Francis Schaeffer "thought it cruel . . . to believe that a homosexual could change by 'accepting Christ.'"[16] In 1970, you could be "a Christian homosexual" and InterVarsity Press would publish your letters.[17] In 1975, Billy Graham said he supported ordaining homosexuals.[18] By the late 1970s, John Stott was emphasizing that homosexuality was part of the believer's "being, a person's identity . . . and constitution." He added, "We cannot blame people for what they are."[19] That is clearly secondary identity language. In 1978, Richard Lovelace encouraged "professing Christians who are gay to have the courage . . . to avow their orientation openly" and called the church to "nurture nonpracticing gay believers in its membership, and ordain these to positions of leadership for ministry."[20] Schaeffer's denomination in 1980 could speak of Christians affectionately as "our homosexual brothers and sisters."[21]

What if our fallen sexual orientation is still homosexual? Can we not find a way to acknowledge the reality and persistence of sexual orientations that seldom change and are part of our lowercase, secondary identities, while still locating homoerotic temptation as an effect of the fall and manifestation of indwelling sin? I think we can and must.

ENDING THE TERMINOLOGY WARS

Mark Yarhouse of Wheaton and Ed Shaw of Living Out have called for an end to the terminology wars. "Descriptive language has been wielded," Yarhouse noted. "It shouldn't be. It was intended as a resource. . . . It was never my intention that it be weaponized."[22] The caution to build one's core identity on Jesus and not on being gay is wise, but we've got to stop weaponizing people's testimonies and shunning people for making word choices we disagree with.

When we enforce the terminology of the ex-gay script, Christians feel emotionally abused. Erased. Unseen or unaccepted unless they use language that feels more familiar and comfortable to us.

Those of us who are church leaders should be careful not to build a fence around God's law. Within my theological tradition, the authority of church leaders is "only ministerial and declarative."[23] That means we can wash your feet and declare to you what the Bible says and what by good and necessary consequence we can deduce from it. That's an incredibly influential role in a believer's life. Even church discipline is merely declaring that sin is sin. Our authority, however, is not legislative. We don't get to make up new rules. We can help our members think things through biblically, but we don't get to make other people's decisions.

We all face the temptation to put a fence around God's law because we're afraid someone might stray into sin. It's well intended, but when people start feeling controlled, they start feeling abused. Some of my worst pastoral regrets are from early in my ministry when my good intentions left people under my care feeling controlled instead of empowered.

And it's not just a feeling of abuse. Whenever a church exceeds its biblical authority, it abuses its power. There is no way those in our flocks will experience that as anything other than emotional abuse. Love always protects. We do well to guard the Christian's freedom.

Yet there is also caution for those of us on the leading edge of these conversations.

Those of us who fancy ourselves more missionally nuanced and sensitive to our broader culture would be wise to learn the wisdom Saint Paul gives when he speaks about being a Jew to reach Jews and being a Gentile to reach Gentiles. Paul was willing to go back into the language and vocabulary of conservative Judaism in order to reach those who inhabited such a space. His charge cuts both ways.

I remember a long conversation with a prominent evangelical leader who was on a different page from me on this question of terminology and identity. He and I spent the better part of two hours respectfully discussing life and sexuality. What struck me afterward was that every time he spoke, he used the term *gay*, and every time I spoke, I used the phrase *same-sex attracted*. It was the opposite of what anyone would have expected. But it was a picture of what it looks like when it's right. He, the stalwart conservative elder statesman, was bending down into a culture I hope to reach, using the language and terminology used by a lot of the people I serve. Similarly, I was adjusting how I might speak in order to avoid placing any stumbling block to understanding in my conversation with him. He was being a Gentile to reach me. I was being a Jew to reach him. And that's what it takes for the church to have unity amid differing perspectives.

Our terminological choices can't be about applying a proud identity label. It can't be about self-expression. It has to be about communicating honestly in love. So if you're using terminology that you find uncomfortable out of sensitivity to someone else, you might be doing it right, provided it's freely offered in love and not done under compulsion.

But for the non-Christian, there are missiological implications of telling gay people, "You cannot be gay and be a Christian." There is only one way a secular audience will hear such a statement. *Gay* to them means their sexual orientation, not their sexual ethic. When you tell someone they can't be gay and be a Christian, they will hear that as, "The gospel of Jesus Christ does not apply to you, because you are sexually attracted to members of the same sex." In our attempt to reinforce the script of a dead movement, we risk obscuring the gospel to gay people.

Surely, these things must come. But woe to the one through whom they come.

EMOTIONAL ABUSE AND CONTROL

I know a man who, when considering a possible call to ministry, was asked explicit and detailed questions about his sexual sin history in front of a committee of people. This ministry never questioned straight candidates about their sexual history, at least not in front of a roomful of people.

I have known Christian women who are afraid to tell people at church about their sexuality for fear that someone in their church will say it was because they were abused.

I knew a man who was put on trial and barred from the Lord's Supper for masturbating, when the only reason his elders knew about it was because he approached them, asking for help.

Believers who are sexually attracted to members of the same sex have been barred from serving their churches.

A friend of mine and his wife and kids were shunned by all their friends because of his honesty about his sexual orientation. Their lives were devastated.

I remember one young celibate gay man in a Captain America T-shirt who came to a conference at my church. The first night, I found him sitting alone out in the narthex, weeping silently. I sat down next to him. Eventually, through sobs, he explained that it was the first time he had ever felt safe in a church.

Abuse in the church is more than just efforts to police the ex-gay script.

Fear and shame are powerful realities that gay people experience when they step into conservative religious spaces. Emotional abuse is often unintended, and Christians often don't recognize abuse when they see it. And when they do recognize it, they may be tempted to be complicit by their silence.

When we look at the experience of nonstraight people in the church, we see obvious forms of abuse, but there are forms that may seem less obvious to the well-meaning Christian who unknowingly inflicts it. When an acquaintance was asked not to come back to his Presbyterian church in Canada because he'd done decades of reparative therapy and still wasn't straight, that's obvious abuse. I'd like to ask that pastor not to come back for still being attracted to his neighbor's wife.

Let me give you an illustration of emotional abuse by using a struggle with which many people are familiar. Let's talk about the temptation to overeat.

The Bible has more passages about the sin of overeating than about homosexual sin. Being overfed. Gluttony. It's one of the seven deadly sins.

Imagine you've put on a few pounds. Over the next six months (just once each week), I'll post on your Facebook wall a reminder about how sinful overeating is. It's a sin listed in the Bible (Proverbs 23; Proverbs 28; Philippians 3; Titus 1). It's even listed as one of the sins of Sodom in Ezekiel 16.

You sodomite.

I'm serious. God hates overeating.

But I'm not going to post about the *actual* sin of *actually* overeating. I'm going to post about how sinful it is to be *tempted* to overeat. Any internal pull toward something sinful is indwelling sin, we say. Now imagine you feel shame about your temptation to overeat. Some people do. Imagine you were teased as a child—not for overeating but for being tempted to overeat. Imagine you have spent your life trying to no longer feel that pull toward french fries, which everyone seems to think makes you a freak. Let me flood your Facebook wall with repeated posts written by people who have never been tempted by french fries. The posts will explore at what point noticing that french fries look or smell pleasant becomes a gluttonous pull of indwelling sin tempting you not only to desire food God hasn't given you but also to consider acting out on such a sinful longing to overeat. Then let's zero in on the smell of french fries and make sure those tempted by the smell of fries—fries that aren't yours and aren't good for you—feel enough shame about it. We just need to know you're really dealing with your sin and not making a halfway house for iniquity. Then let's talk about how the temptation to overeat is itself a sin, and if you were repenting deeply enough, you'd no longer feel the temptation to desire fries or overeating. Your attractions would change if you were repenting deeply enough. Then let's post testimonies of people who say they no longer are tempted to overeat. They've been delivered. They say they don't even like the smell of fries anymore. And let's use those testimonies as normative to further shame those still tempted to grab seconds.

Then let's bemoan the Slippery Slope™ posed by the presence of these people sinfully oriented to ordering supersized french fries. If we're not vigilant, we may find that *actual* overfed people start making their way into our churches. Sooner or later we'll even have overfed pastors and elders . . . even *openly* overfed pastors.

These are signs of the end times, friends.

Then let's pounce on anyone who admits publicly to being tempted to overeat, posting in blogs and online reports about them. After all, it's a sin to identify with your sin. Once you admit you're tempted to be an overeater, it's a slippery slope toward actual overeating. Then let's have churches pass resolutions about overeaters. Then let's have groups of churches post talks in which "former gluttons" denounce people like you. Then let's threaten to split the church over it and blame the one person who admits they're tempted to overeat but who weighs only 130 pounds because they've never overeaten in their life.

Does this sound like emotional abuse?

I'm asking for a friend.

Let's go back to my Canadian Presbyterian friend. The particular temptation was different in his case, but it was a similar fallen condition—feeling an internal longing for something God doesn't want us to have. We all have our disordered desires.

When we treat the temptation to overeat differently than we treat the sexual attraction to a person of the same sex, it's the ex-gay movement walking dead among us.

Perhaps you might get a sense for how it feels when a gay person is born again and steps into a conservative Christian space of people fixated on his or her sexual orientation. If the topic were overeating—which is far more pervasive in our churches—it might also leave you thinking, "You know, let's just focus on helping each other have healthy eating habits. Maybe our focus on becoming no longer attracted to eating too many fries is the wrong focus. Maybe the focus on what term we use to describe hunger is misplaced. Let's just not supersize the order, and keep not supersizing it over and over again, choosing to trust and obey God moment by moment. Maybe we just need to trust God with our fallen affections." Then, when someone blows it, we love them, remind them of the gospel, and help them back up on their feet.

That is love. Love is the opposite of abuse. Love is a posture.

POSTURE

Christians who are straight can take one of two postures toward their siblings who are not. My friend Misty Irons explained this to me.

You can view us as believers exactly like yourself, just with a sexuality that is disordered differently from your own, such that marriage may be out of reach for many of us. Seeing our loss, you want to grieve with us and move closer to us. You want to support us on our difficult cross-bearing journey.

Alternately, you can view us as people who live in a unique and continual state of disordered sexual desire, flattening us into that. With this posture, the only point of connection you have with us is when you experience guilt and repentance over some heinous sexual sin on your part. You apply that paradigm to our sexual orientation. Your relationship with us therefore revolves around our repenting of sexual sin, which for you is seemingly occasional but for us must be repeated every time we're still sexually attracted to the wrong sex. So you're constantly trying to make sure we're dealing with our sin. Trying to make sure we don't harden our heart against the need to repent. Trying to "help" us all the time. It can lead to a morbid introspection that leaves the non-straight believer feeling only one level up from being the church's pedophile.

Look at Jesus. He identified with sinners and rebuked the pastors who "tie up heavy, cumbersome loads and put them on other people's shoulders, but they themselves are not willing to lift a finger to move them" (Matt. 23:4).

We love to say that Jesus loves people. Jesus loves sinners. Jesus loves little children. Jesus loves you. Jesus loves everybody.

Only gay people hear, "Jesus loves you, *but . . .*"

That has to change.

Fear, distrust, and combativeness never ushered anyone into the kingdom. People don't typically fall in love with Jesus because religious people try to fix them. People don't typically get ignored into eternal life. Not many folks get criticized into new life. The gospel requires us to take those who are at the margins of our spiritual communities and bring them into the center. "The parts that we think are less honorable we treat with special honor" (1 Cor. 12:23).

A path to care requires believers and especially Christian leaders to identify closely with their same-sex-oriented members. To be their friend and advocate. To listen to them. To enter into their world and help carve out a place of spiritual and emotional safety within the church. To develop their gifts and invest in their spiritual growth. No path to care can be formed until the emotional abuse stops. That requires Christians to stand up and defend their siblings from those who would shun them, gossip about them, fail to defend them, or go on criticizing their terminology. Then do it over and over again. The path of care cannot flourish until the emotional abuse comes to an end and those who fostered the abuse humble themselves and learn instead to love.

Let's be honest. Fighting for our nonstraight siblings is often hardest for pastors and others in ministry leadership. Gently rebuking a faithful tither for an unkind gay joke can have consequences. People can get mad and leave. Two of the most common ways church members manipulate their leaders are by withdrawing their presence and withdrawing their financial support. If you are going to foster a safe place for a gay person to follow Jesus, you're going to have to be willing to lose members who insist on continuing in patterns of self-righteousness and emotional abuse.

"There is a level playing field at the foot of the cross," writes Bill Henson of Posture Shift Ministries, Inc., an evangelical organization training churches and Christian leaders in how to reach out to the LGBT community. "In the culture war years, we fell into the false premise of *us versus them*. It was comfortable because it allowed us to cover up the truth. In the last decade, it has become impossible to cover up. The truth is this: we are part of one mass of humanity that falls short of God's glory. The things *they* do—guess what? *We* do those same things. Our focus must be on our own need for repentance."[24]

That means repenting of the self-righteousness that drove so many sermons, books, and blog posts about "the gays" and continues to make too many churches scary places for some of our siblings in Jesus.

For every church member who walks away because you defended your repentant sister or brother who is same-sex oriented, there will be many others who will see their own faith grow as a result. When I started sharing my story publicly, the most noticeable result I saw was straight men taking their own sexual sin more seriously. Some of the nonstraight members of my church are among the most godly men and women I know. They are walking miracles whose very presence reminds us all of the beauty of the gospel. Their faith cost them more than a tithe. They are the man who saw a field and sold everything he had to buy it. They remind us that Jesus is worth it.

We want our church to be a safe place to be a sinner loved by Jesus. That's the bottom line. Because that's the gospel—that Jesus saves sinners. We all bring our various disordered desires to Jesus. The gospel is the same for all of us. You are no exception. And Jesus loves to open the doors of his house to bid the bruised and the broken come and find rest.

I recently stayed at a vacation home with an amazing pool, which is where I spent most of my time with a book. Invariably, as soon as I got comfortable, a bee or wasp would find itself drowning in the pool, struggling and unable to fly. Every time, without thinking, I would get out of the pool, grab the net, and rescue the poor thing. Now, if I'm a totally different species and a sinner at that, and I could get stung, but I still feel compassion for this insect that needs rescue, do we think God is any less compassionate toward his children?

The posture of Jesus is one of embrace. There is no difference, for all have sinned. But he's a friend of sinners. And he loves to throw his arms around the gay kid in youth group and tell him he loves him. He does that through his people, his family, his church.

nineteen

Picking Up the Ball We Dropped Forty Years Ago

Often we are not able to cure, but we are always able to care.
—Henri Nouwen

The church today is facing a profound cultural and generational shift. This is partly because of our own failures over the past four decades—the legacy of a failed attempt to cure homosexuality and of what was perceived (rightly or wrongly) as a decades-long culture war against "the gays." As a result, a driving narrative in Western culture is that anyone who holds to a biblical view of sexuality hates gay people.

As a historical and theological retrospective on the ex-gay movement, my analysis leads me to ask a few questions.

Did we love gay people well?

Did we learn what it was like to be them? Did we learn what it was like to be them . . . with us? Did we even ask them?

Often we treated gay people as cultural enemies. When they came to faith in Jesus, we outsourced them to separate parachurch ministries to fix them. By and large, that part failed abominably. Some Christians got help with sexual addictions. Some found a safe community. A small minority developed healthy marriages and raised families. But others felt increased shame and despair because of the movement. It fostered impossible expectations that set people up to fail. Many abandoned hope and walked away. Those who remained had to hide behind a mask or use euphemisms that suggested their sexual orientation had changed or was changing when it was not.

Is there a better way to bring Jesus' welcome to our siblings who are trying to submit their sexuality to him, our Lord?

In the absence of a cure, what does care look like?

I long have wondered whether Dutch priest and theologian Henri Nouwen might have had his own homosexuality in mind when he wrote of the difference between care and cure. Nouwen had tried psychiatric and religious methods at orientation change, but to no avail. The cures all failed. Nouwen knew he couldn't let himself engage in sexual relationships, out of obedience to God. But his path was filled with loneliness and unfulfilled longings and many tears.

He wrote, "Care is being with, crying out with, suffering with, feeling with. Care is compassion. It is claiming the truth that the other person is my brother or sister, human, vulnerable, like I am. . . .

"Often we are not able to cure," he insisted, "but we are always able to care."[1]

What does care look like for our siblings who aren't straight?

As we sift through the crumbled ruins of the ex-gay movement, I believe there is a path forward. The way forward is to step back into the world of Lewis, Graham, Schaeffer, and Stott, picking up the ball they tossed us that we dropped forty years ago. The question then, as now, was not how to cure gay people. The question was how to care for gay people who want to follow Jesus, who promises us abundant life.

This is so urgent at this cultural moment. The world is watching. Our children and grandchildren are watching. They are already second-guessing their faith because they hear all around them that Christians hate gay people, and they can't point to anyone in their congregation who is gay and who is loved and accepted as such. Maybe they can point to someone who uses the language of same-sex attraction. But even that is rare. Not many feel comfortable being open about such matters at church. It's still not safe.

I am not saying we are at risk of losing Christians who are attracted to members of the same sex.

That's a given.

I am saying we are at risk of losing the next generation.

RENEWED EFFORTS AT CARE

In the 1990s, an online forum called Bridges Across the Divide made the effort to foster respectful dialogue between two very different groups of people. It was here where the categories of "Side A" and "Side B" Christians were coined. Side A (affirming) participants believed that God did not consider the sex or gender of a life partner to be significant to the morality of the relationship. Side B people believed that God intended for sex to be only between a husband and a wife. Both Side A and Side B people rejected as ineffective ex-gay ("Side X") efforts at orientation change.

In 2003, Side A (affirming) Gay Christian Network (GCN) founder Justin Lee invited his Side B (nonaffirming) friend Ron Belgau to join him in writing essays mapping out their case for and against committed gay sexual relationships. Both had honed their skills as part of Bridges. Justin Lee mapped out the affirming Side A case, while Ron Belgau mapped out the Side B position, arguing for the traditional view that homosexual activity is wrong and that those unable to marry a person of the opposite sex are called to celibacy. They termed it the Great Debate.[2] In 2014, Side B participants formed a centralized online community for Side B believers. Independent of GCN, A Side B Community grew and continues to provide online support for Side B Christians.

In 2006, Bill Henson founded Posture Shift and soon began providing an alternative leadership curriculum to an ex-gay approach. Anne Paulk accused the ministry of heresy for abandoning the focus on orientation change. Exodus got Henson knocked off the speaking circuit at several evangelical conferences. Nevertheless, the organization—originally Lead Them Home—trained more than 30,000 church and ministry leaders by the time Exodus closed in 2013. That number doubled in the following four years. Alan Chambers later apologized to Henson for trying to squash the ministry.

In 2010, Wesley Hill published *Washed and Waiting*, chronicling his experience as a Christian and a gay man committed to the biblical sexual ethic but aware that sexual orientation rarely changes. "Washed and waiting. That is my life," he wrote, "my identity as one who is forgiven and spiritually cleansed and my struggle as one who perseveres with a frustrating thorn in the flesh, looking forward to what God has promised to do."[3] The book sold a lot of copies. After researching the stories of hundreds of gay celibate Christians, Mark Yarhouse commented that reading *Washed and Waiting* could have been listed as a standard milestone event in the lives of the believers Yarhouse was studying. Hill's book wrestled with what God requires of believers like us and how the gospel makes that possible. It addressed the deep loneliness and crippling shame we experience, and sought for the first time in decades to cast a positive—and not ex-gay—biblical vision for gay people who follow Jesus.

In 2011, Wesley Hill and Ron Belgau started a private blog that went public the following year under the name Spiritual Friendship. In contrast to the ex-gay movement's focus on transferring sexual temptation from members of the same sex to members of the opposite sex, Spiritual Friendship explored how to foster healthy, committed friendships, including friendships with people of the same sex. Drawing inspiration from twelfth-century monk Aelred of Rievaulx's *De spirituali amicitia* (or *Spiritual Friendship*), contributors helped foster a renewal of interest in celibacy, in Christian friendship, and in the value of the single life. Belgau explained the issues that interested him most. "How can I deepen my relationship with God? How can I live a joyful celibate life? How do I cultivate friendships which honor God and grow in intimacy?"[4] Hill added questions of his own. "Should celibate gay Christians think of friendship as some kind of 'replacement' for marriage? If that's the wrong way to think of it, what should we expect from friendship? What kind of thing is friendship? How does *philia* differ from *eros*? Can friendship be a form of sublimated *eros*?"[5]

Across the pond, church leaders Ed Shaw, Sam Allberry, and Sean Doherty founded Living Out in 2013. All of them were same-sex attracted, and they sought to spread the stories of Christians choosing to live with their sexualities under the lordship of Christ. Living Out continues to train and equip church leaders as well as provide resources for Christians grappling with their sexuality.

In 2017, Preston Sprinkle founded the Center for Faith, Sexuality and Gender to equip Christian leaders to cultivate a more robust biblical sexual ethic and—in their words—"create a safe and compassionate environment for LGBT+ people, their families, and anyone wrestling with their sexuality or gender identity."[6]

Then, five years after the last Exodus International conference had gently pivoted from cure to care, another conference was launched.

The first Revoice conference was held at Memorial Presbyterian Church (PCA) in Saint Louis in July 2018 under the leadership of Nate Collins, whose keynote at the last Exodus conference had followed Alan Chambers' announcement that Exodus was closing. Revoice was a unique experience for me. I'll never forget standing in that gothic sanctuary with 450 Christians just like myself singing Horatio Spafford's "It Is Well with My Soul." Everyone was belting out the lyrics. Many hands were raised. We came to the line "My sin, not in part but the whole, is nailed to the cross, and I bear it no more, praise the Lord, praise the Lord, O my soul." A spontaneous cheer overtook the participants—applause, hallelujahs, and more hands in the air. I was weeping tears of joy. Hundreds of followers of Jesus had brought their shared pain, tears, and suffering to Jesus in that space, and he met with them there.

An army of volunteers from local churches provided lunch, kept bathrooms clean, and gave directions through the labyrinthine corridors of the building. Eve Tushnet, a lesbian Jewish atheist who later fell in love with Jesus—she is also author of *Gay and Catholic: Accepting My Sexuality, Finding Community, Living My Faith*[7]—commented afterward about how struck she was by all these straight Christians showing so much love and service to their nonstraight siblings. She had never before seen that happen.

Upon the collapse of Exodus International in 2013, Mark Yarhouse had speculated in *Christianity Today* about whether there would ever be support for a successor organization focused on discipleship and not orientation change. "Is there room in a diverse and pluralistic culture for a Christian ministry to retain its beliefs and values about sexuality and marriage while moving away from the expectation of change? . . . Is there an audience for that kind of ministry?"[8]

Revoice18 answered that question with a resounding yes. Workshops explored how to address the shame we feel. How to walk along a path of healing from abuse. Celibacy, including the particular challenges women face in celibacy. Should I explore marriage to a person of the opposite sex, and how can that be done in a way that actually works? What does the Bible say about sexuality? How can I set up appropriate boundaries? How can I keep same-sex friendships healthy? How can we reach the secular LGBT community? How can I navigate being (1) gay or same-sex attracted and (2) a Christian and (3) a racial or ethnic minority, when I feel like an outsider on all three counts?

Wesley Hill declared in *First Things*, "It was the first theologically conservative event I've attended in which I felt no shame in owning up to my sexual orientation and no hesitation in declaring my sexual abstinence. At Revoice there was no pressure to obfuscate the probable fixity and exclusivity of my homosexuality through clunky euphemisms. Nor was there any stigma attached to celibacy."[9]

Revoice19 drew a yet larger crowd.

Revoice20, while forced online because of the COVID-19 pandemic, drew two thousand participants from thirty-nine countries.

Yes, there are gay or same-sex-attracted people who want encouragement and support in living out new life in Jesus Christ. My own Revoice18 talk to church and ministry leaders addressed what—alongside loneliness—remains the biggest burden that many nonstraight disciples of Jesus carry.

Shame.

My Revoice20 talks focused on the importance of active involvement in a local church and—once again—how the gospel addresses our shame.

FOSTER A GOSPEL CULTURE
TO COMBAT SHAME

In preparation for a seminar at Revoice20, Bekah Mason asked her gay friends, "What was your experience growing up in a church? What do you wish church leaders had said or done?" One nineteen-year-old answered, "I didn't feel safe being out at church. Only at school." Another respondent said, "I felt like I was one step up from a leper. Someone to be pitied, but not someone you want to sit next to." Another replied, "I wish leaders talked about LGBT people in a positive way." The comments continued. "Does God know about me? Does he love me?" "It was terrifying for me to grow up in a church." "I'm still in the closet because I'm not sure my church is equipped to deal with me." "I knew I could never talk to any church leader or family member." "I wished someone would acknowledge it's real." "I wanted someone to take time to know me as a unique individual and not as a project." "I wanted someone to say God loves me. I wished my pastor had said it." Yet another respondent commented, "I wish they would create an aroma of acceptance before I come out."[10]

Mason explains, "There is a wake of trauma" in every nonstraight believer.

Notice what no one was asking for. No respondent was asking for a different sexual ethic. Rather they were looking for an emotionally safe and supportive environment in which they were told that God sees them and loves them.

How can churches address the pastoral reality of what Alan Downs calls the "velvet rage" of shame and self-loathing?[11] We gay men in particular decorate our lives in a constant attempt to cover our shame. Gay men are at the top of every field in an effort to accomplish enough, climb high enough, or make enough to make ourselves lovable. The shame behind our body issues leaves so many gay men spending too many hours in the gym trying to build a body to make themselves lovable. It leaves us having to have the most amazing condo, the most over-the-top cocktail party, the most youthful appearance, and the most fashionable wardrobe. There's a reason they say a gay man's forty is a straight man's twenty-seven. We're driven by our shame and just want to become lovable. Even when we throw off morality and declare that there's nothing wrong with our sexuality—a secular culture's poor solution to shame—the reality is that the shame is still strongly present. If it were not so powerfully driving us, we wouldn't still be trying to make ourselves lovable.

Many of us once thought that the feeling of shame came from homophobia, but it's deeper than that. In cultures that now celebrate all things queer, the shame is still there. The suicide rate hasn't evened out. Others speculate that the shame flows from the internal sense of being different that many of us experienced since childhood, long before puberty. Perhaps in part. But it's still deeper than that. It's the shame that flows from being damaged by the fall.

Shame is different from guilt. Guilt says I did something bad. Shame says I am a defective person.

Our sexuality is damaged, as is—just as with everyone—the totality of our being. We are bent. Like all humans, we remain a shattered visage. A glorious ruin. We are all so much less than the best of humanity, so much less than what humanity was before the fall. Only after the fall did Adam know he was naked and feel ashamed. We need God to clothe us with his eyes.

At Revoice18, I spoke about making the church a haven for sexual minorities. In that talk, I explained that there is one thing without which no church or ministry can become a haven. If there is one thing that is essential, it is this.

The church must be permeated by a gospel culture.

It's the only thing that can speak to our shame.

Because we don't need to become lovable. We need to be loved. That's so much better than being lovable.

Jesus sees you all the way down and still wants to be in relationship with you. When that captures your heart, it changes you. There is an emotional space that only the gospel creates. The traditionalist voice on sexuality works only within this context of radical grace, within churches and families in which there is that gospel cycle of full disclosure and complete acceptance.

The Difference between Forgiveness and Righteousness

Paul writes, "Accept one another, then, just as Christ accepted you" (Rom. 15:7). In the gospel, I see a God who clothes my shame in the righteousness of his Son so that I might be "found in him, not having a righteousness of my own that comes from the law, but that which is through faith in Christ" (Phil. 3:9). That's a lot better than just forgiveness. Forgiveness alone cannot heal me of the deep well of shame that makes me constantly try to make myself lovable.

Imagine I've defaulted on my mortgage. All my credit cards are maxed out, and I've defaulted on three other loans. I'm in debt up to my eyeballs. I have nothing in my bank account; it's a negative balance. I have no savings, half a dozen checks overdrawn. And then I've got all these fees on top of that. So I walk into Bank of America, and I go up to the teller. The teller points me over to this desk in a cubicle in the corner, and the gentleman says, "Okay, Mr. Johnson ... ahem, Reverend Johnson. I see you've made rather a mess of this. But we're going to forgive you all of these debts and cancel everything out. Don't worry about the loans and fees. We'll zero those out for you and take care of those overdrafts as well."

Now, you're probably thinking that's really good service for Bank of America. Yet as I'm walking out the door of the bank, two things are true about me. First, I am bankrupt. Second, Bank of America doesn't ever want to see my face again.

That's forgiveness. A lot of people like me know we're forgiven, but we're stuck there. We think we're bankrupt and that God doesn't ever want to see our face again.

Righteousness is something altogether different.

Righteousness is when I look up and see the CEO of Bank of America waving her arms and rushing up to me. She's grabbing me and pulling me back inside, saying, "I'm so, so sorry, Dr. Johnson. He's new here and didn't understand. He made a terrible mistake." The CEO ushers me up the elevator to her back-corner office with the windows and the big, plush couch and the sleek walnut desk. She motions me into the chair behind her desk. A lawyer stands to attention with a big stack of papers. The CEO explains, "I'm so sorry, it was all a mistake. We're just going to sign over the bank and all its assets to you now. If you don't mind initialing, we have an artist down in the lobby who is waiting with some oil paints and a canvas so we can capture your framed likeness for the boardroom."

That's righteousness. God has not left us naked. The Bible says he has clothed us in Christ's righteousness.

Forgiveness says, "You can go." Righteousness says, "You can come." Forgiveness speaks to our guilt. But being clothed in the righteousness of Christ speaks to our shame.

A Reformation slogan was *Simul justus et peccator.* Simultaneously big, shameful sinners and righteous in the eyes of our heavenly Father. Again, this means Jesus' resume has been transferred to you. God your Father is looking it over and thinking, "I love how you kept your cool before Pilate. And reattaching that soldier's ear was beautiful. Those temptations you faced with such single-minded devotion really put the devil in his place. You're my child whom I love. With you I am well pleased." There is nothing you can do to embellish that resume.

Only the gospel creates a space in which it's safe to be a damaged sinner loved by Jesus. It's the limitless validation of radical grace that grows in my heart a blood-bought love and loyalty to my Savior. My heavenly Father isn't an angry ogre shaking a stick at me. He's my Dad. He delights over me with song.

I am not lovable. I am loved. That is better than being lovable.

When that gospel captivates a whole church, then no one is judging anybody for what terms they use to describe their sexuality. Nobody is trying to fix people; we can't even fix ourselves. Like the apostle Paul, we all assume we're the biggest sinner in the room. And we find ourselves amazed that we don't notice other believers' faults so much as we notice the goodness of God's grace in them.

When a church is shaped by the gospel, then everyone begins to feel safe. The negativity dissipates. The scrutiny lifts. It's not just a sexuality thing. People struggling with infertility start to feel safe. People who can't pay their bills start to feel safe. People with mental illnesses. People with addictions to drugs, alcohol, or porn. People who don't often feel safe in churches. Obviously, these situations are not all analogous. Infertility is morally neutral in a way that a porn addiction is not. Once the church becomes a safe place to be a sinner loved by Jesus, the shame of any situation—whether morally neutral or not—begins to lift, and we can all stop living undercover.

That then allows us to be known—to have intimacy—and to be loved as we are. A gospel culture allows us to minister the gospel to each other's weaknesses. Love builds up. That's the healing balm of the gospel.

It's not enough to have a gospel-centered pulpit. That's essential but insufficient. It's when the people in the pews are giving grace to one another that the church has a gospel culture. That culture makes the church a safe place to be open about our brokenness.

Martin Luther cried out, "May a merciful God preserve me from a Christian Church in which everyone is 'good.' I want to be in a church of the fainthearted, the failed, the feeble and the ailing . . . who believe in the forgiveness of sins."

That kind of gospel culture opens the door to church as family.

Let Jesus Redefine Family

Alongside shame, the soul-crushing reality of loneliness is the largest challenge faced by many gay people. It's a challenge that often becomes even more troubling after Christian conversion. As a celibate forty-eight-year-old virgin who's never so much as held hands, I know loneliness well. I know what it's like to sit alone at home on Christmas Day because I have no family of my own. Even before the fall, God said it was not good to be alone. Loneliness is brutal.

Loneliness is particularly challenging for single people. Within my orientation, sexual attraction to members of the same sex is only one component. Another very large component is an absence of sexual attraction to members of the opposite sex. For many that is the much more painful reality. Sexual temptation is something we all have to deal with. But a lack of sexual desire for members of the opposite sex is the reality that puts marriage out of reach for so many of us.

You say, "Greg, just because you don't have sexual desire doesn't mean you couldn't marry a woman." True. But I feel toward women as I feel toward a sister or mother (1 Tim. 5:1–2). Would you want to make love to your sister? Or to someone of the same sex? Whether the flaw is in my hardware or my software, I'm not sure. But the flaw has had big repercussions for me. It has meant living permanently uncoupled.

That can occasion a lot of loneliness.

Imagine what it's like for the teenager who realizes she's gay. The thought of being alone for an entire lifetime can be crippling.

Think of the older woman in your church as it dawns slowly on her over the years that she will probably never marry. Think of all the pain, sorrow, and despair that might fill her heart at such a loss. And then take the couple in your church in their midforties who have tried for fifteen years to conceive a child, only to realize that every promise ends in failure and every new hope becomes a dead end. Think of how hard it is for them to watch the baptism of a child or a Christmas program or to pass by the nursery at church. Think of how hard it is for them to come to church on Mother's Day. Think of the heartache they experience when they attempt genuinely to be happy every time another couple announces they're expecting a baby. Enter into the pain of realizing God is denying you something for which your body was made. Now take all of that pain and all of that sorrow, heartache, and loss which is spread out very slowly over decades. Take all of that sorrow and loss—both of that couple with infertility and that older woman in your church who will never marry. Combine all that pain. Then front-load all of it—all at once—onto a sixteen-year-old girl in your youth group.

That is her reality.

Weep with her. Make sure she is not alone in that.

How can you address this beast of loneliness? You have a vital role to play.

It all goes back to something Jesus did that turned the world upside down.

When Jesus' mother, Mary, and his brothers were wanting a word with Jesus, someone reminded Jesus that they—his family—were waiting on him. This was a serious matter. To be family in the ancient world brought all kinds of mutual commitments and obligations. Family included more than just the modern Western nuclear family. Family included aunts and grandmothers and cousins. Jewish society in the first century still had its tribal structure. As a son and a brother—as a family member—Jesus owed it to his family to honor them. Snap to attention, Jesus, your family demands your attention!

And that's when Jesus did something truly radical. Jesus asked the crowd, "Who is my mother, and who are my brothers?" He then pointed to his disciples and said, "Here are my mother and my brothers. For whoever does the will of my Father in heaven is my brother and sister and mother" (Matt. 12:48–50).

Don't miss what Jesus just did. Jesus just redefined family for his followers. The church is family with all its mutual duties and obligations to one another.

In doing so, Jesus bound himself to honor us with the mutual obligation of our older brother. He has obliged himself to be there with and for us because of his duties to us as a family member. But he has also defined the church—not the nuclear family—as the foundational new community for his people. This means we have the obligation to make sure that every believer has a seat at the dinner table. No one eats alone unless they want to. God sets the lonely people in families. Surely, John Stott nailed it on the head when he said, "At the heart of the human condition is a deep and natural hunger for mutual love, a search for identity and a longing for completeness. If gay people cannot find these things in the local 'church family,' we have no business to go on using that expression."[12]

For a church to care for its nonstraight siblings, church has to become family, with all the mutual responsibilities that family entailed in a first-century, clan-based family network. What does it look like for the church to function as the chosen family for gay people who follow Jesus? It means making sure people are known. Making sure someone knows when they're out of town. Someone notices when they don't show up. Someone knows when their plane is landing. Someone knows to check in on their pets. It means they have refrigerator rights in someone's home—they don't have to ask permission to open your refrigerator door.

Church as Worship Service Is Not Enough

It means making sure they have community with a level of depth. Yet it also means making sure they have community with a level of fixity.

And that kind of community is an increasingly daunting challenge in modern Western societies. For most of human history, people have lived in extended families, whether as nomads or in villages. If for any reason a person did not marry, they still had family. They still had aunts and uncles and nephews and cousins and grandmothers and nieces and brothers and sisters. And they all lived very close together. They all saw each other every day. An unmarried person would still be known. An unmarried person would still have a tightly knit live-in community. An unmarried person would still have daily opportunity both to give and to receive love.

We moderns—at least the white ones—have destroyed that by our separation of the nuclear family from the extended family. And we have destroyed it by our geographic transiency. We move around a lot. Add to that the busyness and all the things we do on our phones to kill time. It can leave us isolated.

For married people, you can maintain a level of fixity in your community by keeping the nuclear family together during a move. But for single people, it's more challenging. Finding a church with a gospel culture is enough of a challenge, but we also have to find one in which it's not all twentysomethings who plan to move away in a couple years. Churches have to transition from being worship services with programs to being actual spiritual family. Christians have to start putting down roots again.

You need a church that will support your commitment to follow Jesus with your sexuality. And one that will not try to fix you, which always leads to spiritual abuse. Those two needs will rule out many churches on the left and on the right. What if there is no safe church where you live? Sometimes the best hope is to move to a city where you know believers who share your convictions, and put down roots there. People move for jobs all the time. Spiritual family is a higher priority than a job.

And having spiritual family makes it so much easier for all of us to deal with our sin.

Help with Sexual Addictions

Realize that a believer's biggest struggle may not be with sexual sin, whatever their orientation. As Eve Tushnet has written, our biggest struggle may be with our ability to give and receive love.

Christians who are attracted to members of the same sex wait on average seven years before disclosing that reality to another person.[13] Seven years is a long time for a youth to feel alone with that secret. It's a long time to hide behind a mask. It's a long time to let shame intensify. And it's a long time for loneliness to become overwhelming. Because sex offers the illusion of intimacy, loneliness can be a powerful temptation to sexual sin, whether private fantasies, pornography, or sexual acting out.

As with any other sin, when there is disobedience, our Father welcomes us into his presence to confess our sins. He delights to see our faces bringing all our sin to him. And where there are sexually addictive patterns, our spiritual siblings may need support in addition to a reminder of the gospel. While they may need encouragement at first, men typically do better in a group with other (mostly straight) men. It helps them realize that the struggle for sexual integrity is something we all share. And it may also mean they hear fewer stories that might trigger or tempt them. The same is true of women. There may be a time to segregate people according to sexual orientation, so they can process common challenges and experiences and offer personal support. But the dynamics of sexual sin and sexual addiction don't vary much by sexual orientation. My struggle with sexual sin is no different than my straight brother's. Look the other way, don't take a second look, try not to save an image for later retrieval, have accountability on my internet, meet regularly with other guys. None of this differs on account of my attractions.

Often, accountability can help. I've been off porn for something like fifteen years—I've lost track. But that has been possible only because my internet usage is monitored by a friend and elder in my church who gets my accountability report. We've been meeting together weekly for coffee since 2002 to pray for each other. I am not capable of walking faithfully on my own. I wasn't designed to be able to do that. We all need a band of brothers. Or sisters.

While accountability can help, often the bigger need is at the heart level. I remember one woman who had been hiding her sexuality for decades. She had been kicked out of Bible college when someone found out. And she had developed powerful patterns of sexual sin. Her previous church had done everything possible externally to try to change her. They had set up the accountability. They had installed apps on the phone. They tracked her movements.

Seriously.

They sat her down and talked to her. She had meetings with pastors. They got her into counseling.

And at heart level, her foundational problem was not a lack of personal discipline. That's never the deeper issue. Jesus says it's whether we love him that determines if we will obey his commands (John 14:15). If I'm honest, whenever I sin, it's because at that moment I'm loving something more than Jesus. I'm trusting something more than Jesus. How can we reach a place where we're ready to do the hard work to confront a deeply rooted sin pattern head-on?

I'm pretty sure we've all been there at some point.

It takes a greater love—what nineteenth-century Scottish theologian Thomas Chalmers called the expulsive power of a new affection. Only a greater love can push out lesser loves.

And that's exactly how Jesus says this works. Jesus tells us the way to grow in love for him. He says that those who are forgiven much love much. Those who are forgiven little love little (Luke 7:47–48). The counterintuitive economics of spiritual growth show us that loving God requires a deeper experience of his grace. As we grow in awareness of his deep and passionate commitment to us, that develops in us a loyalty to him and a love for him that makes us willing to offer the sacrifice of obedience. Grace makes us willing to sit down with others and work through our wreckage. It's the grace of God that "teaches us to say

'No' to ungodliness and worldly passions, and to live self-controlled, upright and godly lives in this present age" (Titus 2:12). It's the gospel, in its radical power, that can foster such an expulsive new affection.

So I watched this sister in Christ as she became immersed in a gospel culture. She marinated in the radical gospel of Jesus Christ and the love of God her Father. In Christ's passion for sinners as the only class of people he came to save. In God's self-sacrificial love for messed-up rebels like us. And it took months and months. But I remember one day she was weeping during Communion. And then again the next week. I'd later learn that this was the beginning of a new obedience in her life. She still stumbles and falls from time to time. But she now has a heart that is sensitive to God, and she is doing the hard work of putting to death her sexual immorality (Col. 3:5). The motivation came only after she had been smitten by the love of Jesus.

And for many of us, that means celibacy.

twenty

Celibacy and Hope

Christian hope is not about wishing that all things will get better.... Hope is hope because it knows it has become part of a realm, a kingdom, which endures, where evil is doomed and will be banished.

—David F. Wells

At Advent, we have a different family light the Advent wreath during the worship service each week. And every year, we ask a handful of our celibate members to come forward one of those Sundays to light the candle together. They too are family. We're intentional to include them, not as a concession but because we are honored to serve alongside them.

EMBRACE CELIBACY

In 1 Corinthians 7:38, the apostle Paul discusses marriage and celibacy and concludes, "He who marries the virgin does right, but he who does not marry her does better." The apostle is clearly and unambiguously promoting celibacy.

It's awkward, I know. But he does use the term *better.*

Paul himself was celibate. He explains, "I wish that all of you were as I am. But each of you has your own gift from God; one has this gift, another has that. Now to the unmarried and the widows I say: It is good for them to stay unmarried" (1 Cor. 7:7–8). You may argue that Paul says this only because of a very special crisis the Corinthians are going through, which Paul mentions in verse 26. That's true. But the crisis of which Paul speaks is this present era between Christ's first and second coming. "What I mean, brothers and sisters, is that the time is short. . . . For this world in its present form is passing away" (vv. 29, 31).

Paul didn't make this teaching up.

Jesus had said, "There are those who choose to live like eunuchs for the sake of the kingdom of heaven. The one who can accept this should accept it" (Matt. 19:12). Jesus made clear that celibacy awaits us all. "At the resurrection people will neither marry nor be given in marriage; they will be like the angels in heaven" (Matt. 22:30).

Think of all the celibate saints in the Bible. The prophet Jeremiah never married (Jer. 16:2). Shadrach, Meshach, and Abednego were likely court eunuchs and, if so, never married. The prophetess Anna was briefly married but spent most of her life without a spouse and never remarried (Luke 2:36–38). The sisters Mary and Martha were likely single adults.

If the early church historian Eusebius was right, the first Gentile convert was not Cornelius the Centurion (Acts 10) but the African eunuch (Acts 8). Here was a man who was a sexual minority, dark-skinned and tall, infertile and unable to marry, having no descendants and employed by a woman, the Kushite warrior queen *(kandake)* Amantitere. Because desert eunuchs typically had lost all of their genitalia, this man couldn't have converted to Judaism if he wanted to. There would have been nothing to circumcise. He could not have been more different from the Jewish Christian deacon Philip, who baptized him. Think about that.

What kind of God would take a person who is infertile—a man sexually altered—and turn him into the father of the Gentile church? What kind of a God makes a celibate person the father of all the other Gentiles who followed him into the kingdom? There is nothing God could have done to make a more inclusive declaration that the path to full and equal participation is open to all people, no matter their background or experience or how poorly they might otherwise fit into the church's then-dominant Jewish culture and ethos.

Remember too that the apostle Paul was celibate.

And I hate to name-drop. But so was Jesus.

Throughout history, God has raised up celibate believers to serve him. We see examples like theologian J. Gresham Machen and biblical scholar John Murray, who married only after he was in retirement. In the early church Augustine was celibate, as were Jerome and John Chrysostom. Macrina—older sister of Cappadocian Fathers Gregory of Nyssa and Basil the Great—was celibate and devoted her life to the study of Scripture and theology. Twelfth-century visionary and polymath Hildegard of Bingen was celibate.

Early twentieth-century Presbyterian pastor Clarence McCartney was celibate. So too in Aberdeen was William Still. C. S. Lewis was single for all but four years of his life. Henri Nouwen, who shared only privately about his homosexuality, was celibate and remained faithful to his vows. Our Protestant Pope John Stott was celibate, as is Dick Lucas. So was their mentor Eric Nash. And Stott's historical mentor Charles Simeon. Missionaries Amy Carmichael and Gladys Aylward, and Grace Mullen, for four decades librarian at Westminster Theological Seminary, served Christ in celibacy all their lives.

To live a life permanently uncoupled and without sex is to declare before a stunned and confused world that there are more important things than sex and romance, more important even than having a life partner. Celibacy is so unthinkable in our culture that historical theologian Michael McClymond humorously dubbed celibacy "the last sexual perversion."[1] There is nothing that calls out the idols of Western culture more powerfully than a person who swears off sex and romance because they love Jesus.

One of the challenges gay people face when they become Christians is the sense that celibacy is discussed only when people like them are the topic of conversation. Pieter Valk of EQUIP, a Nashville-based ministry to help churches love sexual minorities, said, "Straight people doing celibacy is the key lever in churches." The same-sex-oriented believer may feel forced into celibacy, while the heterosexual believer never even considers celibacy an option. Youth in our churches aren't being challenged to consider both celibacy and marriage as equal callings from God. "In no way is celibacy being walked out in the church in a way that's beautiful."[2] For the church to embrace celibacy is to embrace it as a positive potential calling that all its single members are encouraged to consider.

While God calls the majority of Christians to live in light of the ethics of the present era through marriage, he calls others of us to live life in light of the ethics of the coming age, when all will be celibate. It's not some mystical call that some will feel. It's a path of life Saint Paul commends to us all, whatever our sexual orientation.

Celibacy can be a daunting road to travel when we all long for companionship. The thought of having that special someone to walk with us through life's journey can leave even the strongest of us feeling wistful. We look ahead and we wonder. Does celibacy mean we walk through life alone?

RETURN TO CHRISTIAN FRIENDSHIP

In 1951, English poet W. H. Auden wrote to his dear friend Elizabeth Mayer, "There are days when the knowledge that there will never be a place which I can call home, that there will never be a person with whom I shall be one flesh, seems more than I can bear." Auden was gay. He had abandoned Christianity as a young man and had gone through several relationships with men, but they never became anything like a marriage, no matter how much he tried. Auden eventually returned to the Anglican Church, but the depth of his loneliness never relaxed. It seemed more than he could bear.

He continued to Mayer, "And if it wasn't for you, and a few—how few—like you, I don't think I could."[3]

From Auden's perspective, that small network of close, long-term, dependable friendships was the only thing making his life livable. Yet those are the kind of relationships that are so rare today. In an essay on spiritual friendship, Deanna Briody comments that, today, "damaging for Christian and non-Christian alike is the hollowing of friendship and its unqualified subordination to sexual love." She explains, "In contemporary consciousness, a friend is comparable to a secondhand couch: comfortable to have around, disposable upon relocation, and incomparable in importance to one's boyfriend, girlfriend, or spouse."[4]

As I have paraphrased many times through the decades, "For this reason a man will leave his friends and cling to a wife, and the two shall become one flesh." Too often bachelor parties are going-away parties, just with more alcohol.

By contrast, you see modeled in the Christian Scriptures deeply committed friendships. Ruth and Naomi. David and Jonathan. Why was John called the apostle Jesus loved, unless Jesus had a closer friendship with John than with the others? One can argue that David and Jonathan's relationship was less about their friendship than about the house of Saul acknowledging the messianic line of David. But that does nothing to diminish their friendship. These men were warriors, but Jonathan felt fond of David. He had taken a great liking to him (1 Sam. 19:1). There was nothing sexual about this. Jonathan stood up for David. He risked his life for David. He got angry for David. He protected David. They showed physical affection for one another.

And as a single adult who lives alone, let me point out how badly we need that. If you have four small children hanging all over you, and you are wishing you could get a moment alone, this will seem strange to you. But as a single person, it is possible to go through a week without having physical contact with another human being.

C. S. Lewis said, "Friendship is the greatest of worldly goods. Certainly to me it is the chief happiness of life."[5]

Let's just say my friends know I hug. One of my love languages is physical touch. I'm still not sure why God thought it cool to pair that one with celibacy. But whate'er my God ordains is right.

Christian friendship is huge.

RESTORE THE BROTHERHOOD

Yet even more foundational is the biblical paradigm of brotherhood. As the adopted family of Jesus, we who are united to him are kin. That means not only family duties and obligations to one another but also family intimacy. Closeness. We need spiritual siblings who are our sisters and brothers not only spiritually but also experientially. A brother is someone who knows what you smell like in the morning. A brother is someone who knows what you eat for breakfast. A brother is someone who knows what you look like at the end of the day. A brother is someone you don't have to get dressed up for. A brother is someone who knows what you're facing with your health. A brother knows your insecurities. A brother can call you on the carpet when you're wrong. A brother will defend you publicly. A brother will let you borrow his car. A brother is someone you can go off and do something adventurous with. A brother will carry you to your grave as you face your final calling in this life.

But you do not look longingly into your brother's eyes, thinking he will make you whole. You don't really want to see your brother naked. You don't marry your brother. He's family.

Brotherhood is a nonexclusive, nonromantic, nonerotic paradigm for committed, lifelong companionship. You can have incredible intimacy with a brother. Yet being a brother is not exclusive; you can have more than one brother. And brotherhood is by definition nonromantic.

The anonymous author of the 1970 book *The Returns of Love* expressed it well. He explained, "All I want is a brotherhood open-hearted enough to encourage one to open up one's own heart within it. . . . A tremendous help is a wide circle of friendships."[6]

Historically, when God has called believers to celibacy, they often have lived in community—the *cenobium* for common, or communal, living. They were called brothers or sisters because their relationship was a committed family relationship, not as husband and wife but as sisters or brothers. In the Eastern churches, there were even brother-making ceremonies *(adelphopoiesis)* as a legal way to recognize the expansion of kinship obligations. A family could adopt another adult into their family. Sometimes these were business transactions, sometimes they were based on shared interests or concerns, and they were not romantic. It was a way of extending mutual family duties and obligations to another believer, effectively bringing him into your family's network of care and support. I'm not advocating we resurrect the *adelphopoiesis* ceremony. I am saying Christians in the past have sought various ways to forge bonds of kinship among siblings in Christ to foster biblical community.

Western culture has devalued our need for brotherhood, placing all our human needs for intimacy and companionship onto the back of a romantic relationship and marriage. This is especially true for men. But it was not always so. In *The Literal Meaning of Genesis*, Augustine contemplated why God had made both men and women and concluded that women were obviously created to make babies. Why was this so obvious to Augustine? Because, he said, men could much more easily enjoy companionship with other men. He deduced, "How much more agreeably could two male friends, rather than a man and woman, enjoy companionship and conversation in a life joined together."[7] Granted, I think an understanding of the Hebrew in Genesis 2 could have helped him out here (see discussion in ch. 14), but it is nevertheless a striking admission. What makes it so striking is that Augustine assumed it as a truism in order to develop his argument. It's like he was saying, "Everybody knows a couple dudes could get along better."

Augustine was not the last Christian to deeply value the companionship of other men. J. Gresham Machen felt much the same. His biographer Ned Stonehouse writes, "The prevailing impression, however, is that his romantic interests were not highly developed, and that for the most part he preferred the company of men and the opportunity of engaging in the various aspects of his life without encumbrances often attendant upon marriage."[8] Machen was celibate, but he was not alone. For most of his ministry he lived on campus, surrounded by his students and other faculty. His *cenobium*.

I prefer the biblical paradigm of brotherhood and sisterhood over the secular paradigm of partnership. Partnership sounds transactional to me, and it's complicated because gay marriage was called partnership before gay marriage was legalized. Some believers have been able to maintain celibate partnerships that are nonromantic and function as committed long-term friendships.

The main reason I have shied away from the paradigm of partnership is simply because I don't trust myself. I don't want to judge anyone else, and I certainly don't want to police semantics. I just know what I might do. My sinful nature is such that I would walk into a room of a thousand people and unconsciously scan for the three individuals who are closest to my preferred face and body type. And then I'd hope a friendship would break out. I just can't trust myself. I'd probably start looking for a "marriage" without the sex. And I don't want that.

I'm safer with brothers. With sisters. With siblings in Jesus.

Brotherhood can be an incredibly powerful long-term bond. I have two Christian brothers who are particularly close to me. The three of us decided that we will never leave Saint Louis without clear direction from God. One day, we will walk each other to our graves. We hang out together. I've hung out with one of them once a week for sixteen years and counting. I know of marriages that haven't had an uninterrupted two-hour conversation about life every week for sixteen years. The three of us vacation together. We watch each other's pets when we're away. We know each other's weaknesses, and we really see God's grace in each other. There's pretty much nothing these guys don't know about me. We're brothers.

I have another Christian brother with whom I've met for coffee weekly for nineteen years. Another brother and sister moved to Saint Louis seventeen years ago to be involved in my life and ministry. I introduced them to each other back in Virginia, and I've been in their home hundreds of times. She was the second person I told about my sexuality, back in college in the early 1990s. I have coffee weekly with yet another friend, except during summer, when we go to the community pool to hang out. I have several other friends whom I have hung out with off and on for more than a decade. I've been in the same church since 1994—I never left.

I'm happy living alone, but I am dependent on my Christian siblings.

Others do better living in community. But the constant succession of roommates gets old for many, and they feel a need for something longer-term. I know of one house of celibate believers where they move in for a year before deciding whether to make a long-term commitment. Egon Middelmann experimented with something not too different in Saint Louis four decades ago. His Bucer House opened in 1982. One gay friend of mine has lived with another family of believers for years. They've effectively brought him into the family as an equal. They each still also have their private space, but they share their lives together as sisters and brothers.

CHASING ROMANCE = DIMINISHING RETURNS

If you let romantic feelings drive a friendship, even if boundaries are drawn and observed, you're unlikely to make it for decades. Especially for men, romantic feelings seldom live more than a couple years. That's why marriages have to be built on a stronger foundation in order for them to survive. If you chase after feelings of romance, you likely will cycle through numerous two-year relationships, each ending with a mini-divorce. That's why a lot of secular gay people have given up on dating. It's the law of diminishing returns.

Relationships can get messy, especially when feelings come on strong.

Henri Nouwen described the anguish he felt when feelings of infatuation and sexual longing got wrapped up in a friendship with a male L'Arche coworker. "This deeply satisfying friendship became the road to my anguish, because I soon discovered that the enormous space that had been opened for me could not be filled by the one who had opened it. I became possessive, needy, and dependent, and when the friendship finally had to be interrupted, I fell apart."[9]

Possessive, needy, and dependent are pretty good indicators that a friendship has become unhealthy.

Nouwen was left sobbing and broken because the friendship could never be what Henri's fallen soul longed for. He stepped away from the friendship. Over time, including six months of intensive counseling for Nouwen, the friendship was recalibrated into something healthy.[10]

Leading Victorian poet Gerard Manley Hopkins was gay—the term at the time was *Christian Uranian* (*Uranian* predating the term *homosexual*). Hopkins knew the misery of falling for a young man. He was absolutely taken by young Digby Mackworth Dolben, also a Christian Uranian. Hopkins frequently confessed to his priest the degree to which thoughts of Digby distracted him and pulled at his heart. Hopkins was committed to being faithful to Christ with his sexuality, which made the turmoil all the more painful. He wrote letters to Digby, but soon his letters went unanswered. When word eventually came back to Hopkins that Digby had drowned, he was devastated.[11]

I find the biblical paradigm of brotherhood much more helpful at the heart level. Having a web of Christian siblings whom you know and by whom you are known, a web of siblings who provide daily opportunity to give and receive love, can enable you to bypass the emotional confusion of looking for that special someone.

Brotherhood is powerful. Every other relationship is temporary. Even marriage lasts only through this life, since "at the resurrection people will neither marry nor be given in marriage" (Matt. 22:30). A relationship between Christian brothers and sisters is a permanent relationship and carries through to the other side. When Jesus spoke of his Father's house (*oikos*) in heaven in John 14, his meaning was not likely limited to a physical structure. Rather he spoke of his Father's household, his Father's heavenly family and their dwelling. In the coming age, we who know Jesus Christ will maintain our kinship bond. God will still be our Father. Spiritual brotherhood is therefore eternal. Death cannot destroy it.

A relationship with siblings may never reach the depth of intimacy that can be attained in a truly healthy marriage. But when David was confronted with the death of Jonathan, he called Jonathan not his friend but something stronger. At that point, he called him his brother. "I grieve for you, Jonathan my brother; you were very dear to me. Your love for me was wonderful, more wonderful than that of women" (2 Sam. 1:26).

SUPPORT MIXED-ORIENTATION MARRIAGES

Plenty of men and women who are sexually attracted to members of the same sex have been able to develop a healthy marriage with a person of the opposite sex. They have gone on to have children and grandchildren and lead a fulfilling life with their spouse. Many Christians will prefer to think of such relationships simply as heterosexual marriages, in that both partners are committed to heterosexual functioning. In the clinical literature, they are classified as mixed-orientation marriages.

Mixed-orientation marriage is probably not something everyone would consider. It brings real challenges on top of the normal challenges of Christian marriage. And people should never enter into marriage in the hope that it will make them straight. It won't.

When is marriage to a person of the opposite sex a possibility? There currently are more people with bisexual orientations than with homosexual orientations, and Christians in the bisexual spectrum have a greater potential to marry, because of their sexual attraction to members of the opposite sex. Similarly, I have known men who, while tempted only by members of the same sex, have developed sexual desire for just one person of the opposite sex—a "one-woman orientation"—whom they are able to marry. A 2002 study found that most of those who entered into a mixed-orientation marriage did so because it "seemed natural" to them and they "wanted children and family life."[12]

But there are strong headwinds working against such marriages. The biggest one involves honesty. Was there full disclosure before the marriage? If not—if a spouse hid his or her sexuality—then only about one in three such marriages will survive the disclosure, according to one study. And of that third, half divorce within three years.[13] That's an 83 percent failure rate. The deception occasions feelings of betrayal and devastation and a lack of trust, which are very hard to overcome. It has brought many tears to all involved, often with wounded children in the wake.

But with full disclosure early in the relationship, mixed-orientation marriage will be an option for some. If both partners love each other, are absolutely honest from the beginning, maintain healthy communication and relational intimacy, and make Christ the center of their relationship, such marriages can be a beautiful display of God's grace.

Since these marriages historically have had a high failure rate, what factors can help build a mixed-orientation marriage that works? Studies of such marriages in which both partners report a high level of satisfaction have certain hallmarks. Both partners have a high commitment to God. They both love their spouses and children. They maintain a high level of trust. And they genuinely desire to remain committed to their partner.[14]

In one study of 267 individuals who were at the time or previously had been in mixed-orientation marriages, about half of participants identified as committed Christians. Participants described companionship and friendship as being among the best aspects of their marriages. Most nonstraight spouses acknowledged their sexual orientation privately to a spouse or friend but kept the matter private. The study found little change in their degree of overall sexual orientation since marriage.

There were challenges as well. Participants listed sex, intimacy, and distrust among the most difficult aspects of their marriages. Infidelity was a challenge too. Of straight spouses, 19.2 percent had had an extramarital affair. Of the nonstraight spouses, 42 percent had been unfaithful, their affair(s) beginning on average 7.43 years into the marriage.[15]

These are pastoral issues that Christian leaders need to be prepared for in coming alongside such families. Furthermore, the straight spouse may often feel lonely. They may feel rejected by their spouse. They may want to feel more desired or more pursued. When things get difficult, either spouse may be tempted to immediately assume it's because of their sexual orientation, even when it's not. The nonstraight spouse may struggle with same-sex fantasies during lovemaking.

And how open should a couple be about their mixed-orientation marriage? Surely, they need to be known in this by a pastor and some close friends, but the two spouses need to agree upon a plan they can both support. I have seen various couples take very different approaches with good results. Ideally, a couple will have friends who also are in mixed-orientation marriages, so they can process the experience with people who know. They also ideally have straight couples as friends, people who can say, "No. That's normal. We all go through that. Let's talk about it."[16]

Both Christian celibacy and marriage to a person of the opposite sex are opportunities to grow in Jesus. Both have their sorrows. But both can be a wellspring of grace and blessing.

REKINDLE CHRISTIAN HOPE

Years ago J. I. Packer preached at my church. I recall eagerly grabbing a bulletin to see what he would be preaching about. I was hoping for something juicy. I looked down at the print, and my heart sank.

He was preaching on hope.

I thought, "Well, that sounds boring."

Obviously, I hadn't yet suffered enough. Within my spirit, the topic of hope has since come alive. So alive, it's where I want to end this chapter.

Often when I have honestly explained how rare sexual orientation change is, straight Christians look at me with a puzzled stare and quietly ask me the same question: "Then where do you find hope?"

The question is sincere, but it says a lot about Christianity in America. It leaves me concerned about where we've been putting our hope.

When you're straight and Christian, if you are particularly blessed, you can spend most of your life eagerly looking forward to the next big thing. When you're young, you look forward to dating. While dating, you look forward to engagement. While engaged, you look forward to marriage. While married, you look forward to building your life together. Getting that first home. Getting pregnant. The baby arriving. Each baby milestone. Rolling. Crawling. Cruising. Walking. First word. First sentence. Then you can look forward to a second child. Then school, summer, school, summer, repeat. Then the graduations. Then marrying them off. Then the grandkids. If you are particularly blessed, you can spend an entire lifetime looking forward to the next life stage.

One of celibacy's challenges is not having that next thing to look forward to in this life. It's a reality that can force us to confront the inner hopelessness of this life in a way that a married person might be too distracted to see. I don't have that next thing. For me, I just am. I'm here. Nothing is really changing about my family life until I die. "The life of mortals is like grass, they flourish like a flower of the field; the wind blows over it and it is gone" (Ps. 103:15–16).

Celibacy can leave us with a lot of time to sit alone with only our thoughts and God, should we be so daring. It can provide a perspective that invites me to contemplate meaning and eternity and what is really true and lasting. It can also be a doorway into a godly hopelessness, because there is no locus of hope in this life. Celibacy has removed all the temporal hopes. No date. No special someone. No engagement or marriage or first child or grandkids. "What is your life? You are a mist that appears for a little while and then vanishes" (James 4:14).

When celibate, you live with the reality that you will have to have a traditional burial someday, because no one will want your ashes on their fireplace mantel.

Who would want their pastor's ashes? It's sick.

You say, "It seems cruel of God to consign someone to such a fate."

It's not cruel of God. He created humanity in true knowledge, righteousness, and holiness and walked with us in the garden. We then betrayed him, declaring our independence. Thus the cosmos was shattered. God had promised our first parents that they would die on the day they ate the fruit of that tree. That's what we all deserved: immediate death. That is holy justice.

The fact that I'm still alive means I have been given a tremendously merciful stay of execution. I am not entitled to an unfallen existence in this life.

And there is a divine mercy even within the pain of this life.

This is why physicians don't treat pain without first looking for its underlying cause. If you go to the doctor complaining of severe pain below your left rib and he puts you on an opiate to take away your pain, he has not done you a favor. Rather he has done something very unkind to you. Because that pain is saying something crucial about your existence. That pain may very well be telling you that you have an early stage of pancreatic cancer. If, instead of dulling the pain, the doctor does the work to identify the cause of the pain and treat the underlying condition, then that's your salvation. God allows us to feel the pain in this life to tell us that there is something fundamentally wrong with human existence, fundamentally wrong with the cosmos itself. Our pain is screaming at us, telling us that the world is not the way it was meant to be. It is fallen. It is in need not of an opiate but of a redeemer who can raise it from death and make it new again. And that is the message of Jesus. He is that redeemer. He is that rescuer.

My fallen sexuality is the thing more than any other that God has used to keep me broken and humble and dependent on him. If that's the price of knowing his love, I wouldn't trade it. Jesus is everything.

I get the joy of knowing Jesus, resting in his care, and living in community with Christian siblings who will remain my family forever.

So I go through life undistracted by that next big thing. And in all this I am tremendously hopeful.

I have had an opportunity to know God and to cultivate a hope that is far more lasting and powerful than anything this life might otherwise have given me. A hope that is real. A hope that cannot be taken even by death.

Celibacy has been a gift that God has used to help me think on his Word and invest his Word in others in this brief moment I occupy before the coming of everlasting joy. Last Father's Day, a friend messaged me: "Happy Father's Day to you, who have been a spiritual father to so many. 'For more are the children of the desolate than of the one who has a husband.'"

It was a touching reminder.

Where does Christian hope come from? Theologian David F. Wells says it well.

Christian hope is not about wishing that all things will get better, that somehow emptiness will go away, meaning will return, and life will be stripped of its uncertainties, its psychological aches and anxieties. Nor does it have anything to do with techniques for improving fallen human life, be they therapeutic or even religious. Hope, instead, has to do, biblically speaking, with the knowledge that "the age to come" is already penetrating "this age," that the sin, death, and meaninglessness of the one is being transformed by the righteousness, life and meaning of the other, that what has emptied out life, what has scarred and blackened it, is being replaced by what is rejuvenating and transforming it. More than that, hope is hope because it knows it has become part of a realm, a kingdom, which endures, where evil is doomed and will be banished.[17]

It's a world of brokenness, betrayal, and sin, but with grace and glory breaking in.

This life is fleeting. We're supposed to be disappointed with it. Even relatively healthy marriages include lots of loneliness, disappointment, and sorrow. There is gospel comfort in this life, and the joy of knowing and being known by God. But Jesus calls us to look beyond our present pain. True Christian hope is that the meaningfulness and goodness and joy of the coming age are already breaking into this age on account of Jesus. And what we can taste now of that meaningfulness and love will become a reality when God wipes every tear from our eyes in the coming age. "There will be no more death or mourning or crying or pain, for the old order of things has passed away" (Rev. 21:4). Jesus says "the renewal of all things" is coming (Matt. 19:28).

And even now, I have Jesus. He is my life's positive vision. He rescued me. He forgave all my sin. He clothed me in his righteousness. He took me on as his little brother. He has given me family among his people, the church. Jesus is everything.

Jesus says, "The kingdom of heaven is like treasure hidden in a field. When a man found it, he hid it again, and then in his joy went and sold all he had and bought that field" (Matt. 13:44).

Jesus is that treasure.

I've been walking with Jesus in celibacy as a Christian adult for more than thirty years. I'm here to say it's worth it.

Jesus is worth it.

And the best is yet to come.

Conclusion

I really wanted the ex-gay movement to succeed. And in some ways it did. Through it, many lives were blessed, many friendships made, many lives transformed—just not in quite the way we had hoped. The church's attempt to cure homosexuality failed.

This failure is an opportunity. We learned that sexual orientation is real. It's not an addiction. And any shifts within it are fairly rare and incremental. We learned that the biblical sexual ethic calls us away from homoeroticism to holiness, but that holiness doesn't mean heterosexuality. We learned that the same-sex-oriented believer's biggest struggle may be not with sexual sin but with a need to give and receive love. We learned that the Lord designed the church to be our family. We learned that God calls many believers, including many straight ones, to celibacy for the kingdom. We learned that when we police people's terminology—*gay, same-sex attracted*, whatever—they experience it as emotional abuse. We learned that we can't fake it 'til we make it. We learned that honesty is not a threat to the gospel. We learned that the longing gay people have to make themselves lovable is truly fulfilled not by becoming lovable but by becoming loved. Loved by God. Loved by his family, the church.

It was a rough forty years, but coming out of the ex-gay movement, I can say we have learned a lot.

This is our opportunity. When a piano has been producing a bad sound, you have it revoiced to change its tone or sound quality. Christians have an incredible opportunity to revoice this conversation on sexuality, to shift it from cure back to care. And then to go and care, smothering our nonstraight siblings with love, support, respect, affection, and family intimacy.

We, as the church, have an opportunity here to win the next generation. The world is convinced that Christians hate gay people. The next generation is already leaving because they look around and don't see any gay people in their church. They've noticed that the only time gay people are mentioned, the tone is negative. They haven't seen the costly obedience of gay people telling them, "Jesus is worth it!" You can change that.

The world is saying Christians hate gay people. Your children and grand-children need to see you prove them wrong.

The path forward is not a new sexual ethic. It is a new love.

Because Jesus loves gay people.

I'm still baffled when Christians find it so hard to say that. It was easier to say in the 1970s, before the ex-gay movement, before the culture wars.

Here we return to the double repentance about which Richard Lovelace wrote in 1978. He longed for the surrounding culture to see "Christians who are gay ... avow their orientation openly" while committing themselves to obey the biblical sexual ethic. He envisioned a commitment of "the church to accept, honor, and nurture nonpracticing gay believers in its membership, and ordain these to positions of leadership for ministry." When that happens, the world will see "a profound witness to the world concerning the power of the Gospel to free the church from homophobia and the homosexual from guilt and bondage."[1]

Only the gospel can create the emotionally safe space for all of us both to be defective and to own our failings without shame. The gospel creates the con-text in which believers of any sexual orientation can find the care they deserve as children adopted by the Father. The gospel also creates the context in which the church can find the grace it will need to face the hundreds of thousands of survivors—survivors of excessive scrutiny and emotional abuse, survivors of reparative therapy, survivors of false hope. Some are still seated in our pews. Others walked away. Others have felt chased away.

The gospel can help us do the work of reconciliation that God is setting before us. Gay people who come to Jesus can repent of sexual sins. Seriously, it's a path of life. I don't want you to miss out.

And we, as the church, can finally turn to gay members and former mem-bers and say we're sorry for the harm done by reparative therapy and the ex-gay movement. We're sorry for fostering false hope. We're sorry for farming out your spiritual care. We're sorry for treating you differently. We're sorry for put-ting politics over people like you. We're sorry for the times we didn't speak up in your defense.

For all involved, the gospel is the way forward.

I hope we are not too proud or too fearful or too self-righteous to begin making this right. What I am asking for is not a change in theology or a change in ethics. To make such changes would be to shipwreck the souls of people who need both truth and love. What I'm asking for is a change in posture.

Jesus said, "By this everyone will know that you are my disciples, if you love one another" (John 13:35).

Jesus will lead us.

With Simon Peter, let us turn together to Jesus and say, "Lord, to whom shall we go? You have the words of eternal life. We have come to believe and to know that you are the Holy One of God" (John 6:68–69).

Notes

Introduction

1. Alan Medinger, "Is Anyone Ever Totally Healed?" Regeneration Ministries, March 1, 2006, *https://www.regenerationministries.org/is-anyone-ever-totally -healed/*.
2. Christy Mallory et al., *Conversion Therapy and LGBT Youth* (Los Angeles: UCLA, 2018).
3. Alan Downs, *The Velvet Rage: Overcoming the Pain of Growing Up Gay in a Straight Man's World*, 2nd ed. (New York: Da Capo, 2012).
4. Parts of this introduction were originally published in *Christianity Today*. Used by permission. Greg Johnson, "I Used to Hide My Shame. Now I Take Shelter under the Gospel: How a Gay Atheist Teenager Discovered Jesus and Stopped Living Undercover," *Christianity Today Online*, May 20, 2019, *www.christianitytoday.com /ct/2019/may-web-only/greg-johnson-hide-shame-shelter-gospel-gay-teenager.html*.

Chapter 1: C. S. Lewis and His Gay Best Friend, Arthur

1. J. I. Packer, "Still Surprised by Lewis: Why This Non-Evangelical Oxford Don Has Become Our Patron Saint," *Christianity Today*, September 7, 1998, 54.
2. Michael Hamilton, "The Dissatisfaction of Francis Schaeffer," *Christianity Today*, March 3, 1997, 22.
3. "Reverend John Stott Dies Aged 90," *BBC News*, July 28, 2011, *www.bbc.com/news /uk-14320915*.
4. C. S. Lewis, *Mere Christianity* (New York: Macmillan, 1952), ix.
5. Alister McGrath, *C. S. Lewis: A Life* (Carol Stream, IL: Tyndale, 2013), 61–62.
6. C. S. Lewis, *Surprised by Joy* (New York: Houghton Mifflin Harcourt, 1956), 97.
7. C. S. Lewis, *They Stand Together: The Letters of C. S. Lewis to Arthur Greeves (1914–1963)*, ed. Walter Hooper (London: Collins, 1979).
8. C. S. Lewis, *The Collected Letters of C. S. Lewis*, vol. 1, ed. Walter Hooper (San Francisco: HarperCollins, 2009), ccliii.
9. McGrath, *C. S. Lewis: A Life*, 72.
10. Ibid., 142.
11. Lewis, *Surprised by Joy*, 104.

12. C. S. Lewis, *The Collected Letters of C. S. Lewis*, vol. 3, ed. Walter Hooper (San Francisco: HarperCollins, 2009), 471. Also quoted in Sheldon Vanauken, *A Severe Mercy* (San Francisco: Harper and Row, 1980), 148.

13. Lewis, *Collected Letters*, vol. 3, 471.

14. C. S. Lewis, *Yours, Jack: Spiritual Direction from C. S. Lewis*, ed. Paul F. Ford (New York: HarperOne, 2008),181.

15. Arthur Greeves abandoned his family's Brethren faith, experimenting with Unitarianism and Bahai before becoming a Quaker.

16. Lewis had had no intention of ever marrying, until his friendship with poet Joy Davidman became threatened by fear of her deportation. A Jewish atheist member of the American Communist Party, Davidman experienced a Christian conversion and became Presbyterian in 1948. Corresponding with and then meeting Lewis, Davidman fell madly in love with him. But these were feelings he did not share. Lewis valued her friendship, her intellect, and her wit, and so he helped support her financially after her move to England. When her visa was not renewed, Lewis married her in a civil ceremony rather than let her be deported. Claiming the marriage was a "pure matter of friendship and expediency," they continued to live apart. Six months later Joy was diagnosed with terminal cancer. It was only then that Lewis realized his feelings for Davidman. Only then did Lewis seek out a church wedding. He was in his late fifties, and the next three years with Joy became among the best of his life.

17. C. S. Lewis, *The Four Loves* (London: Geoffrey Bles, 1960), 75.

18. Lewis, *Collected Letters*, vol. 3, 1154.

19. Lewis, *Mere Christianity*, 101–2.

20. Ibid.

Chapter 2: Evangelicalism before the Ex-Gay Movement

1. Michael Hamilton, "The Dissatisfaction of Francis Schaeffer," *Christianity Today*, March 3, 1997, 22.

2. Ibid.

3. Francis Schaeffer, *The God Who Is There* (Downers Grove, IL: InterVarsity, 1968), 57.

4. Francis A. Schaeffer, *Letters of Francis Schaeffer* (Westchester, IL: Crossway, 1985), 193–95.

5. Ibid. By "natural," Schaeffer does not mean in accordance with God's creational intent or natural law. Rather he speaks of nature in its fallen condition. Schaeffer has in view those who engage in sexual violence while in prison, though heterosexual. He also would be familiar with the English public school tradition of buggering, or pederasty.

6. Schaeffer, *Letters*, 195. This is a phrase characteristic of Schaeffer. See for example, ibid, 157.

7. Ibid., 194.

8. Ibid.

9. Ibid.

10. Ibid.

11. Ibid., 195. Italics original.

12. Ibid.

13. Ibid., 194–95.

14. Ibid.

15. Frank Schaeffer, "Pro-Life—And in Favor of Keeping Abortion Legal," interview by Terry Gross, NPR, December 9, 2008, *www.npr.org/2008/12/09/97998654/pro -life-and-in-favor-of-keeping-abortion-legal.*

16. Frank Schaeffer, *Crazy for God* (New York: Da Capo, 2007), 77.

17. Ibid.

18. Ibid.

19. Francis Schaeffer and Udo Middelmann, *Pollution and the Death of Man* (London: Hodder and Stoughton, 1970). Middelmann authored the concluding chapter.

20. We see in this report all the things we would expect to see from a theologically conservative, confessionally minded Reformed denomination. Many in the RPCES worried about joining the PCA in 1982, because they perceived the PCA to be less theologically conservative, less confessional, and less Reformed. Philosopher and theologian Gordon Clark ultimately refused to transfer his credentials into the PCA.

21. Egon Middelman, et al, "Pastoral Care for the Repentant Homosexual," in Minutes of the 158th General Synod of the Reformed Presbyterian Church, Evangelical Synod, 4 July 1980, 43–50.

22. Overture 11 to the General Assembly of the Presbyterian Church in America, 1977. "In light of its sinfulness, a practicing homosexual continuing in this sin would not be a fit candidate for ordination or membership in the Presbyterian Church in America."

23. The report explains, "Our sensitivity to the holiness of God can easily become a problem to us if it overshadows our relating to one another as sinners saved by grace." The report continues, "It will be important to be aware of the danger of creating an atmosphere in which the individual member finds it more and more difficult to reveal himself."

24. One section of the report was not approved. This section discusses various approaches that Christians might take in response to the secular gay political agenda. One option it presents is for the Christian to focus on evangelism and ignore politics. With this approach, "the Christian should not get involved in this particular political question in order not to prejudice his active personal evangelistic and friendship outreach to the gay community." Christians are called to bring the welcome of Jesus to our gay neighbors, and this model highlights that supreme calling. Another approach points to Jesus' teaching about divorce in Matthew 19 as allowing leeway where civil matters are concerned. Jesus says that not even the Mosaic civil laws in Exodus and Deuteronomy reflect God's perfect moral law. These laws were not the way it was in the beginning. All human law is a concession to the reality of human sin. To soften political laws on homosexuality in the secular sphere, this approach contends, is no different than the Mosaic code

softening laws on divorce on account of the people's hardness of heart. Of those Christians who seek to criminalize homosexual behaviors—another approach—the RPCES study report presses the question of the minority status of nonstraight people. It questions why those arguing for criminalization impose biblical morality on the activity of gay people but do not criminalize more prevalent sins like divorce, child abuse, and spousal abuse. The report continues, "Should political expediency be a major motivating force, then Christians would be open to the charge that they only legally pursue those who are a minority." The final words of the RPCES study report (before the bibliography) discuss option C, which if taken requires the Christian to "be committed to protecting the homosexual from harassment in the area of his political, economic and social life."

25. Lyndon B. Johnson and Billy Graham, recorded phone call, October 20, 1964, Miller Center archive, University of Virginia, citation 5926.

26. Billy Graham, "My Answer: Homosexual Perversion a Sin That's Never Right," *Lakeland Ledger*, November 30, 1973, 5D.

27. UPI, "Billy Graham Backs Ordaining Homosexuals," *Atlanta Journal-Constitution*, July 25, 1975, 21.

28. Rae Ansley, "Graham Statement," letter to the editor, *Atlanta Journal-Constitution*, August 1, 1975, 5. Italics original.

29. Billy Graham, interview by Larry King, *Larry King Live*, CNN, December 22, 1994.

30. In 2014, when Graham was ninety-three years old, ads ran in North Carolina newspapers quoting him asking voters to oppose the state's Amendment 1 on gay marriage. I have no doubt that the ads reflected Graham's values. There was little doubt at the time, though, that the force behind the ads was not Billy Graham but in fact his son Franklin.

31. Hank Arends, "Graham Pushes 9 Aside," *Statesman Journal*, September 22, 1992, 1A.

32. Lisa Daniels, "God's Judgment and Graham's Judgment," *Hampton Roads Daily Press*, October 6, 1993.

33. Manny Fernandez et al., "Ailing Billy Graham Inspires S.F. Crowd: He Welcomes Gays, All Believers," *San Francisco Chronicle*, October 10, 1997.

Chapter 3: John Stott: Architect of the Paradigm of Care

1. Alex Davidson, *The Returns of Love: Letters of a Christian Homosexual* (London: InterVarsity, 1970).

2. Billy Graham, "Heroic Icons: John Stott," *Time*, April 18, 2005, 103.

3. Think J. I. Packer, Alister McGrath, David Wenham, Os Guinness, J. Alec Motyer, Michael Green, Derek Kidner, Leon Morris.

4. John Stott et al., "Attitudes to Homosexual People," *Third Way*, February 1981, 13–14. Participants included a very young Dr. Richard Winter, later head of the counseling program at Covenant Theological Seminary in St. Louis and a close friend of Schaeffer's L'Abri.

5. Ibid., 14.

6. John Stott, *Issues Facing Christians Today* (Basingstoke, UK: Marshalls, 1984). The chapter on homosexuality was also published separately under the title *Same Sex Relationships*.

7. Ibid., 322.

8. Ibid., 301.

9. Ibid.

10. Ibid., 311.

11. Ibid., 302.

12. Note that the 1980 study report of the Reformed Presbyterian Church, Evangelical Synod concludes that believers are responsible not only for our active choices in word, thought, and deed but also for the degree to which our constitution itself fails to measure up to God's ideal. Such theological nuance makes sense within the denomination's radical grace theology, in which—to quote Jonathan Edwards—the believer contributes nothing to his or her salvation except the sin.

13. Stott, *Issues Facing Christians Today*, 303.

14. Ibid., 301.

15. Ibid.

16. Ibid., 315.

17. Ibid., 305.

18. Ibid., 317.

19. John Stott and Al Hsu, "John Stott on Singleness: 'Uncle John' Explains Why He Stayed Single for 90 Years," *Christianity Today Online*, August 17, 2011, *www.christianitytoday.com/ct/2011/augustweb-only/johnstottsingleness.html*.

20. A later edition of Stott's *Issues* continues, "The person who cannot marry and who is living a celibate and chaste life, whatever his or her sexual orientation, is living a life which is pleasing to God."

21. Stott, *Issues Facing Christians Today*, 316–22.

22. A term coined by early twentieth-century sexologist Havelock Ellis.

23. Stott, *Issues Facing Christians Today*, 320.

24. Ibid.

25. Ibid., 319.

26. Ibid., 321.

27. Ibid.

28. Hugh Evans Hopkins, *Charles Simeon of Cambridge* (Eugene, OR: Wipf and Stock, 2012), 12–13.

29. Ibid., 69.

30. From a historical perspective, the modern era's tendency to categorize people by the relative sexual proclivities of one's indwelling sin does seem a little bizarre.

31. Tim Chester, *Stott on the Christian Life: Between Two Worlds* (Wheaton, IL: Crossway, 2020).

32. Marcus Loane, "Reaching Out to Touch the Ends of the Earth for God," in Christopher Wright, ed., *Portraits of a Radical Disciple: Recollections of John Stott's Life and Ministry* (Downers Grove, IL: InterVarsity, 2011), 97–99.

33. Stott and Hsu, "John Stott on Singleness."

34. David W. Bebbington, *Evangelicalism and Fundamentalism in the United Kingdom during the Twentieth Century* (Oxford: Oxford Univ. Press, 2013), 192–93.

35. Andrew Brown and Linda Woodhead, *That Was the Church That Was: How the Church of England Lost the English People* (London: Bloomsbury, 2016).

36. Ian Paul, "Is Church Decline the Fault of Poor Leadership?" *Psephizo*, November 3, 2016, *www.psephizo.com/reviews/is-church-decline-the-fault-of-poor-leadership/*.

37. Brown and Whitehead, *That Was the Church That Was*, 38.

38. Similar speculation has ensued concerning Dietrich Bonhoeffer. Though engaged to be married at the time, Bonhoeffer died a virgin. His correspondence with his best friend and confidant, Eberhard Bethge, shows a deep infatuation with Bethge. A 2014 biography suggested that Bonhoeffer was gay. The conclusion is possible but not necessary. Bethge did feel uncomfortable with the intensity of Bonhoeffer's interest in him, but Bethge did not think the interest was sexual in nature. See Charles Marsh, *Strange Glory: A Life of Dietrich Bonhoeffer* (New York: Knopf, 2014).

39. Stott, *Issues Facing Christians Today*, 317.

40. Davidson, *Returns of Love*, 29.

41. Ibid., 65, 89.

42. Ibid., 22.

43. Ibid., 40. For the record, I might nuance this discussion differently. My goal here is to fairly present Alex Davidson's perspective, not my own.

44. The 1980 report of the Reformed Presbyterian Church, Evangelical Synod offered a somewhat different nuance. That report sees human beings as morally responsible before God not only for their choices but also for the degree to which their constitution fails to measure up to God's ideal.

45. The Westminster divines had distinguished between internal corruption and actual sins centuries earlier.

46. Davidson, *Returns of Love*, 80.

47. Ibid., 49.

48. Ibid., 29–30.

49. Ibid., 22.

50. Ibid., 20–21. Italics original.

51. Ibid., 16. Italics original.

52. Ibid.

53. Ibid., 54.

54. Ibid., 83.

55. Ibid., 90.

56. Ibid., 51. Italics original.

Chapter 4: A Positive Gospel Vision

1. Wesley Hill, "Revoice and a Vocation of Yes," *First Things*, August 7, 2018, *www.firstthings.com/web-exclusives/2018/08/revoice-and-a-vocation-of-yes*. Hill here develops a theme championed by celibate gay Roman Catholic author Eve Tushnet. See Eve Tushnet, *Gay and Catholic: Accepting My Sexuality, Finding Community, Living My Faith* (Notre Dame, IN: Ave Maria, 2014).

2. John Stott, *Same Sex Relationships*, rev. ed. (Epsom, Surrey, UK: Good Book, 2017), 81. Note that the 1984 language has been updated, replacing the word *homosexual* with *gay*, in line with modern usage.

3. Bill Henson, *Posture Shift* (Acton, MA: Posture Shift, 2018), 9.

4. Richard F. Lovelace, *Homosexuality and the Church: Crisis, Conflict, Compassion* (Old Tappan, NJ: Revell, 1978), 125.

Chapter 5: The Birth of a Movement

1. Frank Worthen, "Looking for a Father," Exodus Global Alliance, (n.d.), *www .exodusglobalalliance.org/lookingforafatherp3.php*. There are various accounts of the precise wording and whether the tape was a free loaner tape or an eight-dollar purchase. This could be on account of the wording changing from issue to issue. For a discussion of Worthen's shifting testimony, see Mark D. Jordan, *Recruiting Young Love: How Christians Talk about Homosexuality* (Chicago: Univ. of Chicago Press, 2011), 150–57.

2. John Evans, "The History of Love in Action," *Ex-Gay Watch*, August 5, 2005, *https://exgaywatch.com/2005/08/co-founder-sick/*.

3. Kent Philpott, quoted in Wayne Beesen, *Anything But Straight* (New York: Harrington Park, 2003), 65.

4. Michael Bussee comment, July 18, 2008, in Jeremy Hooper, "Chambers Sheds Light on Those Who've Shed Orientation," *Good as You*, June 22, 2007, *www.good asyou.org/good_as_you/2007/06/chambers-sheds-.html*.

5. Michael Bussee, "Statement of Apology by Former Exodus Leaders," *Beyond Ex-Gay*, June 27, 2007, *https://beyondexgay.com/article/busseeapology.html*.

6. Frank Worthen, quoted in Nate Collins, *All But Invisible* (Grand Rapids, MI: Zondervan, 2017), 273.

7. Tanya Erzen, *Straight to Jesus* (Berkeley, CA: Univ. of California Press, 2006), 5.

8. E. W. Kenyon, *A New Type of Christianity* (Amazon Digital Services, 2010), 18–19.

9. E. W. Kenyon and Don Gossett, *His Word Is Now* (New Kensington, PA: Whitaker House, 2016), 16.

10. See D. R. McConnell, *A Different Gospel* (Peabody, MA: Hendrickson, 1995).

11. Charles Farah, *From the Pinnacle of the Temple* (Plainfield, NJ: Logos, 1979).

12. Harold Lindsell, "Editor's Note," *Christianity Today*, March 4, 1977, 30, 5.

13. Peter T. Chattaway, "Documentary of a Hippie Preacher," *Christianity Today Online*, April 19, 2005, *www.christianitytoday.com/ct/2005/aprilweb-only/david disabatino.html*.

14. Sigmund Freud, *The Psychogenesis of a Case of Homosexuality in a Woman* (1920; London: Hogarth, 1955), 145–72.

15. Irving Bieber et al., *Homosexuality: A Psychoanalytic Study* (New York: Basic, 1962); C. W. Socarides, *The Overt Homosexual* (New York: Grune and Stratton, 1968).

16. "Homosexuals Can Be Cured," *Time*, February 12, 1965, 40–41.

17. Eric Johnson and Stanton Jones offer an enlightening history in "A History of Christians in Psychology," in Eric Johnson and Stanton Jones, eds., *Psychology and Christianity: Four Views* (Downers Grove, IL: InterVarsity, 2000), 11–53.

18. Johnson and Jones, "A History of Christians in Psychology," 36.

19. Clyde Narramore, *The Psychology of Counseling* (Grand Rapids, MI: Zondervan, 1960), 234.

20. Quoted in Harmon Leon, "Gay Conversion Therapy Got Its Start on the Golden Gate Bridge," *Timeline*, February 22, 2017, *https://timeline.com/amp/p/7c6944d6a57c*.

Chapter 6: "From Gay to Straight"

1. Advertisement, *The Living Church*, vol. 174 (May 8, 1977), 3.

2. Ibid.

3. Gary R. Collins, ed., *The Secrets of Our Sexuality* (Waco, TX: Word, 1976).

4. Guy Charles, "Gay Liberation Confronts the Church," *Christianity Today*, September 12, 1975, 14–17.

5. Ronald Lawson, "The Troubled Career of an 'Ex-Gay' Healer: Colin Cook, Seventh-Day Adventists, and the Christian Right" (paper, American Sociological Association, August 27, 1998, updated October 14, 2007, based on interview with "Eddy," 1994–95).

6. Ibid.

7. Wayne Besen, *Anything But Straight* (New York: Harrington Park, 2003), 95.

8. Bruce Buursma, "AIDS May Be Churches' Ministry of the '80s," *Chicago Tribune*, November 16, 1985, *https://www.chicagotribune.com/news/ct-xpm-1985-11-16 -8503190311-story.html*.

9. Christopher Reed, "The Rev. Jerry Falwell: Rabid Evangelical Leader of America's 'Moral Majority,'" *Guardian*, May 17, 2007, *https://www.theguardian.com/media /2007/may/17/broadcasting.guardianobituaries*.

10. John J. Smid, "To the Parents—I'm So Sorry!" *Grace Rivers*, September 20, 2018, *www.gracerivers.com/parents/*.

11. Sy Rogers, in *One Nation Under God*, directed by Teodoro Maniaci and Francine Rzeznik (Hourglass, 1993), film.

12. Interview with Blake Smith, April 20, 2020.

13. CBS Reports, "The Homosexuals," anchored by Mike Wallace, aired March 7, 1967, on CBS.

14. Ibid.

15. "The Homosexual in America," *Time*, January 21, 1966, 40–41.

16. Kent Demaret, "In His Beloved Key West, Tennessee Williams Is Center Stage in a Furor over Gays," *People*, May 7, 1979, 32–35.

17. Ibid.

18. George Weinberg, *Society and the Healthy Homosexual* (New York: St. Martin's Press, 1972).

19. Joseph Bayly, *Out of My Mind: The Best of Joe Bayly*, ed. Timothy Bayly (Grand Rapids, MI: Zondervan, 1993), 154.

20. Andrew Marin, *Us versus Us: The Untold Story of Religion and the LGBT Community* (Colorado Springs: NavPress, 2016), 135.

21. Michael Bussee, "Statement of Apology by Former Exodus Leaders," *Beyond Ex-Gay*, June 27, 2007, *https://beyondexgay.com/article/busseeapology.html*.

22. Quoted in Jan Gelech, *"Such Were Some of You": Crisis and Healing in the Lives of Same-Sex-Attracted Christian Men*, PhD Diss. (University of Saskatchewan, 2015), 133, 135–36.

23. Interview with A. R. D., February 16, 2020.

24. Michael Bussee, quoted in Ray Ruppert, "EXIT: Special Ministry for Gays," *Seattle Times*, December 3, 1977, A8.

25. Interview with Richard Holloman, June 8, 2020.

26. Interview with Roger Jones and Scott Kingry, July 29, 2020.

27. Interview with Jill Rennick, July 28, 2020.

28. Nate Collins, "Developments at Exodus International, Part I—The Apology," *Life in HD*, June 2013, *https://www.hollanddavis.com/developments-at-exodus-international-part-i-the-apology/*.

29. Alan Chambers, letter to Exodus leaders, April 3, 2012.

30. Frank Worthen, quoted in Nate Collins, *All But Invisible* (Grand Rapids, MI: Zondervan, 2017), 273.

Chapter 7: Conversion Therapies

1. Interview with Josh Proctor, October 17, 2020.

2. A. Dodd and E. Nutt, *Plain Reasons for the Growth of Sodomy in England* (London: Royal Exchange, 1728.)

3. Quoted in Ralph Blair, *Etiological and Treatment Literature on Homosexuality*, Otherwise Monograph Series, vol. 5 (New York: National Task Force on Student Personnel Services and Homosexuality, 1972), 1.

4. Robert Rodale, *Prevention*, October 1968, reported in Blair, *Etiological and Treatment Literature*, 1.

5. Charles H. Hughes, "The Gentleman Degenerate: A Homosexualist's Self-Description and Self-Applied Title. Pudic Nerve Section Fails Therapeutically," *Alienist and Neurologist: A Journal of Scientific, Clinical and Forensic Neurology and Psychology, Psychiatry and Neuriatry* 25 (February 1904): 62–70.

6. Thomas Schlich, *The Origins of Organ Transplantation: Surgery and Laboratory Science, 1880–1930* (Rochester, NY: Univ. of Rochester Press, 2010), 112–15.

7. Hans Neumann, *Die Männer mit dem Rosa Winkel* (Hamburg: Merlin-Verlag, 1972).

8. Matthew Caruchet, "When the U.S. Used Lobotomies to Create Gay Auschwitz," *Economic Opportunity Institute*, June 27, 2019; Joseph Friedlander and Ralph Banay, "Psychosis Following Lobotomy in a Case of Sexual Psychopathy: Report of a Case," *Archives of Neurology and Psychiatry* 59, no. 3 (1948): 303–11, 315, 321.

9. Bill Lipsky, "Vacaville, 1956: California's First Gay Rights Protest," *San Francisco Bay Times*, January 11, 2008, *http://sfbaytimes.com/vacaville-1956-californias-first-gay-rights-protest/*. See also Alex Ross, "Love on the March," *New Yorker*, November 4, 2012, *https://newyorker.com/magazine/2012/11/12/love-on-the-march/amp*.

10. John LaStala, "Atascadero: Dachau for Queers?" *Advocate*, April 26, 1972, 11, 13.

11. Lillian Faderman, "LBGTQ in San Diego: A History of Persecution, Battles and Triumphs," *Journal of San Diego History* 65, no. 1 (Spring 2019).

12. Robert Colvile, "The 'Gay Cure' Experiments That Were Written Out of Scientific History," *Mosaic*, July 4, 2016, *https://mosaicscience.com/story/gay-cure-experiments/*.

13. Jamie Scot, "Shock the Gay Away: Secrets of Early Gay Aversion Therapy Revealed," *Huffington Post*, December 6, 2017, *https://m.huffpost.com/us/entry /us_3497435*. See also Joseph R. Cautela, "Covert Sensitization," *Psychological Report* 20, no. 2 (1967): 464–65.

14. William Backus, quoted in Wilmar Thorkelson, "Homosexual Desire Can Be Changed, Counselors Say," *Minneapolis Star*, November 25, 1977, 37.

15. Jeremy Gavins, quoted in Patrick Strudwick, "This Gay Man Was Given Repeated Electric Shocks by British Doctors to Make Him Straight," *BuzzFeed*, September 30, 2017, *www.buzzfeed.com/amphtml/patrickstrudwick/this-gay-man -was-given-repeated-electric-shocks-by-british*.

16. Joseph Nicolosi, quoted in Decca Aitkenhead, "Going Straight," *Guardian*, April 2, 2004, *https://www.theguardian.com/lifeandstyle/2004/apr/03/weekend.deccaaitkenhead*.

17. Joseph Nicolosi, *Reparative Therapy of Male Homosexuality: A New Clinical Approach* (Northvale, NJ: Jason Aronson, 1991), 3. Chapter one is titled "Non-Gay Homosexuals: Who Are They?"

18. Gabriel Arana, "My So-Called Ex-Gay Life," *American Prospect*, April 11, 2012, 54.

19. Janet Chrismar, "Out of Bondage: Helping Homosexuals Who Want to Change," *Christian Headlines*, August 26, 2002, *www.christianheadlines.com/articles/out-of -bondage-helping-homosexuals-who-want-to-change-1163154.html%3famp=1*.

20. Richard Fitzgibbons, "Origin and Healing of Homosexual Attractions and Behaviors," paper presented at the Second Pan American Conference on Family and Education, Toronto, May 1996.

21. Charles Socarides, Benjamin Kaufman, Joseph Nicolosi, Jeffrey Satinover, and Richard Fitzgibbons, "Don't Forsake Homosexuals Who Want Help," *Wall Street Journal*, January 9, 1997, 1.

22. George Rekers, *Growing Up Straight: What Every Family Should Know about Homosexuality* (Chicago: Moody, 1982).

23. Ryan Owens and Melia Patria, "From Gay to Straight? Controversial Retreat Helps Men Deal with 'Unwanted Attraction,'" *ABC News*, October 29, 2010, *https:// abcnews.go.com/Nightline/gay-straight-retreat-helps-men-deal-unwanted-feelings /story?id=12005242*.

24. Erik Eckholm, "'Ex-Gay' Men Fight Back against View That Homosexuality Can't Be Changed," *New York Times*, October 31, 2012, *https://www.nytimes.com /2012/11/01/us/ex-gay-men-fight-view-that-homosexuality-cant-be-changed.html*.

25. Interview with Blake Smith, April 20, 2020.

26. Owens and Patria, "From Gay to Straight?"

27. Jamie Ross, "Attorney Objects to Bizarre Seminar for Guys," *Courthouse News*, September 3, 2010, *https://www.courthousenews.com/attorney-objects-to-bizarre -seminar-for-guys/*.

28. Westminster Shorter Catechism Q.88.

29. Warren Throckmorton, "The Reparative Therapy Makeover Continues: No Naked Therapy?" *Warren Throckmorton.com*, December 6, 2016, *https://www*

.wthrockmorton.com/2012/12/06/the-reparative-therapy-makeover-continues-no
-naked-therapy/.

30. "Frequently Asked Questions," *ManKind Project*, https://mankindproject.org
/frequently-asked-questions/.

31. Barry Yeoman, "Gay No More?" *Psychology Today*, March 1, 1999, 26–29.

Chapter 8: The Ex-Gay Script

1. Leanne Payne, *The Broken Image: Restoring Personal Wholeness through Healing Prayer* (Grand Rapids, MI: Baker, 1995), 9.
2. Leanne Payne, *Healing Homosexuality* (Grand Rapids, MI: Baker, 1996).
3. Scott Bixby, "Meet the Man Who Helped Create the 'Ex-Gay' Movement—And Now Works to Save Its Victims," *Mic*, June 3, 2015, *www.mic.com/articles/120029 /meet-the-man-who-helped-create-the-ex-gay-movement-and-now-works-to-save-its -victims*.
4. Samantha Allen, "Meet the Conversion Therapists Who Turned against Conversion Therapy," *Daily Beast*, March 20, 2019, *www.thedailybeast.com/meet -the-conversion-therapists-who-turned-against-conversion-therapy*.
5. Darlene Bogle, "I Was Delivered from Lesbianism," *Christian Life*, reproduced in digital format in *New Hope in the Lord Ministries* (n.d.), *https://newhopeinthelord .com/lesbianism.php*.
6. Joseph P. Laycock, *Spirit Possession around the World* (Santa Barbara, CA: ABC-CLIO, 2015), 132.
7. John Smid, "Was Love in Action Double Minded?" *GraceRivers*, February 18, 2019, *www.gracerivers.com/double-minded/*.
8. Frank Worthen, quoted in Nate Collins, *All But Invisible* (Grand Rapids, MI: Zondervan, 2017), 273.
9. *Love in Action: The Source Residential Program Application* (Memphis, TN: Love in Action, 2010), 1.
10. Smid, "Was Love in Action Double Minded?"
11. Dana Kennedy, "Group Aims to Help Gays Lead Straight Life," *News Leader*, January 3, 1988, 17.
12. Jim Scott, quoted in Lindsay Melvin, "Beyond Ex-Gay Blogger Leads Parade," *Memphis Commercial Appeal*, June 15, 2008, B6.
13. Tanya Erzen, *Straight to Jesus* (Berkeley, CA: Univ. of California Press, 2006), 5.
14. Interview with Jill Rennick, July 28, 2020.
15. Jim Venice, "I'm a Brand New Man," First Stone Ministries, March 20, 2002, *www .firststone.org/articles/post/im-a-brand-new-man*.
16. Mario Bergner, *Setting Love in Order* (Grand Rapids, MI: Baker, 1995), 77–78, 200–201.
17. Andrew Comiskey, *Pursuing Sexual Wholeness: How Jesus Heals the Homosexual* (Lake Mary, FL: Siloam, 1989), 188. Italics original.
18. Ibid., 178.
19. Jan Gelech, *"Such Were Some of You": Crisis and Healing in the Lives of Same-Sex -Attracted Christian Men*, PhD Diss. (University of Saskatchewan, 2015), 126.

20. Alan Medinger, *Growth into Manhood* (Colorado Springs: Waterbrook, 2000).

21. Sy Rogers, *The Man in the Mirror* (Lindale, TX: Last Days Ministries, 1984).

22. McKrae Game, in "Garrard Conley and McKrae Game Face to Face on Conversion Therapy," interview by Garrard Conley, *Logo TV*, February 20, 2020, *www.logotv .com/video-clips/c8g252/face-to-face-garrard-conley-and-mckrae-game-face-to-face-on -conversion-therapy.*

23. Interview with George Ontko, former director of First Light, April 15, 2020.

24. Christine Bakke, "In Mesh," *Rising Up Whole*, October 1, 2007, *https://rising-up .blogspot.com/2007/10/in-mesh.html?m=1.*

25. James Davis, "Local Groups Help Gays Go 'Straight,'" *South Florida SunSentinel*, July 5, 1986.

26. See Colin Cook, et al., "The Fourteen Steps," *Homosexuals Anonymous* (archived September 12, 2009), *https://web.archive.org/web/20090205095656/http://ha-fs .org/14-steps.htm.*

27. From the Fourteen Steps:

> 5. We came to perceive that we had accepted a lie about ourselves, an illusion that had trapped us in a false identity.
>
> 6. We learned to claim our true reality that as humankind, we are part of God's heterosexual creation and that God calls us to rediscover that identity in Him through Jesus Christ, as our faith perceives Him.
>
> 7. We resolved to entrust our lives to our loving God and to live by faith, praising Him for our new unseen identity, confident that it would become visible to us in God's good time.

28. Home Page, *Homosexuals Anonymous*, *https://homosexuals-anonymous-com.webs .com*. Retrieved February, 2020. The quote has since been removed.

29. Colin Cook, "Homosexual Healing," *Ministry*, September 1981, 4–13.

30. Colin Cook, *Homosexuality: An Open Door?* (Boise, ID: Pacific, 1985).

31. Homosexuals Anonymous, "Statement on Philosophy," archived February 5, 2009, *https://web.archive.org/web/20090205095449/http://ha-fs.org/philosophy.htm.* This version of the statement has recently been shortened. See *https://homosexuals -anonymous-com.webs.com/statement-on-philosophy.*

32. Cook, *Homosexuality*.

33. Homosexuals Anonymous, *www.homosexuals-anonymous.com/faqs.*

34. Cook, "Homosexual Healing," 4–13.

35. Ronald Lawson, "The Troubled Career of an 'Ex-Gay' Healer: Colin Cook, Seventh-day Adventists, and the Christian Right" (paper, American Sociological Association, August 27, 1998, updated October 14, 2007, based on interview with "Eddy," 1994–95).

36. Interview with Jeff Johnson, July 22, 2020.

37. John J., *Lord, Set Me Free: A Workbook on the Fourteen Steps* (Reading, PA: Homosexuals Anonymous Fellowship Services, 1994).

38. Rosa Salter, "At Homosexuals Anonymous, Christian Principles Are Used to Break the 'Addiction' of a Gay Lifestyle," *Morning Call*, September 25, 1986, *https://www .mcall.com/news/mc-xpm-1986-09-25-2532823-story.html.*

39. "Group's Goal Is Decrease in Homosexuality," *Oklahoman*, January 12, 1986, *https://oklahoman.com/article/2134008/groups-goal-is-decrease-in-homosexuality*.

40. Kimberly Durnan, "Homosexuals Anonymous Chapter Founded in Valley," *Valley Morning Star*, April 12, 1995.

41. Rob Hiaasen, "A Question of Conversion. Their Quest Was the Same: To Be Healed of Their Homosexuality; The Results Were Different, but Both Thank God for Who They Are Today," *Baltimore Sun*, November 1, 1998, *https://www .baltimoresun.com/news/bs-xpm-1998-11-01-1998305166-story.html*.

42. "Mill Valley Church Opens Doors to Homosexuals Anonymous," *Marin Independent Journal*, January 22, 2007.

43. Interview with Mike Rosebush, April 4, 2020.

44. While Courage encourages its participants to use the language of same-sex attraction, its 2020 revised handbook states, "No one should be excluded or marginalized from the chapter because of the terms they use to refer to themselves."

45. Tim Stafford, "An Older, Wiser Ex-Gay Movement: The Thirty-Year-Old Ministry Now Offers Realistic Hope for Homosexuals," *Christianity Today*, September 13, 2007, 48.

46. Gelech, *"Such Were Some of You,"* 122.

47. Interview with Roger Jones and Scott Kingry, July 29, 2020.

48. Ibid.

49. We will discuss in a later chapter what the clinical literature terms *mixed-orientation couples*, including some discussion of what factors mark those marriages that are successful.

50. See Erzen, *Straight to Jesus*, ch. 2.

51. Ralph Blair, "Ex-Gay," address to the national convention of the Christian Association for Psychological Studies, held at the Homosexual Community Counseling Center, New York, April 1982.

52. Alan Medinger, "Is Anyone Ever Totally Healed?" Regeneration Ministries, March 1, 2006, *https://www.regenerationministries.org/is-anyone-ever-totally-healed/*.

53. Bogle, "I Was Delivered from Lesbianism."

54. See Cook, *Homosexuality*. Quoted in Ralph Blair, "Review of *Homosexuality: An Open Door?* By Colin Cook," *Evangelicals Concerned Inc.*, March 9, 1986, *https:// ecinc.org/review-spring-1986-vol-11-no-2/*.

55. Joseph Nicolosi, quoted in Decca Aitkenhead, "Going Straight," *Guardian*, April 2, 2004, *https://www.theguardian.com/lifeandstyle/2004/apr/03/weekend.deccaaitkenhead*.

56. Bixby, "Meet the Man Who Helped Create the 'Ex-Gay' Movement."

57. Frank Worthen, "Looking for a Father," *Exodus Global Alliance* (undated testimony), *https://www.exodusglobalalliance.org/lookingforafatherp3.php*.

58. Alex Davidson, *The Returns of Love: Letters of a Christian Homosexual* (London: InterVarsity Press, 1970).

59. UPI, "Billy Graham Backs Ordaining Homosexuals," *Atlanta Journal-Constitution*, July 25, 1975, 21.

60. Richard F. Lovelace, *Homosexuality and the Church: Crisis, Conflict, Compassion* (Old Tappan, NJ: Revell, 1978), 125.

61. C. S. Lewis, *The Collected Letters of C. S. Lewis*, vol. 3, ed. Walter Hooper (San Francisco: HarperCollins, 2009), 471. Also quoted in Sheldon Vanauken, *A Severe Mercy* (San Francisco: Harper and Row, 1980), 148.

62. Francis A. Schaeffer, *Letters of Francis Schaeffer* (Westchester, IL: Crossway, 1985), 193–95.

63. Egon Middelmann et al., "Pastoral Care for the Repentant Homosexual," Reformed Presbyterian Church, Evangelical Synod, 1980.

64. John Stott, *Issues Facing Christians Today* (Basingstoke, UK: Marshall, 1984), 303. The chapters were derived from Stott's 1978 lecture series.

Chapter 9: Fissures from the Beginning

1. Frank Worthen, quoted in Nate Collins, *All But Invisible* (Grand Rapids, MI: Zondervan, 2017), 273.

2. Joel French and Jane French, *Straight Is the Way* (Minneapolis: Bethany Fellowship, 1979).

3. Cited in Blair, "Ex-Gay," address to the national convention of the Christian Association for Psychological Studies, held at the Homosexual Community Counseling Center, New York, April 1982.

4. Jeffrey Satinover, *Homosexuality and the Politics of Truth* (Grand Rapids, MI: Baker, 1996), 49–51.

5. Michael Bussee, "Statement of Apology by Former Exodus Leaders," *Beyond Ex-Gay*, June 27, 2007, *https://beyondexgay.com/article/busseeapology.html*.

6. Tony Campolo, "A Christian Sociologist Looks at Homosexuality," *Wittenburg Door* 39 (November 1977): 16–17.

7. Kenneth Gangel, *The Gospel and the Gay* (Nashville: Nelson, 1978).

8. Robert K. Johnston, "Book Briefs," *Christianity Today*, July 20, 1979, 28–29.

9. Gangel, *Gospel and the Gay*. Ralph Blair quoted this same passage in his early critique of the movement. See Blair, "Ex-Gay."

10. Ibid.

11. Bussee, "Statement of Apology."

12. Jeff Ford, quoted in Ralph Blair, "The Real Changes Taking Place in the Ex-Gay Movement," *Open Hands* 2, no. 2 (Fall 1986).

13. Mark, "Survivor Narrative," *Beyond Ex-Gay*, *https://beyondexgay.com/narratives/mark.html*.

14. Sharon Kuhn, "Hope for Homosexuals," *Worldwide Challenge*, September 1980, 40.

15. Quoted in Randy Frame, "The Homosexual Lifestyle: Is There a Way Out?" *Christianity Today*, August 9, 1985, 34.

16. Tanya Erzen, *Straight to Jesus* (Berkeley, CA: Univ. of California Press, 2006), 34.

17. Greg Reid, quoted in Blair, "Real Changes."

18. Joe Dallas, "Homosexuality and Modern Ministry: Examining Old Approaches and Assessing New Ones—Part One: A History of Missions and Missteps," Christian Research Institute, December 10, 2018, *www.equip.org/article/homosexuality-and-modern-ministry-examining-old-approaches-and-assessing-new-ones-part-one-a-history-of-missions-and-missteps/*.

19. Erzen, *Straight to Jesus*, 35.

20. John Smid, quoted in Wayne Besen, "Former 'Ex-Gay' Activist Admits Gay People Don't Change," *Falls Church News Press*, October 12, 2011.

21. Anthony Venn-Brown, "The Sy Rogers Story (An Anthony Venn-Brown Perspective)," *Ambassadors and Bridge Builders International*, December 1, 2007, *www.abbi.org.au/2007/12/sy-rogers/*.

22. Sy's Posts, *Sy Rogers*, *https://syrogers.com/archives/*.

23. McKrae Game, quoted in Joshua Bote, "Conversion Therapy Organization Founder Comes Out as Gay: 'Please Forgive Me,'" *USA Today*, September 4, 2019, *https://www.usatoday.com/story/news/nation/2019/09/04/mckrae-game-founder -conversion-therapy-group-comes-out-gay/2210789001/*.

24. John Smid, quoted in Sam Ashworth et al., *The Pernicious Myth of Conversion Therapy* (Washington, DC: Mattachine Society of Washington, DC, 2018), 31–32.

25. Stanton Jones and Mark Yarhouse, *Ex-Gays? A Longitudinal Study of Religiously Mediated Change in Sexual Orientation* (Downers Grove, IL: IVP Academic, 2007).

26. Interview with Richard Holloman, June 8, 2020.

27. Interview with Josh Proctor, October 17, 2020.

28. Michael Ybarra, "Going Straight: Christian Groups Press Gay People to Take a Heterosexual Path," *Wall Street Journal*, April 21, 1993, A1.

29. James Peron, *Homosexuality and the Miracle Makers* (Glen Ellyn, IL: privately printed, 1978).

30. Bussee, "Statement of Apology." Italics original.

31. Jeanette Howard, *Dwelling in the Land* (Oxford: Monarch, 2015), 15.

32. Ibid., 19–21.

33. McKrae Game, quoted in Bote, "Conversion Therapy Organization Founder Comes Out."

34. McKrae Game, in "Garrard Conley and McKrae Game Face to Face on Conversion Therapy," interview by Garrard Conley, *Logo TV*, February 20, 2020, *www.logotv .com/video-clips/c8g252/face-to-face-garrard-conley-and-mckrae-game-face-to-face-on -conversion-therapy*.

35. Michael Bussee, quoted in Scott Bixby, "Meet the Man Who Helped Create the 'Ex-Gay' Movement—And Now Works to Save Its Victims," *Mic*, June 3, 2015, *www.mic.com/articles/120029/meet-the-man-who-helped-create-the-ex-gay -movement-and-now-works-to-save-its-victims*.

36. Ibid.

37. Joni Eareckson Tada, *A Place of Healing: Wrestling with the Mysteries of Suffering, Pain, and God's Sovereignty* (Colorado Springs: Cook, 2010), 35.

38. American Psychological Association, *Report of the American Psychological Association Task Force on Appropriate Therapeutic Responses to Sexual Orientation* (2009), 51.

39. Interview with J. J. B., February 13, 2020.

40. Ibid.

Chapter 10: The Movement Matures

1. Interview with Jeff Johnson, July 22, 2020.

2. Ibid.

3. Alan Medinger, "Is Anyone Ever Totally Healed?" Regeneration Ministries, March 1, 2006, *https://www.regenerationministries.org/is-anyone-ever-totally-healed/*.

4. Andrew Comiskey, quoted in Tim Stafford, "An Older, Wiser Ex-Gay Movement: The 30-Year-Old Ministry Now Offers Realistic Hope for Homosexuals," *Christianity Today*, September 13, 2007, 51.

5. Andrew Comiskey, letter to ministry supporters, Desert Stream Ministries, April 2012.

6. Robbi Kenney, untitled article, *Outpost News*, September 1981.

7. Tanya Erzen, *Straight to Jesus* (Berkeley, CA: Univ. of California Press, 2006), 33–34.

8. "Christian Ex-Gay Ministry Hosts Chicago Conference," *Charisma*, July 1999.

9. "Our Position (Same-Sex Counseling)," *Focus on the Family* (2008), *http://www.focusonthefamily.com*. It has since been removed. The content can be found in B. A. Robinson, "Changes in Beliefs about Gays, Lesbians, and Bisexuals (GLB) among Conservative Christians," *Religious Tolerance*, March 21, 2010, *http://www.religioustolerance.org/homevanchg.htm*.

10. American Association of Christian Counselors, AACC Code of Ethics (2014), 15.

11. Sarah Pulliam Bailey, "Gay, Christian and Celibate: The Changing Face of the Homosexuality Debate," *Washington Post*, August 4, 2014, *https://www.washingtonpost.com/national/religion/gay-christian-and-celibate-the-changing-face-of-the-homosexuality-debate/2014/08/04/65a73d6c-1c1a-11e4-9b6c-12e30cbe86a3_story.html*.

12. Richard Fitzgibbons, quoted in Mike Aguilina, "Daring to Speak Its Name," *Our Sunday Visitor*, November 22, 1998, 14–15.

13. See Richard Fitzgibbons, "The Origins and Therapy of Same-Sex Attraction Disorder," in Christopher Wolfe, ed., *Homosexuality and American Public Life* (Dallas: Spence, 1999), 86–97.

14. David Morrison, *Beyond Gay* (Huntington, IN: Our Sunday Visitor, 1999).

15. A 2021 Google *n*-gram search of the phrase "same-sex attraction" showed almost no use of the term in volumes within Google Books before 1981. The phrase got a little use in the 1990s but then spiked in the year 2000, remaining in high use after that time.

16. Erin Eldridge, *Born That Way? A True Story of Overcoming Same-Sex Attraction* (Salt Lake City: Deseret, 1994).

17. Garrick Hyde and Ginger Hyde, *A Place in the Kingdom: Spiritual Insights from Latter-day Saints about Same-Sex Attraction* (Salt Lake City: Century, 1997).

18. Tom Gledhill, *The Message of the Song of Songs* (Downers Grove, IL: InterVarsity, 1994).

19. Joseph Nicolosi, *Reparative Therapy of Male Homosexuality: A New Clinical Approach* (Northvale, NJ: Jason Aronson, 1997).

20. Editorial, "Walking in the Truth: Winning Arguments at Church Conventions Is Not Enough without Compassion for Homosexuals," *Christianity Today*, September 4, 2000, 46. The article uses homosexual as a noun and as an adjective, but for the first time it speaks of a Christian who "struggles with same-sex attraction."

21. Anne Paulk, *Restoring Sexual Identity: Hope for Women Who Struggle with Same-Sex Attraction* (Eugene, OR: Harvest House, 2003).

22. Joe Dallas, *When Homosexuality Hits Home* (Eugene, OR: Harvest House, 2004).

23. Mark Yarhouse, "Same-Sex Attraction, Homosexual Orientation, and Gay Identity: A Three-Tier Distinction for Counseling and Pastoral Care," *Journal of Pastoral Care and Counseling* 59, no. 3 (Fall 2005): 201–11.

24. Interview with Richard Holloman, June 8, 2020.

25. "'Ex-Gay' Label to Be Retired," *Vigilance*, August 18, 2006, *http://vigilance.teachthe facts.org/2006/08/ex-gay-label-to-be-retired.html?m=1*.

26. Stafford, "An Older, Wiser Ex-Gay Movement," 51.

27. Randy Thomas, quoted in Jim Burroway, "Former Exodus Vice President Issues Open Apology to LGBT Community," *Box Turtle Bulletin*, July 23, 2013, *www .boxturtlebulletin.com/2013/07/23/57578*.

28. Alan Chambers, *My Exodus: From Fear to Grace* (Grand Rapids, MI: Zondervan, 2015), 191.

29. Alex Williams, "Gay Teenager Stirs a Storm," *New York Times*, July 17, 2005, Style section, 1.

30. Tom Otteson, quoted in Casey Sanchez, "Memphis Area Love in Action Offers Residential Program to 'Cure' Homosexuality," *Intelligence Report*, January 1, 2003, *https://www.splcenter.org/fighting-hate/intelligence-report/2003/memphis -area-love-action-offers-residential-program-"cure"-homosexuality*.

31. Chambers, *My Exodus*, 191.

32. Sanchez, "Memphis Area Love in Action."

33. Garrard Conley, *Boy Erased: A Memoir of Identity, Faith, and Family* (New York: Riverhead, 2016), 24.

34. Stanton Jones and Mark Yarhouse, *Ex-Gays? A Longitudinal Study of Religiously Mediated Change in Sexual Orientation* (Downers Grove, IL: IVP Academic, 2007).

35. Caitlin Ryan et al., "Parent-Initiated Sexual Orientation Change Efforts with LGBT Adolescents: Implications for Young Adult Mental Health and Adjustment," *Journal of Homosexuality* 67, no. 2 (November 7, 2018): 159–73.

36. The Trevor Project, *National Survey on LGBTQ Youth Mental Health*, 2019, *www .thetrevorproject.org/survey-2019/*.

37. Mark Yarhouse, "What the White House's Opposition to 'Conversion Therapy' Means," *First Things*, April 29, 2015, *https://www.firstthings.com/web-exclusives /2015/04/what-the-white-houses-opposition-to-conversion-therapy-means*.

38. Robert Knight, quoted in Laurie Goodstein, "The Architect of the 'Gay Conversion' Campaign," *New York Times*, August 13, 1998, A10.

39. "First Annual Ex-Gay Lobby Days on Capitol Hill a Success," *Seattle Catholic*, May 16, 2003, *https://seattlecatholic.com/pr_20030516.html*.

40. Randy Thomas, "Former 'Ex-Gay' Lobbyist to 'Marry a Dude': The Randy Thomas Story," *Truth Wins Out*, July 15, 2020, *https://m.youtube.com/watch?v=Hb1IylOTjxU*.

41. Chambers, *My Exodus*, 186.

42. Stafford, "An Older, Wiser Ex-Gay Movement," 49.

43. Chambers, *My Exodus*, 187.

44. Roger Jones, quoted in Eugene Wagner, "'Where Grace Abounds' Latest to Leave Exodus International," *ExGay Watch*, April 25, 2008, *https://exgaywatch.com/2008 /04/where-grace-abounds-latest-to-leave-exodus-international/*.

45. Interview with Roger Jones and Scott Kingry, July 29, 2020.

46. Chambers, *My Exodus*, 187.

47. Ibid.

48. Interview with MNC, July 8, 2020.

49. Chris Norton, "Willow Creek Splits with Exodus International," *Christianity Today Online*, July 21, 2011, *www.christianitytoday.com/news/2011/july/willowcreek exodus.html*.

Chapter 11: Questioning the Paradigm

1. Ronald Lawson, "The Troubled Career of an 'Ex-Gay' Healer: Colin Cook, Seventh-day Adventists, and the Christian Right" (paper, American Sociological Association, August 27, 1998, updated October 14, 2007, based on interview with "Eddy," 1994–95).

2. Virginia Culver, "Sessions with Gays Criticized: Former Minister's Counseling Methods Brought Reprimands," *Denver Post*, October 27, 1995, 1A, 8A–9A.

3. UPI, "Colorado Minister Accused of Phone Sex," *UPI*, October 27, 1995, *https:// www.upi.com/Archives/1995/10/27/Colorado-minister-accused-of-phone-sex/54698 14766400/?spt=su*.

4. Ibid.

5. Lawson, "Troubled Career of an 'Ex-Gay' Healer."

6. By 2007, Cook had set up an online ministry, FaithQuestRadio.com.

7. "Frequently Asked Questions," *Love Won Out*, December 17, 2008, *https://web .archive.org/web/20081217080150/http://www.lovewonout.com/questions/*.

8. John Paulk, *Not Afraid to Change: The Remarkable Story of How One Man Overcame Homosexuality* (Mukilteo, WA: WinePress, 1998).

9. Ibid.

10. John and Anne Paulk, *Love Won Out: How God's Love Helped Two People Leave Homosexuality and Find Each Other* (Carol Stream, IL: Tyndale, 1999).

11. *Newsweek*, August 1998, cover.

12. Timothy Kinkaid, "The Newly Refurbished Michael Johnston," *Ex-Gay Watch*, January 17, 2007, *https://exgaywatch.com/2007/01/the-newly-refur/*.

13. Warren Throckmorton, "Exodus Makes Public Statement Regarding Richard Cohen," *Warren Throckmorton* (March 22, 2007), *https://www.wthrockmorton .com/2007/03/22/exodus-makes-public-statement-regarding-richard-cohen/*.

14. "Ex-Gays Purge Leader," *Between the Lines*, April 12, 2007, *https://pridesource.com /article/24407/*.

15. Randi Kaye and CNN Wire Staff, "Anti-Gay Rights Activist Resigns after Trip with Male Escort," *CNN*, May 14, 2010, *https://www.cnn.com/2010/US/05/12 /anit.gay.activist.resigns/index.html*.

16. Robert Downen, "More Men Accuse Former Texas Judge, Baptist Leader of Sexual Misconduct," *Houston Chronicle*, April 13, 2018, *https://www.houstonchronicle .com/news/houston-texas/houston/article/More-men-accuse-former-Texas-judge -Baptist-12831892.php*; Meagan Flynn, "Houston Man's Lawsuit Alleges Retired Judge Sexually Assaulted Him," *Houston Chronicle*, December 27, 2017, *https://*

www.houstonchronicle.com/news/houston-texas/houston/article/Lawsuit-accuses
-retired-Texas-justice-of-sexual-12458341.php.

17. Christopher White, "Courage Founder Pushed Bishops to Resist Zero Tolerance on Abuse," *Crux*, October 8, 2018. The article can now be accessed here: *http:// www.bishop-accountability.org/news2018/09_10/2018_10_08_Christopher_Crux _Courage_tolerance.htm.*

18. Ibid.

19. Amanda Holpuch, "Man Who Worked as Top 'Conversion Therapist' Comes Out as Gay," *Guardian*, January 25, 2019, *https://www.google.com/amp/s/amp.the guardian.com/world/2019/jan/25/david-matheson-former-gay-conversion-therapy -advocate-comes-out.*

20. Alex Davidson, *The Returns of Love: Letters of a Christian Homosexual* (London: InterVarsity, 1970), 20–21.

21. Warren Throckmorton, "Documentary 'I Do Exist' to Premiere Nationwide October 8–11," *PRWeb*, September 20, 2004, *https://www.prweb.com/releases/2004 /09/prweb159361.htm.*

22. Warren Throckmorton, quoted in Jon Ward, "The Evangelical Professor Who Turned against 'Reparative Therapy' for Gays," *Yahoo News*, December 2, 2017, *www.yahoo.com/amphtml/news/evangelical-professor-turned-reparative-therapy-gays -174326663.html.*

23. Warren Throckmorton, quoted in Matthew Cullinan Hoffman, "Grove City College Psychologist Warren Throckmorton Blasted for Backpedaling on Homosexuality," *Life Site News*, March 22, 2010, *https://www.lifesitenews.com/news /grove-city-college-psychologist-warren-throckmorton-blasted-for-backpedalin.*

24. Warren Throckmorton, "The Reparative Therapy Makeover Continues: No Naked Therapy?" *Warren Throckmorton*, December 6, 2016, *https://www.wthrockmorton .com/2012/12/06/the-reparative-therapy-makeover-continues-no-naked-therapy/.*

25. Mark Yarhouse, interview by Warren Throckmorton, *YouTube*, July 19, 2020, *https://youtu.be/4zWlFflyuIc.*

26. Alan Chambers, quoted in Jonathan Merritt, "The Downfall of the Ex-Gay Movement: What Went Wrong with the Conversion Ministry, According to Alan Chambers," *Atlantic*, October 6, 2015, *https://www.theatlantic.com/politics/archive /2015/10/the-man-who-dismantled-the-ex-gay-ministry/408970/.*

27. Tim Stafford, "An Older, Wiser Ex-Gay Movement: The 30-Year-Old Ministry Now Offers Realistic Hope for Homosexuals," *Christianity Today*, September 13, 2007, 51.

28. *The Montel Williams Show*, "Homosexuality . . . Can It Be Cured?" hosted by Montel Williams, aired March 15, 2007, on CBS.

29. Alan Chambers, quoted in Bobby Ross Jr., "No Straight Shot: More Evangelical Therapists Move from Changing Orientation to Embracing Faith Identity for Gays," *Christianity Today*, September 14, 2009, 10–11.

30. Stephanie Simon, "Approaching Agreement in Debate over Homosexuality," *Los Angeles Times*, June 18, 2007, *https://www.latimes.com/archives/la-xpm-2007 -jun-18-na-exgay18-story.html.*

31. Interview with Jill Rennick, July 28, 2020.

32. Interview with Richard Holloman, June 8, 2020.

33. "Wendy Gritter of Exodus Member Ministry New Direction," *Ex-Gay Watch*, February 25, 2008, *https://exgaywatch.com/2008/02/wendy-gritter-of-exodus -member-ministry-new-direction/*.

34. Interview with Roger Jones and Scott Kingry, July 29, 2020.

35. Interview with Mike Rosebush, April 4, 2020.

36. Tobin Grant, "Exodus from 'Day of Truth,'" *Christianity Today Online*, October 15, 2010, *www.christianitytoday.com/ct/2010/octoberweb-only/51-51.0.html*.

37. David Roberts, "Exodus International Shuts Down 'Day of Truth,'" *Ex-Gay Watch*, October 6, 2010, *https://exgaywatch.com/2010/10/ exodus-international-shuts-down-day-of-truth/*.

38. Alan Chambers, quoted in Grant, "Exodus from 'Day of Truth.'"

Chapter 12: The Death of Cure

1. Jamie Dean, "2011 Daniel of the Year: Alan Chambers: Change We Can Believe In," *WORLD*, December 5, 2011, *https://world.wng.org/2011/12/2011_daniel_of _the_year*.

2. Alan Chambers, *My Exodus: From Fear to Grace* (Grand Rapids, MI: Zondervan, 2015), 195.

3. Ibid.

4. Ibid., 196.

5. Quoted in Patrick Condon, "Christian Group Backs Away from Gay 'Cure,'" *NBC News*, June 27, 2012, *https://www.nbcnews.com/id/wbna47975787*.

6. Mark Yarhouse and Olya Zaporozhets, *Costly Obedience: What We Can Learn from the Celibate Gay Christian Community* (Grand Rapids, MI: Zondervan, 2019), 16.

7. Tim Stafford, "An Older, Wiser Ex-Gay Movement: The Thirty-Year-Old Ministry Now Offers Realistic Hope for Homosexuals," *Christianity Today*, September 13, 2007, 48.

8. Misty Irons, "The Failure of Ex-Gay Ministries," *Commonplace Holiness*, December 2013, *www.craigladams.com/archive/files/misty-irons-where-at-ex-gay-ministries .html*.

9. Jeffrey C. Billman, "Healthier, Happier and Heterosexual," *Orlando Weekly*, July 24, 2003, *https://m.orlandoweekly.com/orlando/ healthier-happier-and-heterosexual/Content?oid=2260595*.

10. Ralph Blair, "'Ex-gay' Leader Frank Worthen and His Wife Anita Led a Workshop on 'Making Your Marriage Work' at This Summer's Exodus 'Ex-Gay' Conference in Virginia," *Evangelicals Concerned Inc.*, Summer 2005, *https://ecinc.org/summer -2005/*.

11. Chambers, *My Exodus*, 144.

12. John J. Smid, "To the Parents—I'm So Sorry!" *Grace Rivers*, September 20, 2018, *www.gracerivers.com/parents/*.

13. John Smid, "Was Love in Action Double Minded?" *GraceRivers*, February 18, 2019, *www.gracerivers.com/double-minded/*.

14. John Paulk, quoted in Sunnivie Brydum, "John Paulk Formally Renounces, Apologizes for Harmful 'Ex-Gay' Movement," *Advocate*, April 24, 2013, *https:// www.advocate.com/politics/religion/2013/04/24/john-paulk-formally-renounces -apologizes-harmful-ex-gay-movement*.

15. Interview with Jill Rennick, July 28, 2020.

16. Debra Bary shares her story at *https://sswh.wordpress.com/*.

17. Jan Gelech, *"Such Were Some of You": Crisis and Healing in the Lives of Same-Sex-Attracted Christian Men, PhD Diss. (University of Saskatchewan, 2015)*, 140, 144.

18. Warren Throckmorton, "The Jones and Yarhouse Study: What Does It Mean?" *Warren Throckmorton* (blog), October 27, 2011, *www.wthrockmorton.com/2011/10 /27/the-jones-and-yarhouse-study-what-does-it-mean/*.

19. Ibid.

20. Robert R. Reilly, *Making Gay Okay: How Rationalizing Homosexual Behavior Is Changing Everything* (San Francisco: Ignatius, 2014).

21. "Study Shows Change Is Possible for Homosexuals," Citizenlink, September 28, 2011, *http://www.citizenlink.com/2011/09/28/study-change-is-possible-for-homo sexuals/*. Citizenlink, formerly Focus on the Family Action, has since been renamed Family Policy Alliance. See discussion on the article in Throckmorton, "The Jones and Yarhouse Study."

22. Throckmorton, "The Jones and Yarhouse Study."

23. Ibid.

24. Will Dahlgreen and Anna-Elizabeth Shakespeare, "One in Two Young People Say They Are Not 100% Heterosexual," YouGov, August 16, 2015, *https://yougov.co .uk/topics/lifestyle/articles-reports/2015/08/16/half-young-not-heterosexual*.

25. Laura Kann et al., "Youth Risk Behavior Surveillance—United States, 2017" (Washington, DC: Centers for Disease, Control and Prevention, 2018), table 4, 125.

26. Lisa Diamond, *Sexual Fluidity: Understanding Women's Love and Desire* (Cambridge, MA: Harvard Univ. Press, 2008).

27. Throckmorton, "The Jones and Yarhouse Study."

28. Christy Mallory et al., *Conversion Therapy and LGBT Youth* (Los Angeles: UCLA, 2018).

29. Frank Worthen, quoted in Nate Collins, *All But Invisible* (Grand Rapids, MI: Zondervan, 2017), 273.

30. Interview with Richard Holloman, June 8, 2020.

31. Frank Worthen, message to Exodus ministry leaders, March 10, 2012.

32. Discussion among Exodus ministry leaders, March 11, 2012.

33. Alan Chambers, letter to ministry leaders, April 3, 2012.

34. Andy Comiskey, "Statement by Andy Comiskey Expressing Concern about Exodus International and Alan Chambers," Desert Stream Ministries, April 2012.

35. Stephen Black, letter to Exodus International, April 20, 2012.

36. Joe Dallas, "Homosexuality and Modern Ministry: Examining Old Approaches and Assessing New Ones—Part One: A History of Missions and Missteps," *Christian Research Institute*, December 10, 2018.

37. *Our America with Lisa Ling,* "Pray the Gay Away?" hosted by Lisa Ling, aired March 8, 2011, on the Oprah Winfrey Network.

38. Jennie Rothenberg Gritz, "Sexual Healing: Evangelicals Update Their Message to Gays," *The Atlantic,* June 20, 2012, https://www.theatlantic.com/national /archive/2012/06/sexual-healing-evangelicals-update-their-message-to-gays/258713/.

39. Clark Whitten, *Pure Grace: The Life Changing Power of Uncontaminated Grace* (Shippensburg, PA: Destiny Image, 2012), 20, 26. Whitten writes, "My new nature is not a sin nature but a sinless nature! I can sin, but I am not a sinner. All of us are either in Adam (with a sin nature) or in Christ (with a sinless nature). There are no other categories! A state of being! Saints or sinners." Ironically, Whitten's construction here is not far from that of modern exgay proponents, with their insistence on identifying only with Christ and not also with your fallen condition. This is far from Martin Luther's *simul justus et peccator*—that the Christian is simultaneously a saint (righteous in Christ) and a sinner.

40. Chambers, *My Exodus,* 197–98.

41. Interview with Nate Collins, May 27, 2020.

42. Was it a conspiracy? Some critics on the change side of the Exodus discussion suspected conspiracy in the actions of Chambers and the board. They watched Chambers and his pastor and Exodus board chair Clark Whitten put control of the ministry squarely in the hands of Chambers. Exodus had started out as a member ministry, with the various affiliates electing the board members. Early in the 2000s, however, there was a push to get outside expertise onto the board. Eventually the board voted for its own members. The Exodus board went through constant reshuffling during the ministry's final years. The board that would ultimately close the ministry was handpicked by Chambers and Whitten. None of the board members from early 2011 remained in 2013. This raises a serious question of Alan's intention. Clark Whitten had been teaching that Christians can engage in unrepentant lifelong homosexual practice without it affecting their assurance of salvation, and by 2013 that was clearly Alan's perspective as well. Exodus vice president Randy Thomas also attended Whitten's church and eventually moved in with a gay partner and became executive director of Thrive LGBT+. By 2010, conservative voices within Exodus had already begun voicing concerns about Alan's intentions. Was it all a conspiracy to turn Exodus into an organization with a very different vision for gay people who come to Jesus? A vision of a salvation in which gay sexual relationships are an option, even if not strictly God's ideal? It's an intriguing possibility. Remember, though, that Alan Chambers was a nineteen-year-old self-loathing Baptist kid with a history of anonymous gay hookups when in 1990 he first showed up at an Exodus meeting. Just eleven years later, Exodus International made Alan their president. Over the next fifteen years, his views clearly changed. That should surprise no one. For those fifteen years, he sat under the preaching of Clark Whitten. He considered Whitten a mentor. Whitten said Chambers was like a son to him. The reality was likely complex.

43. Interview with Richard Holloman, June 8, 2020.

44. Chambers, *My Exodus,* 211.

45. Ibid., 212.
46. Nate Collins, "Developments at Exodus International, Part I—The Apology," *Life in HD*, July 15, 2013, *https://www.hollanddavis.com/developments-at-exodus -international-part-i-the-apology/*.
47. Dorothy and Christopher Greco, "Our Eulogy for Exodus International," *Christianity Today Online*, June 24, 2013, *www.christianitytoday.com/ct/2013/june -web-only/eulogy-for-exodus-international.html*.

Chapter 13: Postmortem

1. John Calvin, *Institutes of the Christian Religion* 3.3.13.
2. Westminster Confession of Faith 6.5.
3. William Beveridge, *Private Thoughts* (London: Taylor, 1720), 52.
4. Samuel Bolton, *The True Bounds of Christian Freedom* (London: Banner of Truth Trust, 1964), 26.
5. Charles Hodge, "Sermon on Romans 7," in Joseph Exell, ed. *Biblical Illustrator*, vol. 5 (Harrington, DE: Delmarva, 2015).
6. John Murray, *Redemption Accomplished and Applied* (Grand Rapids, MI: Eerdmans, 1955), 145.
7. Al Mohler, address given to the Southern Baptist Convention Ethics and Religious Liberty Commission, 2014.
8. R. Albert Mohler Jr., "Sexual Orientation and the Gospel of Jesus Christ," *Albert Mohler* (website), November 13, 2014, *https://albertmohler.com/2014/11/13/sexual -orientation-and-the-gospel-of-jesus-christ*.
9. See Laurie and Matt Krieg, *An Impossible Marriage: What Our Mixed-Orientation Marriage Has Taught Us about Love and the Gospel* (Downers Grove, IL: InterVarsity, 2020).
10. John Piper, "'Let Marriage Be Held in Honor': Thinking Biblically about So-Called Same-Sex Marriage," Gospel Coalition, June 16, 2012, *https://resources.the gospelcoalition.org/library/let-marriage-be-held-in-honor-thinking-biblically-about -so-called-same-sex-marriage*.
11. I heard R. C. Sproul say this decades ago, and it might be a direct quote, but I'm not sure where he said it.
12. Al Mohler, *We Cannot Be Silent* (Nashville: Nelson, 2015), 155.
13. Nate Collins, *All But Invisible* (Grand Rapids, MI: Zondervan, 2017), 221.
14. A. N. Groth and H. J. Birnbaum, "Adult Sexual Orientation and Attraction to Underage Persons," *Archive of Sexual Behavior* 7 (1978): 180.
15. National Research Council, Division of Behavioral and Social Sciences and Education, Commission on Behavioral and Social Sciences and Education, Panel on Research on Child Abuse and Neglect, *Understanding Child Abuse and Neglect* (Washington, DC: National Academies Press, 1993), 143.
16. For a scholarly critique of the Family Research Council's counterargument (by Timothy J. Dailey, titled *Homosexuality and Child Abuse*), see discussion at University of California, Davis, at *https://psychology.ucdavis.edu/rainbow/html /facts_molestation.html*.

17. Mohler, *We Cannot Be Silent*, 157.
18. For an overview of current research as of 2020, see Yan Wang et al., "The Biological Basis of Sexual Orientation: How Hormonal, Genetic, and Environmental Factors Influence to Whom We Are Sexually Attracted," *Frontiers in Neuroendocrinology* 55 (October 2019): article 100798.
19. Ivanka Savic and Per Lindström, "PET and MRI Show Differences in Cerebral Asymmetry and Functional Connectivity between Homo-and Heterosexual Subjects," *PNAS* 105, no. 27 (July 8, 2008): 9403–08.
20. L. S. Allen and R. A. Gorski, "Sexual Orientation and the Size of the Anterior Commissure in the Human Brain," *PNAS* 89, no 15 (August 1, 1992): 7199–202.
21. M. L. Lalumiere et al., "Sexual Orientation and Handedness in Men and Women: A Meta-Analysis," *Psychological Bulletin* 126, no. 4 (July 2000): 575–92.
22. A. Ganna et al., "Large-Scale GWAS Reveals Insights into the Genetic Architecture of Same-Sex Sexual Behavior," *Science* 365, no. 6456 (August 30, 2019).
23. Niklas Långström et al., "Genetic and Environmental Effects on Same-Sex Sexual Behavior: A Population Study of Twins in Sweden," *Archives of Sexual Behavior* 39, no. 1 (February 2010): 75–80.
24. K. S. Kendler et al., "Sexual Orientation in a U.S. National Sample of Twin and Nontwin Sibling Pairs," *American Journal of Psychiatry* 157, no. 11 (November 2000): 1843–46.
25. Michael Balter, "Can Epigenetics Explain Homosexuality Puzzle?" *Science* 350, no. 6257 (October 9, 2015): 148.
26. C. C. Cohen-Bendahan, "Prenatal Sex Hormone Effects on Child and Adult Sex-Typed Behavior: Methods and Findings," *Neuroscience and Biobehavioral Reviews* 29, no. 2 (April 2005): 353–84.
27. Louise Frisén et al., "Gender Role Behavior, Sexuality, and Psychosocial Adaptation in Women with Congenital Adrenal Hyperplasia Due to CYP21A2 Deficiency," *Journal of Clinical Endocrinology and Metabolism* 94, no. 9 (September 1, 2009): 3432–39; Heino F. L. Meyer-Bahlburg et al., "Sexual Orientation in Women with Classical or Non-Classical Congenital Adrenal Hyperplasia as a Function of Degree of Prenatal Androgen Excess," *Archives of Sexual Behavior* 37, no. 1 (February 2008): 85–99; Kenneth J. Zucker et al., "Psychosexual Development of Women with Congenital Adrenal Hyperplasia," *Hormones and Behavior* 30, no. 4 (December 1996): 300–318.
28. R. Blanchard and A. F. Bogaert, "Homosexuality in Men and Number of Older Brothers," *American Journal of Psychiatry* 153, no. 1 (January 1996): 21–32; J. M. Cantor, R. Blanchard, A. D. Paterson et al., "How Many Gay Men Owe Their Sexual Orientation to Fraternal Birth Order?" *Archives of Sexual Behavior* 31, no. 1 (March 2002): 63–71; Scott W. Semenyna, "Birth Order and Recalled Childhood Gender Nonconformity in Samoan Men and Fa'afafine," *Developmental Psychobiology* 59, no. 3 (April 2017): 338–47.
29. Andrea Roberts et al., "Does Maltreatment in Childhood Affect Sexual Orientation in Adulthood?" *Archives of Sexual Behavior* 42, no. 2 (February 2013): 161–71.

Chapter 14: Did We Get the Biblical Sexual Ethic Wrong?

1. Daniel Cox, Juhem Navarro-Rivera, Robert P. Jones, "A Shifting Landscape: A Decade of Change in American Attitudes about Same-Sex Marriage and LGBT Issues," Public Religion Research Institute, February 16, 2014, *https://www.prri .org/research/2014-lgbt-survey/*.

2. Bob Witeck, "Cultural Change in Acceptance of LGBT People: Lessons from Social Marketing," *American Journal of Orthopsychiatry* 84, no. 1 (2014): 19–22.

3. Elahe Izadi, "'They Remain Puppets': 'Sesame Street,' Once Again, Shuts Down Speculation over Bert and Ernie's Sexual Orientation," *Washington Post*, September 19, 2018, *https://www.washingtonpost.com/news/arts-and-entertainment /wp/2018/09/18/they-remain-puppets-sesame-street-once-again-shuts-down-speculation -over-bert-and-ernies-sexual-orientation/*.

4. Interview with Ralph Blair, February 20, 2020.

5. Ralph Blair, *Looking Back: Evangelicals and Homosexuality* (New York: Evangelicals Concerned, 2015).

6. Robert K. Johnston, *Evangelicals at an Impasse: Biblical Authority in Practice* (Atlanta: John Knox, 1979), 113.

7. Ralph Blair, *The Bible Is an Empty Closet* (New York: Evangelicals Concerned, n.d.).

8. Interview with Ralph Blair, February 20, 2020.

9. "Homosexual Ordination: Bishops Feel the Flak," *Christianity Today*, March 4, 1977, 54.

10. Edward Tivnan, "Homosexuals and the Churches," *New York Times*, October 11, 1987, sec. 6, 84.

11. Derrick Sherwin Bailey, *Homosexuality and the Western Christian Tradition* (London: Longmans, Green, 1955).

12. Mark Vasey-Saunders, *The Scandal of Evangelicals and Homosexuality: English Evangelical Texts, 1960–2010* (Farnham, UK: Ashgate, 2015).

13. Bailey, *Homosexuality and the Western Christian Tradition*, 169.

14. James Brownson, *Bible, Gender, Sexuality: Reframing the Church's Debate on Same-Sex Relationships* (Grand Rapids, MI: Eerdmans, 2013).

15. Ibid., 36.

16. Ibid.

17. Ibid., note 27. He writes, "The Hebrew phrase translated by the NRSV as 'as his partner' *(kenegdo)* is usually understood as 'corresponding to him' or 'in front of, or beside him.' The phrase certainly allows for the notion of difference as well. Yet this aspect of difference remains undeveloped in the remainder of the passage."

18. Ibid., note 39.

19. Ibid., 261.

20. Ibid., 281.

21. See Wayne Grudem, "Should We Move beyond the New Testament to a Better Ethic? An Analysis of William J. Webb, Slaves, Women and Homosexuals: Exploring the Hermeneutics of Cultural Analysis," *JETS* 47, no. 2 (June 2004): 299–346.

22. See Grudem, "Should We Move beyond the New Testament?"

23. Leviticus 18:22; 20:13. Both David Wright and William L. Pedersen have made this argument. See David Wright, "Homosexuals or Prostitutes? The Meaning of ARSENOKOITAI (1 Cor. 6:9, 1 Tim. 1:10)," *Vigiliae Christianae* 38, no. 2 (1984): 125–53. See also William L. Pedersen, "On the Study of 'Homosexuality' in Patristic Sources," in Jan Krans and Joseph Verheyden, *Patristic and Text-Critical Studies: The Collected Essays of William L. Petersen* (Leiden: Brill, 2011), 110–16.

24. Brownson, *Bible, Gender, Sexuality*, 274.

25. William Loader, *Sexuality in the New Testament: Understanding the Key Texts* (Louisville: WJK, 2010), 31.

26. Brownson, *Bible, Gender, Sexuality*, 275.

27. Judith P. Hallett, *Fathers and Daughters in Roman Society: Women and the Elite Family* (Princeton, NJ: Princeton Univ. Press, 1984), 142.

28. See Wright, "Homosexuals or Prostitutes?" 125–53.

29. Loader, *Sexuality in the New Testament*, 31.

30. Eusebius, *Preparation for the Gospel* 6.10.26. Translation in Robert Gagnon, *The Bible and Homosexual Practice: Texts and Hermeneutics* (Nashville: Abingdon, 2001).

31. See Wright, "Homosexuals or Prostitutes?" 134–35. Gagnon follows Wright in noting Origen, Theodoret of Cyrrhus, a homily ascribed to Cyril of Alexandria, Nilus of Ancyra, and a work attributed to John of Damascus.

32. Pseudo-Macarius, *Fifty Spiritual Homilies*.

33. Hippolytus, *Refutation of All Heresies* 5.11. For Greek text and modern translation, see Hippolytus, *Refutation of All Heresies*, trans. M. David Litwa (Atlanta: SBL, 2016), 344–45.

34. Virgil, *Aeneid* 1.28.

35. Elizabeth Bartman, "Eros's Flame: Images of Sexy Boys in Roman Ideal Sculpture," *Memoirs of the American Academy in Rome, Supplementary Volumes 1* (2002): 249–71.

36. Wright, "Homosexuals or Prostitutes?" 144–45.

Chapter 15: Tackling the Argument from Cultural Distance

1. James Brownson, *Bible, Gender, Sexuality: Reframing the Church's Debate on Same-Sex Relationships* (Grand Rapids, MI: Eerdmans, 2013), 44.

2. Karen Keen, *Scripture, Ethics, and the Possibility of Same-Sex Relationships* (Grand Rapids, MI: Eerdmans, 2018), 355.

3. Plato, *Symposium* 191e–192e, in *Plato*, trans. Harold Fowler, vol. 9 of 12 (Cambridge, MA: Harvard Univ. Press, 1925).

4. Ibid.

5. Ibid.

6. There were a lot of Gamaliels, and we cannot know for certain which generation is here meant.

7. F. F. Bruce, *Paul: Apostle of the Heart Set Free* (Grand Rapids, MI: Eerdmans, 2000), 127.

8. Aristotle, *Problems* 4.26, in Thomas K. Hubbard, *Homosexuality in Greece and Rome* (Berkeley, CA: Univ. of California Press, 2003), 262–64.

9. Phaedrus, *Liber Fabularum* 4.16. See also Bernadette Brooten, *Love between Women: Early Christian Responses to Female Homoeroticism* (Chicago: Univ. of Chicago Press, 2009), 50.

10. Soranus, *On Chronic Disorders*, Latin translation by Caelius Aurelianus, 10.5.134–37, in Hubbard, *Homosexuality in Greece and Rome*, 463–65.

11. Polemon, *On Physiognomy* 61, in Hubbard, *Homosexuality in Greece and Rome*, 466.

12. Firmicus Maternus, *Mathesis* 3.6.4–6; 6.31.39; 7.25.3–5, in Hubbard, *Homosexuality in Greece and Rome*, 531–32.

13. Firmicus Maternus, *De errore profanarum religionum*, c. AD 346.

14. Brooten, *Love between Women*, 13.

15. Pindar, *Tenth Pythian Ode* 55–68, in Hubbard, *Homosexuality in Greece and Rome*, 48–49.

16. Ovid, *The Art of Love* 2.683–84, in Hubbard, *Homosexuality in Greece and Rome*, 373.

17. Suetonius, *Galba* 22, in Hubbard, *Homosexuality in Greece and Rome*, 422.

18. Hubbard, *Homosexuality in Greece and Rome*, 5, also figs. 12a, 12b, 12c, 12d.

19. Beryl Rawson, *The Roman Family in Italy* (Oxford, UK: Oxford Univ. Press, 1999), 21.

20. Walter Scheidel, "Roman Funerary Commemoration and the Age at First Marriage," Princeton/Stanford Working Papers in Classics, Princeton University, 2005.

21. Sabine R. Huebner and Christian Laes, *The Single Life in the Roman and Later Roman World* (Cambridge, UK: Cambridge Univ. Press, 2019), 49.

22. Hubbard, *Homosexuality in Greece and Rome*, 5. Hubbard points to Theodotus, Timarchus, and Aristion as examples.

23. Theognis of Megara, *Theognid Collection*, in Hubbard, *Homosexuality in Greece and Rome*, 46.

24. Hubbard, *Homosexuality in Greece and Rome*, 11.

25. Pindar, fragment 123 Snell–Maehler, in Hubbard, *Homosexuality in Greece and Rome*, 48.

26. Hubbard, *Homosexuality in Greece and Rome*, 12.

27. Plato, *Protagorus*, 315.

28. Aristotle, *Nicomachean Ethics* 8.4.1–2, in Hubbard, *Homosexuality in Greece and Rome*, 260–61.

29. Philo, *On the Life of Abraham* 135–37, trans. F. H. Colson, Loeb Classical Library, vol. 6 (Cambridge: Harvard Univ. Press, 1984), 71.

30. Tacitus, *Annals* 15.37.

31. Cassius Dio, *Roman History* 62.28–63.12–13.

32. Royston Lambert, *Beloved and God: The Story of Hadrian and Antinous* (New York: Viking, 1984).

33. Eva Cantarella, *Bisexuality in the Ancient World* (New Haven, CT: Yale Univ. Press, 1992), 125.

34. William S. Anderson, *"Lascivia vs. Ira": Martial and Juvenal*, California Studies in Classical Antiquity, vol. 3 (January 1970): 1–34.

35. Christopher Faraone, *Ancient Greek Love Magic* (Cambridge, MA: Harvard Univ. Press, 2001), 147–48.

36. Brooten, *Love between Women*, 56.

Chapter 16: Is the Biblical Ethic Inherently Violent to Gay People?

1. Eliel Cruz, "The Evangelical Right's Theology on LGBT People Is Violence," *Huffington Post*, July 1, 2016, *https://m.huffpost.com/us/entry/us_10721660*.

2. Jonathan Blake, "Man Seeks Euthanasia to End His Sexuality Struggle" *BBC News*, June 9, 2016, *https://www.bbc.com/news/world-europe-36489090*.

3. Anne Harding, "Religious Faith Linked to Suicidal Behavior in LGBQ Adults," *Reuters*, April 13, 2018, *www.reuters.com/article/us-health-lgbq-religion.-suicide -idUSKBN1HK2MA*.

4. Haeyoun Park and Iaryna Mykhyalyshyn, "L.G.B.T. People Are More Likely to Be Targets of Hate Crimes Than Any Other Minority Group," *New York Times*, June 16, 2016, *https://www.nytimes.com/interactive/2016/06/16/us/hate-crimes -against-lgbt.html*.

5. D. M. Barnes and I. H. Meyer, "Religious Affiliation, Internalized Homophobia, and Mental Health in Lesbians, Gay Men, and Bisexuals," *American Journal of Orthopsychiatry* 82, no. 4 (October 2012): 505–15. Cited in Mark Yarhouse and Olya Zaporozhets, *Costly Obedience: What We Can Learn from the Celibate Gay Christian Community* (Grand Rapids, MI: Zondervan, 2019), 29–30.

6. Yarhouse and Zaporozhets, *Costly Obedience*, 18, 20.

Chapter 17: Confronting the Walking Dead

1. Warren Throckmorton, "Is There a War on Psychotherapy?" *Warren Throckmorton* (blog), September 9, 2019, *www.wthrockmorton.com/2019/09/09/is-there-a-war-on -psychotherapy/*.

2. Interview with Richard Holloman, June 8, 2020.

3. "Frequently Asked Questions," Restored Hope Network, *www.restoredhopenetwork .org/frequently-asked-questions*.

4. Stephen Black, *Freedom Realized: Finding Freedom from Homosexuality and Living a Life Free from Labels* (Enumclaw, WA: Redemption Press, 2017), introduction.

5. See for example Stephen Black, "LGBT Infiltration in the Church," *Janet Mefferd Today*, January 11, 2019, *https://m.soundcloud.com/janetmefferdtoday/1-11-19 -janet-mefferd-today*. See also Peter Montgomery, "Religious Right Radio Host Janet Mefferd Is Promoting Extreme Anti-LGBTQ 'Gone Too Far' Group," *Right Wing Watch*, February 11, 2019, *https://www.rightwingwatch.org/post/religious-right -radio-host-janet-mefferd-is-promoting-extreme-anti-lgbtq-gone-too-far-group/*.

6. Black, *Freedom Realized*, "Effectiveness Survey," questions CT-13, CT-19. Also Stephen H. Black, *The Complete First Stone Ministries Effectiveness Survey Report* (Enumclaw, WA: Redemption, 2017), 55, 72.

7. Johanna Goth Finegan, "Defence against the Dark Arts," Spiritual Friendship Preconference, Revoice18, St. Louis, MO, July 26, 2018.

8. Mark Yarhouse, "Same-Sex Attraction, Homosexual Orientation, and Gay

Identity: A Three-Tier Distinction for Counseling and Pastoral Care," *Journal of Pastoral Care and Counseling*, February 2005, 201–11.

9. Mark Yarhouse, *Homosexuality and the Christian* (Bloomington, MN: Bethany, 2010), 37–55.

10. Johanna Goth Finegan, Spiritual Friendship Preconference, Revoice19, St. Louis, MO, June 6, 2019.

11. Greg Johnson, "I Used to Hide My Shame. Now I Take Shelter under the Gospel: How a Gay Atheist Teenager Discovered Jesus and Stopped Living Undercover," *Christianity Today Online*, May 20, 2019, *www.christianitytoday.com/ct/2019/may -web-only/greg-johnson-hide-shame-shelter-gospel-gay-teenager.html*.

12. Jill Rennick, Revoice19, St. Louis, MO, June 7, 2019.

13. Paul David Tripp, *Broken-Down House* (Wapwallopen, PA: Shepherd, 2009), 34–35.

14. Johannes Oecolampadius, *ad Rhomanos* 61v.1623.

15. Frank Worthen, "Introduction to Love in Action," undated (1976–78), cassette tape. Quoted in James Peron, *Homosexuality and the Miracle Makers* (Glen Ellyn, IL: privately printed, 1978).

16. See a helpful essay by Matthew Lee Anderson, "The Trouble with Talking about Our 'Identity in Christ,'" *Mere Orthodoxy*, July 12, 2012, *https://mereorthodoxy .com/trouble-with-talking-about-our-identity-in-christ/*.

Chapter 18: Ending (Unintentional) Emotional Abuse

1. Jan Gelech, *"Such Were Some of You": Crisis and Healing in the Lives of Same-Sex-Attracted Christian Men*, PhD Diss. (University of Saskatchewan, 2015), 143.

2. Lynne Hasher, David Goldstein, and Thomas Toppino, "Frequency and the Conference of Referential Validity," *Journal of Verbal Learning and Verbal Behavior* 16 (1977): 107–12.

3. "The Truth Effect and Other Processing Fluency Miracles," *Science Blogs*, September 18, 2007, *https://scienceblogs.com/mixingmemory/2007/09/18/the-truth -effect-and-other-pro*.

4. Gabriel Blanchard, "Caution: Contents Toxic, Under High Pressure," *Mud Blood Catholic*, June 18, 2019, *http://mudbloodcatholic.blogspot.com/2019/06/caution -contents-toxic-under-high.html?m=1*.

5. See D. A. Carson's endorsement of Gregory Coles' book *Single, Gay, Christian: A Personal Journey of Faith and Sexual Identity* (Downers Grove, IL: InterVarsity, 2017): "To say this book is important is a painful understatement. It is the candid, moving, intensely personal story of a gay young man who wants to live his life under the authority of King Jesus and who refuses to accept the comforting answers proffered by different parts of the culture. Superbly written, this book stands athwart the shibboleths of our day and reminds us what submission to King Jesus looks like, what it feels like. This book needs to be thoughtfully read by straight people and by gay people, by unbelievers and by Christians. It is not to be read with a condescending smirk, but with humility" (D. A. Carson, President, the Gospel Coalition, Research Professor of New Testament, Trinity Evangelical Divinity School).

6. Molly Worthen, *Apostles of Reason: The Crisis of Authority in American Evangelicalism* (Oxford: Oxford Univ. Press, 2016), 24.

7. Matthew Anderson (@mattleeanderson), January 17, 2020, Twitter, *https://twitter .com/mattleeanderson*. Italics original.

8. Council on Biblical Manhood and Womanhood, *https://cbmw.org*. Data retrieved June 22, 2020, courtesy Jeremy Erickson.

9. Denny Burk, et al., "The Nashville Statement," *Council on Biblical Manhood and Womanhood* (August 2017), *https://cbmw.org/nashville-statement*.

10. Alan Medinger, "Is Anyone Ever Totally Healed?" Regeneration Ministries, March 1, 2006.

11. Colin Cook, et al., "The Fourteen Steps," *Homosexuals Anonymous* (archived September 12, 2009), *https://web.archive.org/web/20090205095656/http://ha-fs.org /14-steps.htm*.

12. Interview with Denny Burk, August 13, 2020. See also Alastair Roberts, "The Transgender Question," *Alastair's Adversaria*, July 3, 2014, *https://alastair adversaria.com/2014/07/03/podcast-the-transgender-question/*.

13. I here reference Julie Rodger's presentation at the final 2013 Exodus conference.

14. Southeast Alabama Presbytery (PCA), "Open Letter from Southeast Alabama Presbytery to Missouri Presbytery Regarding Its Investigation of TE Greg Johnson," *Aquila Report*, August 14, 2020, *www.theaquilareport.com/open-letter-from-southeast -alabama-presbytery-to-missouri-presbytery-regarding-its-investigation-of-te-greg-johnson/*.

15. C. S. Lewis, *The Collected Letters of C. S. Lewis*, vol. 3, ed. Walter Hooper (San Francisco: HarperCollins, 2009), 471. Also quoted in Sheldon Vanauken, *A Severe Mercy* (San Francisco: Harper and Row, 1980), 148.

16. Frank Schaeffer, *Crazy for God* (New York: Carroll and Graf, 2007), 77.

17. See Alex Davidson, *The Returns of Love: Letters of a Christian Homosexual* (London: InterVarsity, 1970).

18. UPI, "Billy Graham Backs Ordaining Homosexuals," *Atlanta Journal-Constitution*, July 25, 1975, 21.

19. John Stott, *Issues Facing Christians Today* (Basingstoke, UK: Marshall, 1984), 303.

20. Richard F. Lovelace, *Homosexuality and the Church: Crisis, Conflict, Compassion* (Old Tappan, NJ: Revell, 1978), 125.

21. Egon Middelmann et al., "Pastoral Care for the Repentant Homosexual," Reformed Presbyterian Church, Evangelical Synod, 1980.

22. Mark Yarhouse, interview by Warren Throckmorton, YouTube, July 19, 2020, *https://youtu.be/4zWlFflyuIc*.

23. *Book of Church Order of the Presbyterian Church in America*, Preliminary Principle 7.

24. Bill Henson, *Posture Shift* (Acton, MA: Posture Shift, 2018), 13. Italics original.

Chapter 19: Picking Up the Ball We Dropped Forty Years Ago

1. Henri Nouwen, *Bread for the Journey: A Daybook of Wisdom and Faith* (San Francisco: HarperSanFrancisco, 1997), entry for February 8.

2. As of 2020, Justin Lee's essay can be found at *http://geekyjustin.com/great-debate/*. Ron's essay can be found at *https://ronbelgau.com/great-debate/*.

3. Wesley Hill, *Washed and Waiting: Reflections on Christian Faithfulness and Homosexuality* (Grand Rapids, MI: Zondervan, 2010), 64.

4. Ron Belgau, "Ron Belgau: Why Am I Here?" *Spiritual Friendship*, May 4, 2012, *https://spiritualfriendship.org/2012/04/07/ron-belgau-why-am-i-here/amp/*.

5. Wesley Hill, "Wesley Hill: Why Am I Here?" *Spiritual Friendship*, April 8, 2020, *https://spiritualfriendship.org/2012/04/08/wesley-hill-why-am-i-here/*.

6. "About," Center for Faith, Sexuality and Gender, *https://centerforfaith.com/about*.

7. Eve Tushnet, *Gay and Catholic: Accepting My Sexuality, Finding Community, Living My Faith* (Notre Dame, IN: Ave Maria, 2014).

8. Mark Yarhouse, quoted in Melissa Steffan, "After Exodus: Evangelicals React as Ex-Gay Ministry Starts Over," *Christianity Today Online*, June 21, 2013, *www.christianitytoday.com/ct/2013/june-web-only/exodus-international-alan-chambers-apologize-for-exgay-past.html*.

9. Wesley Hill, "Revoice and a Vocation of Yes," *First Things*, August 7, 2018, *www.firstthings.com/web-exclusives/2018/08/revoice-and-a-vocation-of-yes*.

10. Bekah Mason, Pastors and Leaders Seminar, Revoice20, St. Louis, MO, July 25, 2020.

11. Alan Downs, *The Velvet Rage: Overcoming the Pain of Growing Up Gay in a Straight Man's World*, 2nd ed. (New York: Da Capo, 2012).

12. John Stott, *Same Sex Relationships*, rev. ed. (Epsom, Surrey, UK: Good Book, 2017), 81. Note that the 1984 language has been updated, replacing the word *homosexual* with *gay*, in line with modern usage.

13. Mark Yarhouse and Olya Zaporozhets, *Costly Obedience: What We Can Learn from the Celibate Gay Christian Community* (Grand Rapids, MI: Zondervan, 2019), 116.

Chapter 20: Celibacy and Hope

1. Michael McClymond, "The Last Sexual Perversion: An Argument in Defense of Celibacy," *Theology Today* 57 (2000): 217–31.

2. Pieter Valk, "Arguments Aren't Enough: Pastoral Response to Side A Theology," Revoice20, St. Louis, MO, July 25, 2020. See also Pieter Valk, "The Case for Vocational Singleness," *Christianity Today*, November 25, 2020, *https://www.christianitytoday.com/ct/2020/november-web-only/valk-case-for-vocational-singleness.html*.

3. W. H. Auden, quoted in Wesley Hill, "A Few Like You: Will the Church be the Church for Homosexual Christians?" in Matthew Hundley, ed., *Thinking Christianly about Homosexuality: Essays from the Pages of Critique* (Minneapolis: Ransom Fellowship, 2008), 20–28.

4. Deanna Briody, "What's a Body to Do? The Place of Beauty and the Body in Non-Sexual Loves," *Spiritual Friendship*, January 4, 2018, *https://spiritualfriendship.org/2018/01/04/whats-a-body-to-do-the-place-of-beauty-and-the-body-in-non-sexual-loves/*.

5. C. S. Lewis, *Yours, Jack: Spiritual Direction from C. S. Lewis*, ed. Paul F. Ford (New York: HarperOne, 2008), 46.

6. Alex Davidson, *The Returns of Love: Letters of a Christian Homosexual* (London: InterVarsity, 1970), 16.

7. Augustine, *The Literal Meaning of Genesis* 2.9.5.

8. Ned Stonehouse, *J. Gresham Machen: A Biographical Memoir* (Grand Rapids, MI: Eerdmans, 1954), 389.

9. Henri Nouwen, *The Inner Voice of Love: A Journey through Anguish to Freedom* (New York: Crown, 1997), xv.

10. Michael W. Higgins, "Priest, Writer, Mentor, Misfit: Understanding Henri Nouwen," *Commonweal*, December 16, 2016, 13–16.

11. Robert Bernard Martin, *Gerard Manley Hopkins: A Very Private Life* (London: HarperCollins, 1991).

12. Daryl J. Higgins, "Gay Men from Heterosexual Marriages," *Journal of Homosexuality* 42, no. 4 (February 2002): 15–34.

13. A. P. Buxton, "Works in Progress: How Mixed-Orientation Couples Maintain Their Marriages after the Wives Come Out," *Journal of Bisexuality* 4 (2004): 76–82.

14. Mark Yarhouse et al., "Characteristics of Mixed Orientation Couples: An Empirical Study," *Edification: The Transdisciplinary Journal of Christian Psychology* 4, no. 2 (2011): 41–56.

15. Yarhouse et al., "Characteristics of Mixed Orientation Couples."

16. Pieter Valk of EQUIP offered some very helpful insights. See Valk, "Arguments Aren't Enough."

17. David Wells, *Above All Earthly Pow'rs: Christ in a Postmodern World* (Grand Rapids, MI: Eerdmans, 2005), 206.

Conclusion

1. Richard F. Lovelace, *Homosexuality and the Church: Crisis, Conflict, Compassion* (Old Tappan, NJ: Revell, 1978), 125.